More praise for Amanda Hesser and
COOKING FOR MR. LATTE

"One of the best—if not the best—of the young food writers."

—Jeffrey Steingarten, *Vogue*'s food critic and
the author of *The Man Who Ate Everything*

"Amanda Hesser writes about both food and love in the same passionate, fascinating voice. Her recipes and stories are seductive, simple, and deeply satisfying. I simply cannot get enough."

—Mario Batali, host of "Molto Mario" and
chef/owner of New York's Babbo

"Amanda Hesser's charming personality shines as the reader experiences the life and loves of a gourmet. *Cooking for Mr. Latte* is perfectly seasoned with sensuality and superb recipes."

—Jean-Georges Vongerichten

"*Cooking for Mr. Latte* is proof that great food is truly seductive, and any prospective suitor should make haste to read it and cook from it often. But it is much more than a cookbook for the lovelorn. In a voice that resonates with candor and wit, Hesser dramatizes the curious—often hilarious—ways that food . . . informs all our relationships."

—Matthew Lee and Ted Lee

"If there's anyone writing about food in America today who might someday inherit M. F. K. Fisher's status, it's Amanda Hesser."

—Nancy Harmon Jenkins, author of
The Mediterranean Diet Cookbook

ALSO BY AMANDA HESSER

The Cook and the Gardener:
A Year of Recipes and Writings from the French Countryside

Cooking for Mr Latte

A FOOD LOVER'S COURTSHIP,

WITH RECIPES

Amanda Hesser

ILLUSTRATIONS BY IZAK

W. W. NORTON & COMPANY

NEW YORK · LONDON

Excerpt from "This Is Just to Say" by William Carlos Williams, from *Collected Poems,
1909–1939*, Volume 1, copyright © 1938 by New Directions Publishing Corp. Reprinted by
permission of New Directions Publishing Corp.

For information about permission to reproduce selections from this book, write to
Permissions, W. W. Norton & Company, Inc., 500 Fifth Avenue, New York, NY 10110

Manufacturing by The Haddon Craftsmen, Inc.
Book design by Chris Welch
Production manager: Andrew Marasia
Illustrations by IZAK@TRAFFICNYC.COM

LIBRARY OF CONGRESS CATALOGING-IN-PUBLICATION DATA

Hesser, Amanda.
Cooking for Mr. Latte : a food lover's courtship, with recipes /
Amanda Hesser ; illustrations by Izak.
p. cm.
Includes index.
ISBN 0-393-05196-X
1. Cookery. 2. Courtship. I. Title.
TX652 .H466 2003
641.5—dc21   2002154145

ISBN 0-393-32559-8 pbk.

W. W. Norton & Company, Inc., 500 Fifth Avenue, New York, N.Y. 10110
www.wwnorton.com

W. W. Norton & Company Ltd., Castle House, 75/76 Wells Street, London W1T 3QT

3 4 5 6 7 8 9 0

For Tad

Contents

Acknowledgments

This book requires an unusual set of acknowledgments. Because it is a diary, many friends helped me simply by being themselves, by cooking in front of me and teaching me new techniques in the kitchen, by inviting me for dinner, by telling me about their passion for kumquats or pigs in a blanket, and by debating with me the merits of fine dining.

Along the way, a great number of people—chefs, acquaintances, friends and family—generously shared their recipes with me. My warmest thanks to Helen Getz, Judith Hesser, Neil Fuhrer, Andrea and Tony Manella, Rhonda and Paul Thomson, Luke Thomson, Dean and Leslie Hesser, Elizabeth and Dorie Friend, Timmie Friend, Scott Haskins, Pier and Sara Friend, Baba (aka Margaret Dunn), Jeffrey Steingarten, Caron Smith, Jennifer Steinhauer, Ed Wyatt, Hannah Wyatt, Julia Child, Anne Willan, Mark Cherniavsky, Jonathan Reynolds, Tama Janowitz, Peter Elliott, Heather Schroder, Maiken Baird, Tim Luke, Charles Gepp, the late Nora Norman, Heidi da Empoli, Giuliano da Empoli, Paula Disbrowe, David Norman, Rachel Urquhart, John Herrera, Thomas Canfield, Kelly Alexander, Dan Barber, Irene Hamburger, Tom Colicchio, Rebecca Charles, Adam Platt, Sherry and Mark

Cicero, Nan Wilson, Tony Gomez-Ibañez, Deborah Copaken Kogan, Paul Kogan, Michael Hirschorn, Elizabeth Beier, Aleksandra Crapanzano, John Burnham Schwartz, Prakash Detha, Deborah Needleman, Jacob Weisberg, Wade Graham, Mitie Tucker, Maia Samuel, Joan Thorsen, Lora Zarubin, Geoffrey Drummond, Frances Mayes, Maida Heatter, Marcella Hazan, David Lebovitz, Nancy Silverton, Anna Pump, Mindy Berry, Mario Batali, Emalee Chapman, Diane Kochilas, Ruth Reichl, Paola di Mauro, Jane Smith, Francesca Colombani, Nancy Harmon Jenkins, Gabrielle Hamilton, Pete Ambrose, John Dee, the late Bill Devin, José Andrés, Katie Roiphe, Harry Chernoff, Ginia Bellafante, Andy Borowitz, Michael and Eleanora Kennedy, Liz Berger, Rene Becker, Jessica Abbott, George Polk, Charlotte Mandler, Geoffrey Zakarian, William Mattiello, Jason Denton, Mark Ladner, Joaquín Perez, Juana Perez, Louis Blair, Maya Klaris, Bernadette Cura, Sofia Perez, Alix and David Earle, and Jeanne Courtner.

I have included recipes from many cookbooks and magazines, a somewhat unusual practice. Because this book began as a diary, I wanted to highlight some of my favorite books and publications and showcase them in the way that they are used by cooks like me across the country—as a resource for new dishes, or new styles of cooking. When I followed the original recipe, it is printed and credited in a straightforward manner. At times, I've included the changes that I or my friends have made to the recipe. And in some instances, I've given credit to the book and recipe that led to the creation of a new recipe of my own. In every case, I encourage readers to look up the originals and buy the book or magazine.

This book began as a column in *The New York Times Magazine*, where it was called "Food Diary." The column would not have existed were it not for the exceptional support of Adam Moss, Amy Spindler, and Andy Port. At the magazine, many people devoted their energy and creativity to making each column just right. For this, I thank Maura Egan, Claude Martel, Mary Johnson, Scott Darling and Zoë van Baaren of Formula z/s, and Michael Boodro. I am also grateful for the support I received from my editors at the newspaper, Michalene Busico and Barbara Graustark.

Every author should have an editor like John Barstow, who believes that meetings should take place at the Grand Central Oyster Bar over a dozen Spinney Creeks and a glass of Sancerre. He is a sensitive and sharp-eyed editor, a fine gourmet and an enthusiastic reader. Many at W. W. Norton, like Jeannie Luciano, Nancy Palmquist, Georgia Liebman, Andrew Marasia and Susan Stuck, worked hard and thoughtfully on this book.

My agent, Doe Coover, as always, had a great vision for the book. She was enormously helpful in focusing my ideas and believed from the first that vignettes from my life could be made into a coherent book.

Izak, the illustrator, created the charming, unmistakable portraits for both the magazine columns and the book. Early on, Izak came to my apartment for lunch so we could meet and he could make some sketches. I served lamb stew. He is a vegetarian. I am grateful that he took the job nonetheless.

I owe a special thank you to Mary Johnson, Alta de Lara and to my sister and ever-trustworthy cooking critic Rhonda Thomson. They tested dozens of recipes, making sure that each one read clearly, was appealing to a home cook, and actually produced a tasty dish.

Finally, I want to thank Tad Friend, who allowed his eating habits to be scrutinized in public and his every move documented, and did so wittingly and confidently. Tad has had the unusual role of both muse and mentor. He read and reread every draft of this book, applying his deft and tactful skills as an editor and his thoughtfulness as a partner and dining companion. I am indebted to him.

He still maintains that biscotti, one of my favorite confections, are fragments of the Dead Sea scrolls. But we have years ahead to work out this issue.

Introduction

During the five years that I have been writing about food for *The New York Times*, in whose pages I am often describing four-course meals topped off with Armagnac, there is one question that people always ask me: What do you really eat? Well, some days I'm having lunch at Daniel, and others I'm subsisting on tepid coffee and BLTs as I hunch over my desk writing (or avoiding writing) a story.

The real difficulty in answering that question briefly, I've realized, is that what I eat is inextricably tied to where I eat, when I eat, why I eat and with whom I eat. Eating well is not as much about good food as it is about the people you share that food with, the room you dine in, what you talk about, and the emotional hungers that you bring to the table.

M.F.K. Fisher wrote, "Our three basic needs, for food and security and love, are so mixed and mingled and entwined that we cannot straightly think of one without the others." I know that I certainly cannot. For a year or so, I kept a diary. Out of it came these stories, which I hope will answer that popular question.

Cooking for Mr Latte

Chapter 1

FIRST DATE

We almost didn't make it past the first phone call.

A friend had set us up. I thought she might have mentioned that I wrote about food. He called from L.A. where he was on a business trip. All we needed to do was arrange the date.

After a few awkward minutes, he suggested we meet somewhere on the Upper West Side. Fine. Oh, yes, we both live there. Good, good. We were being dreadfully practical.

"How about Merchants?" he said.

Merchants NY, for those fortunate enough to have been spared it, is the Manhattan equivalent of an Outback Steakhouse. Starbucks decor, loud music and utterly forgettable urban bar food.

"Merchants?" I challenged. He stuck to his plan.

Many people assume that being a food writer and single entitles me to dates at all the top restaurants. They imagine me breezing through Daniel, stopping in for cocktails at Danube, glugging down Champagne and oysters at Le Bernardin.

I wish. This happened only once, I'm afraid. I was on a date at Chelsea Bistro, a dim little place. My date and I began chatting about restaurants with the man who was dining alone at the next table. He was a regular at all the places where I wished I were a regular. When my date went to the bathroom, this man made his move.

A week later we had lunch at Nobu. Nobu is awfully bright in the daylight. When we met in the doorway, we exchanged looks of horror. He was a partner at Goldman Sachs. He wore an Hermès tie and a suit as crisp as a potato chip. I worked in a cubicle and had on shoes I bought in college. He was as old as my father, and my father was dead.

Too late to flee, we bonded over the *tiradito* while he told me about his retirement plans. Then he paid the bill and went off to a gallery to work on his collection. I went back to my cubicle.

Merchants was not the alternative I had in mind.

Merchants has a long front with doors flung open in the summertime and yet manages to make you feel you are entering a black hole. I crept inside. My date was lurking in shadow. He was tall and handsome. He wore glasses and had wavy brown hair with a few defiant curls that hung over his forehead.

We sat at a table outside. He ordered a Budweiser. I thought of an old friend and Francophile, who insists that friends in France often order the same thing to express appreciation of each other. So I ordered one, too. Our waiter brought it in bottles but never offered glasses. Music blared from the black hole. I felt like I was at a frat party.

The bread had the very same texture as my doormat. But, to my astonishment, the meal was not half bad. A tolerable tomato soup and tuna that was acceptably pink.

Things aside from the meal were going very well. He was witty, impossibly smart and very, very funny. Until he told me that if he had to give up one of his senses, he'd give up taste. I drank more Budweiser. Then he ordered a latte. After dinner.

He needed a lot of reform.

Over the next few weeks, we marked our culinary territory. He introduced me to the burgers at All State. I paced him through six courses at Café Boulud.

Then it came time for the meal. That first meal. In my lair.

The first meal you cook for someone is intimate. Not just if it's for a date. And not just because no one cooks anymore—it really has nothing to do with whether you are a good cook or not. It's an entry into the way you think, what you've seen and know, the way you treat others, how you perceive pleasure. Dinner guests can see by how you compose a meal if you are an ungenerous hothead or a nurturer, stingy or clever, fussy or stylish.

Which is probably why I lost sleep over what to cook him. I knew he would see everything; he is a writer, and writers love nothing more than to observe. I was hoping to divert his attention with good food. And yet I had no intention of cooking Babette's feast. I don't cook that way, nor do I have a desire to.

I lived in France for a couple of years. French country food was safe, easy to like and, well, an honest part of me. I didn't want to show off, and I certainly didn't want to fool him into thinking he would be eating foie gras on a daily basis if he stuck with me. I just wanted him to eat well and want to come for dinner again. I wanted him to think I was as wonderful as I thought he was.

I decided on guinea hen, potatoes, a salad and a simple dessert.

The day he was coming, I set the table, then began making the dessert, which involved heating honey and star anise on the stove and keeping a close eye on it. I made the mistake of calling my mother, who has a special way of numbing the brain with point by point details of her tennis game. I scorched the honey, not once but twice. And each time, she said, "You should watch it more carefully."

He arrived with wine. While I finished roasting the guinea hen, I served him some smoked salmon laid in ribbon folds on toasted black bread with a dab of crème fraîche and horseradish. It was a safe starter, I thought: salty, robust, crisp and about as innocuous as chips and dip.

He ate one, then promptly ignored the rest. I asked if he liked the toasts. "Well, actually," he said, "I just don't like smoked salmon. Or any smoked fish, really."

Terrific!

I sucked it up and moved on. With the guinea hen we had mashed celery root and potatoes and haricots verts with crushed walnuts and walnut oil. Then I made a small salad with soft lettuces, and for dessert, ice cream with roasted figs and the vexing honey sauce.

He ate heartily and had seconds of everything. We finished the wine. I made him a latte, even.

A few nights later at a cocktail party, a tray of smoked salmon tartlets passed by while my Mr. Latte was chatting away with a friend. Mr. Latte took one—and then another—and popped them into his mouth.

Humpff!

Dinner for a date

Salmon and Crème Fraîche on Black Bread Toasts

You can make the same recipe with smoked mackerel or smoked trout, pulled into small lumps and piled on top of the crème fraîche. It is also delicious on white Pullman bread. Just be sure that it isn't too fluffy or too sour.

    4 thin slices black or dark pumpernickel bread, crusts removed and cut
        into triangles
    5 tablespoons crème fraîche
    1 tablespoon horseradish, plus more to taste
    1 tablespoon thinly sliced chives
    Sea salt
    1/4 pound thinly sliced smoked salmon
    Coarsely ground black pepper

1. Preheat the oven to 350°F. Place the bread pieces on a baking sheet and bake until lightly toasted but still soft in the center, just a minute or two. Meanwhile, whisk together the crème fraîche, horseradish and chives in a small bowl. Add more horseradish and salt to taste. Cut the salmon into strips (2 inches by 1 inch) or squares, so that you have the same number as triangles of bread.

2. Place the toasts on a serving platter. Spoon a little horseradish cream on each piece. Lay a slice of salmon on top in delicate folds. Grind pepper over the salmon.

16 TOASTS, TO SERVE 2 TO 4.

Roasted Guinea Hen

If you have the time, place the guinea hen on a baking rack, uncovered, in the refrigerator for 24 hours. This dries the skin, and helps it crisp better in the oven. You can do this with any kind of poultry.

    1 guinea hen, about 4 pounds (or a plump chicken), rinsed and patted
        dry
    Olive oil

Coarse sea salt
Coarsely ground black pepper
2 tablespoons fresh thyme leaves
3 cloves garlic, skin left on and lightly crushed with the side of a knife
1 cup chicken broth

1. Preheat the oven to 400°F. Place the guinea hen in an iron skillet large enough for it to fit, or in a heavy roasting dish. (Enameled cast iron is best.) Using your hands, rub olive oil all over the bird, inside and out. Season generously (also inside and out) with salt and pepper. Sprinkle with the thyme leaves. Scatter the garlic around the pan.

2. Place in the oven and roast, basting often, until a thermometer inserted in the thickest part of the thigh reads 160°F; this should take about 40 to 50 minutes.

3. Remove the hen from the oven and transfer to a cutting board. Drain off excess fat (do leave a little to give the gravy body) from the skillet or roasting pan and place over medium-high heat. Pour in the chicken broth. Using a wooden spoon, scrape up the pan drippings and bring to a boil. Reduce until sauce is syrupy. Correct seasoning. Cut the hen into 6 pieces, and pour any juices from the cutting board back into the sauce. Serve the hen on a platter and pass the sauce with a big spoon.

ENOUGH FOR 2 FOR DINNER AND LUNCH THE NEXT DAY.

Haricots Verts with Walnuts and Walnut Oil

This is a recipe that I often make for parties or picnics, when I'm asked to bring a dish. It travels well and people love it. They think they're getting regular green beans, and then the walnut oil kicks in. I've made it with yellow beans mixed in. You could also add some baby potatoes, cut in quarters.

Grains of paradise are available at specialty stores and on line at www.worldspice.com. The small seeds have a heat that resembles that of black pepper, but with a little nuttiness and a hint of citrus. I have been completely seduced by them. I keep them in my peppermill, and when I need real black pepper, I grind it in a mortar and pestle.

1/3 cup walnuts
Sea salt
3/4 pound haricots verts, stems trimmed

3 tablespoons walnut oil, or excellent olive oil
Coarsely ground black pepper, or grains of paradise if you have them

1. Preheat the oven to 350°F. Spread the walnuts in a small baking dish. Bake until you can hear the walnuts sizzling or smell them when you open the oven door, about 5 minutes. (Set your timer!) Remove from the oven and chop coarsely.

2. Meanwhile, bring a large pot of water, seasoned with sea salt so that it tastes like ocean water (not quite, but salty), to a boil. Add the haricots verts and cook until just tender but still firm, about 4 minutes. (Don't overcook: they will continue to cook out of the water.) Drain, then spread out on a kitchen towel to soak up the excess water.

3. Gather the beans while hot and toss in a bowl with the warm walnuts and the walnut oil. Season generously with pepper and perhaps a little more salt. Serve now or later. They're lovely after a few hours, too.

VEGETABLES FOR 2 (SIMPLY DOUBLE OR TRIPLE FOR A FAMILY).

Chapter 2

MR. LATTE HAS A TRICK UP HIS SLEEVE

Everything had been going deliciously well with Mr. Latte. We went to book parties and party parties, readings and movies. We were invited to dinners at friends' apartments. We ate out a lot, too.

He had made a few slips. He'd used the expression "tying on the feed bag" as a teasing reference to eating one too many times and once described a chicken dish as having "pork chop seasoning," whatever that may mean. But in general he was proving to be a big, enthusiastic eater and had even survived a meal with the charming but indomitable gourmand Jeffrey Steingarten.

Then he casually mentioned that he sometimes used Equal instead of sugar in his lattes. The blood in my head did a free fall to my toes. Equal?

It's something I have a difficult time qualifying as a food. Equal is made of dextrose with maltodextrin and aspartame. Sugar, on the other hand, comes from sugarcane. When you taste raw sugar, you can make out the grains on your tongue, and as they melt, your palate gets a gentle, glorious bath of sweetness and caramel.

When you warm white sugar in a pan, it turns into a bitter amber syrup—that lovely little pool of sauce that washes over crème caramel. When you beat sugar with eggs, the eggs thicken and turn pale, forming the foundation for fluffy layer cakes and moist, buttery muffins. When you sprinkle it over custard and broil it, it melts and then hardens like a thin layer of ice that you get to shatter with a spoon.

Equal has no such qualities. It gives you a jolt of sweetness and zero nuance.

I avoid eating foods whose ingredients I can't picture in my head. Eating is a high form of pleasure for me, but it is also a form of nourishment. So I stick to things like seasonal vegetables and fruits, fish caught in the wild, fresh pressed oils, naturally leavened breads, salt from the ocean, raw milk cheese, and fragrant spices.

If I think I've had too much sugar, I simply do not use it. To me, using Equal is like a vegetarian trying to replace meat with veggie burgers and tofu "duck." What's the point? Good coffee does not need sugar, and I would much rather live without dessert than eat one that has the dull veneer of Equal. Call me a snob! I am one.

The more I thought about it, the more fear set in: how could I be seen in public with someone ordering lattes and then swooshing packets of Equal all around?! Would I be grabbing the spent packages and stashing them in my purse? Could I even picture us asking for Equal after five courses at Ducasse? He tried the health argument. But a man who starts off the day with a gigante mocha and ends it with beef knows he's going nowhere with that. Then he mumbled something about there being very little difference in taste. Right.

To tell the truth, I wasn't all that surprised. Most men I've dated have had some kind of food or dining "issue." There was Wade (I have mercifully changed all names), a smart, handsome fellow whose fatal flaw was that he drank five liters of water a day and was philosophically opposed to restaurants with entrées costlier than $12.

And Edward, the novelist and vegan, who fooled himself into believing that restaurant dishes like sautéed spinach and carrot soup had no butter or chicken stock in them. I cooked for him carefully and quietly pitied his pleasureless life, until he started two-timing me and came to my house late one night looking for dinner. I served him leftover pasta with butter, cream, bacon and a smile, and clueless as ever, he ate it.

The winner, though, was Michael, a lawyer, who tricked me into thinking we were going to Rao's then made a last-minute diversion to Gotham Bar and Grill, where he proceeded to have an allergy attack from the veal stock in his sauce, the yeast in the bread or perhaps the sparkling water. He was allergic to everything. What was he thinking asking out someone whose profession is eating? Our only date ended at the emergency room.

The real question is, what was I thinking?

I should have established a set of guidelines long ago. That all potential boyfriends have to be willing to travel to the far reaches of a city to seek out that dark little bar that makes the best fried oysters; that they must like going to restaurants, expensive restaurants. And when they're at one, they should happily linger over the petits fours and savor a good Cognac. If they itch to leave as soon as the desserts are cleared, they've missed the point.

They must eat sushi and offal; they should know what a coat check is

COOKING FOR MR. LATTE 27

and know to tip the attendant, and they must! must! must! be able to open a bottle of Champagne. I couldn't care less if they cook. I am happy to do that.

But I had hoped those days were past—Mr. Latte was terrific in every other way.

Equal, however, had the potential to spark other gastronomic debates. And a recent conversation I'd had with a well-known French chef only added to my worry. The chef was on a diet and told me he was eating carefully. The night before, for instance, he had eaten at Smith & Wollensky. Not my idea of spa food.

"I had steak and lobster and onion rings," he said, "but then I had asparagus with it." I tried hard not to laugh. I began to see Mr. Latte's little Equal problem ballooning into the same mass of self-deception. And since I don't plan on dipping low-sodium crackers in warm skim milk when we're old, we needed to handle it now.

I had in mind a side-by-side taste test. I would make him a latte two ways: one with raw sugar, one with its imposter. I bought supplies of Equal at Gristedes, feeling like I was buying Depends at the pharmacy.

Then I got distracted. A few weeks passed. When I reminded Mr. Latte about the tasting, he looked smug. "I'm not sure we need it," he said.

"What do you mean?"

"Well, you remember the other night when we went to the movies and I got us cappuccinos?"

"Yeah."

"What do you think made them sweet?"

Silence.

Sweets Mr. Latte likes, all made with real sugar

Coffee Caramel Custard

Adapted from Room for Dessert *by David Lebovitz (HarperCollins, 1999)*

This is pudding for an adult palate: pleasingly rich and a little austere.

1 1/4 cups real white sugar
A few drops lemon juice
2 1/2 cups heavy cream
1/2 vanilla bean, split
7 egg yolks
1 tablespoon instant espresso powder dissolved in 1/4 cup water
Sea salt
1/2 teaspoon vanilla extract
A dark bitter, only faintly sweet chocolate, for shaving over the custard

1. Preheat the oven to 350°F. In a deep, heavy saucepan (at least 8 quarts), mix together the sugar, lemon juice and 1/3 cup water. Cook the sugar until it dissolves and begins to darken. Do not stir. Continue caramelizing until the sugar turns a dark amber color and begins to smoke. When it gets just a touch darker, remove it from the heat and immediately add the cream. The mixture will steam violently and bubble up; don't be alarmed.

2. Add the vanilla bean. Put on oven mitts and stir the mixture with a wooden spoon over low heat until the caramel is fully dissolved and the mixture has stopped bubbling.

3. Whisk the egg yolks in a medium bowl, then add the warm caramel cream to them a little at a time, whisking continuously so the yolks don't cook. Then whisk in the espresso, a large pinch of salt and the vanilla. Pour the custard into a large measuring cup or pitcher, then pour into six ramekins.

4. Put the ramekins in a deep baking dish. Fill the dish with warm water until it reaches halfway up the sides of the ramekins. Cover the pan tightly with aluminum foil. Bake until the custards are barely set, about 35 to 45 minutes. They should still be jiggly in the center.

5. Remove the custards from the water bath and set on a baking rack to cool. Cover and chill. Before serving, set out for 15 minutes or so to warm up,

then shave a few curls of chocolate over the surface of the custard. (This can be done with a vegetable peeler.)

6 DELICATE LITTLE CUSTARDS.

Mountain Honey Gingersnaps with Candied Ginger

Adapted from Maida Heatter's Cookies *by Maida Heatter*
(Andrews McMeel Publishing, 1997)

2 1/4 cups sifted all-purpose flour
1 1/2 teaspoons baking soda
1/2 teaspoon salt
1/2 teaspoon powdered ginger
1/2 teaspoon ground cinnamon
1/4 teaspoon ground cloves
6 ounces (1 1/2 sticks) unsalted butter
1 cup moist, fresh light brown sugar, firmly packed
1 egg
1/4 cup mountain honey or herb honey
3 tablespoons chopped candied ginger
36 pecan halves

1. Adjust two racks to divide the oven into thirds and preheat to 350°F. Line cookie sheets with parchment. Sift together the flour, baking soda, salt, ginger, cinnamon and cloves.

2. In an electric mixer fitted with a paddle, cream the butter. Beat in the sugar to mix, then the egg, then the honey, and finally the candied ginger. On low speed, gradually add the sifted dry ingredients, scraping the bowl with a rubber spatula and beating only until thoroughly mixed.

3. Place the dough by well-rounded teaspoonsful on the baking sheets. Space them 3 inches apart. Place a pecan half on top of each cookie, pressing it slightly off to one side.

4. Bake until the cookies are richly browned all over, about 13 to 15 minutes. Reverse the cookie sheets top to bottom and front to back as necessary during baking to ensure even browning. Transfer the cookies to racks to cool. They will flatten and harden as they cool.

5. Store in an airtight container, or they will turn soft and limp.

32 COOKIES, PLUS A FEW FOR TASTING.

Walnut Cake

Adapted from Essentials of Classic Italian Cooking *by Marcella Hazan*
(Knopf, 1992)

This is a great dinner party cake, because you can make it ahead of time. In fact, you should make it a day ahead because it will taste better. It's also well behaved. There's no worry that it will fall apart or get sloppy when you're cutting it. And there are a number of things you can complement it with: crème fraîche ice cream, walnut ice cream, whipped cream, or just a good short espresso.

7 tablespoons unsalted butter, room temperature, plus more for greasing pan
1 cup all-purpose flour, plus more for flouring pan
1/2 pound walnuts
2/3 cup real white sugar
1 egg
2 tablespoons rum
Grated zest of 1 1/2 lemons
1 1/2 teaspoons baking powder

1. Place a rack in the upper third of the oven and preheat to 325°F. Butter and flour an 8-inch springform pan. Spread the walnuts on a baking sheet and place in the middle of the oven. They're ready when you can smell them, usually about 4 or 5 minutes. Take the walnuts out of the oven and increase the heat to 350°F. Let the walnuts cool completely.

2. Pour the walnuts into a food processor with 1 tablespoon sugar and grind, using the pulse button, to fine granules but not to powder. Pour into a bowl and reserve.

3. Place the butter in the processor with the remaining sugar and process until creamy. Add the egg, rum, lemon zest and baking powder and pulse until you have a uniform paste. Transfer to a mixing bowl.

4. Fold the ground walnuts into the butter mixture with a spatula. Sift the flour in small amounts over the batter and fold together. When all the flour is incorporated, pour the coarse and nubbly batter into the cake pan, leveling it off with the spatula.

5. Bake in the upper third of the oven. After 45 minutes, test the center of the cake with a toothpick. If it comes out dry, the cake is done. If not,

bake roughly 10 minutes longer. Remove from the oven and remove the sides of the pan. After the cake has cooled somewhat, invert it onto a plate and carefully lift off the pan base. Invert once more onto a pretty serving plate. Dust with confectioners' sugar. The cake's flavor improves the next day. If you ever make this cake and it seems dry, brush it with sugar syrup infused with whisky or rum. This will brighten it up.

A CAKE FOR 8.

Chapter 3

HIS TURN

Mr. Latte does not talk much in the morning. He might mumble a few monosyllables before we get to Xando, his favored café, but it isn't until after his coffee that he forms full and coherent sentences.

So I was taken by surprise one morning when he looked up from his paper and said, "I'd like to cook dinner for you." I thought it was the caffeine talking.

I'd had boyfriends cook for me, and as good as their intentions were, it was usually a disaster. One, who visited me when I was living in France, whipped up a roasted beef that gave me such a dose of food poisoning that I was in bed for the rest of his visit. But I quickly accepted Mr. Latte's offer. I was very curious. What could come out of a kitchen with a refrigerator containing only an unwrapped block of cheddar cheese, mustard, and a bottle of Moët & Chandon Champagne?

We settled on the following Saturday, and I was mildly dreading the week to come. All the tense questions; the requests for whisks and pots; a Friday evening spent at the grocery store. Of course, I did want to help out. Perhaps bring a side dish. Consult some of my cookbooks for him. And if it all flopped, well, then, we could always crack open that Champagne and call it a night.

Until this point, Mr. Latte hadn't spent much time in the kitchen. He'd made me a ham sandwich once. (Not bad: ham on whole-wheat bread with mayonnaise, thinly sliced tomato and a few basil leaves thrown in to good effect.) And his mother had mentioned a stint of cooking classes years ago, which apparently resulted in a short-lived flurry of dishes, all containing capers. But his kitchen these days was more like an attic; its cabinets held boxes of letters, a hammer, wrapping paper, a set of dusty margarita glasses and a terracotta planter.

The days that followed passed without a single mention of dinner. On Saturday morning we lingered over more mediocre coffee at Xando (my reluctant effort to meet him halfway on his food reform). He flipped the pages of the paper, slugged back his mocha, and caressed my shoulder from time to time, while I stewed over his nonchalance.

We headed downtown for a squash tournament. Mr. Latte played, then hung around to drink a beer with some friends. Shadows were growing long as we parted on Broadway and he headed to Fairway. He said to come over around seven.

At home, I leaned into my refrigerator and stared at a snowy round of goat cheese while a scenario took shape in my head: he wouldn't realize how long it took for a chicken to roast, the vegetables would get overcooked and it would be eleven before we ate dinner. I thought about nibbling on that lovely little cheese before heading over but decided I was being too much of a pessimist.

When I arrived, Mr. Latte kissed me at the door, dressed as always in a crisp shirt with dark dress pants and oxfords. His hands were cool and dry to the touch, and he wore a calm expression as he sat me down with a glass of wine. "I've got a little more cooking to do," he said. I'm sure you do, I thought. He rolled up his sleeves and returned to the kitchen.

The large mahogany dining table, which takes up most of his living room and catches the overflow of books and papers from his desk, had been cleared off. Two damask placemats floated on its surface. His college flatware was gone; antique silver was in its place.

Where had this other side of Mr. Latte been hiding?

I pretended to read, but from the kitchen I could hear gentle chopping, and the suction of the refrigerator opening and then settling closed. There was the tick-tick-tick of the gas igniting on the stove and eventually the light scraping sound of food going into serving dishes. While those little noises were like the cooing of a baby to me, I was still predicting a meat-and-potato extravaganza. When people cook for you, they usually cook what *they* like to eat. One of my sisters, for instance, has endured her husband making, for each of her birthdays, shrimp smothered in garlic and Tabasco sauce.

A few minutes later, Mr. Latte called me to the table, and set plates before us both. I bit my lip. There was chicken breast nestled in what looked to be a smooth velouté, a dollop of puree and couscous. Nary a caper in sight.

The puree was a sweet and peppery cloud of peas and watercress, made fluffy and creamy with a good deal of butter. The couscous was hearty and pleasantly sharp: Mr. Latte had cooked it in beef broth and stirred in red-wine vinegar, safflower oil, celery hearts and chopped parsley. It was like a warm salad and was perfectly seasoned.

He made me guess what was in the shiny yellow sauce on the chicken. It wasn't at all a velouté, which is rich and feels like velvet in your mouth. This had more heft and was tangy, even a little fruity. It was a delicious mystery. "Lemon, I think, and mustard," I said. Not quite.

There was lemon, but it was Meyer lemon. He had whisked the lemon juice with sour cream, Major Grey chutney, curry powder and, of all things, mayonnaise. He spooned it over the chicken and roasted it quickly in a hot oven. It sounds about as promising as green goddess dressing, but it was marvelous. And later, it occurred to me why. It has all the components of a good sauce: cream, egg yolks, lemon juice and salt.

We settled on the sofa and shared a bowl of sliced pineapple. My mind was filled with questions. Where did these recipes come from? How did he learn to cook so well? Why hadn't he seemed anxious about whether I would like it? *Why isn't there more food in his refrigerator?!* But I couldn't quite get them out.

"Thank you for such a lovely dinner," I said, instead.

"You're welcome," he said. "I'll be happy to do it again in 2002."

Mr. Latte's well-planned meal

Chicken Roasted with Sour Cream, Lemon Juice and Mango Chutney

Adapted from Fifteen Minute Meals *by Emalee Chapman*
(101 Productions, 1988)

I have sometimes considered swapping crème fraîche for the sour cream, and homemade mayonnaise for the Hellmann's, but then I resist. It is such a perfect concoction as is.

4 boneless, skinless chicken breast halves
1/2 cup Hellmann's mayonnaise
1/2 cup sour cream
2 tablespoons Major Grey mango chutney
1 teaspoon curry powder
Juice of 1 Meyer lemon or 1 regular lemon
Freshly ground black pepper

1. Preheat the oven to 450°F. Lay the chicken flat in a roasting dish (either Pyrex or enamel) that's large enough to fit the pieces in one layer. Whisk together the mayonnaise and sour cream. Drop in the chutney and curry powder and keep whisking until smooth. Add the lemon juice a little at a time and taste as you go. It should be quite tangy. Stop when it is to your liking.

2. Spoon the sauce over the chicken. Place in the oven and roast until the chicken is just cooked through, about 15 minutes. After you take it out of the oven, grind fresh pepper over top.

DINNER FOR 2.

Puree of Peas and Watercress

Adapted from Loaves and Fishes Cookbook *by Anna Pump*
(Macmillan Publishing, 1985)

This is also excellent with roasted duck and sautéed fish—red snapper and sole come to mind.

4 cups frozen peas
2 1-pound bunches watercress, trimmed of all but top 2 to 3 inches
4 tablespoons unsalted butter, cut into small pieces
1/2 teaspoon freshly ground black pepper
3/4 teaspoon sea salt

1. Fill a large saucepan with water and bring to a boil. Pour in the peas. When it returns to a boil, turn off the heat. Add the watercress tops to the peas and place a cover on the saucepan. Let sit for 5 minutes, so that the watercress wilts.

2. Drain the peas and watercress and transfer to a food processor. Add the butter, pepper and salt and process until smooth. Taste and adjust seasoning. Spoon into a pretty bowl.

A SIDE DISH FOR 4 (OR 2, WITH LEFTOVERS).

Couscous with Celery, Parsley and Red-Wine Vinegar

Mr. Latte has made this many times since. He served it with baked blue-fish when we were on vacation with his family and as an accompaniment to a Middle Eastern dish of chicken with prunes for a party. It's the kind of recipe that can slip in under many guises, and still be memorable. You may want to double it, as I have begun encouraging Mr. Latte to, because you will want leftovers.

    2 cups beef broth
    1 cup couscous
    5 tender inner stalks celery
    4 large sprigs parsley, stems removed
    1/4 cup safflower oil
    2 tablespoons red wine vinegar
    Sea salt
    Freshly ground black pepper

1. In a small saucepan, bring the beef broth to a boil. Place the couscous in a medium serving bowl. Pour the boiling broth over the couscous, cover with a lid or plastic wrap (Mr. Latte uses a dinner plate) and let stand for 5 minutes.

2. Finely chop the celery and parsley, then scrape them over the couscous. Sprinkle with the oil and vinegar, then stir until the couscous glistens. Season to taste with salt and pepper. Let sit for 5 minutes, then taste and adjust seasoning once more before serving.

COUSCOUS FOR 4 (OR 2, WITH LEFTOVERS).

Chapter 4

COOKING WITH JULIA

My mother likes to claim that I became a food writer because she used to feed me applesauce in my highchair while she watched Julia Child on TV. I don't remember this. (My mother also watched the tipsy Galloping Gourmet, and now I like wine, so who's to say?) My first conscious impression of Julia came almost a decade later when I saw Dan Aykroyd impersonate her, hacking a chicken to bloody bits on "Saturday Night Live."

Since then, it has been my peculiar good fortune to have crossed paths with Julia many times.

The first time I met her was a few years ago. I was living in Burgundy, where I was the cook for Anne Willan, the owner of École de Cuisine La Varenne. Anne is a friend of Julia's, so when Julia came to France to visit, I got the job of picking her up at Orly airport in Paris and driving her to Dijon. After peeling beans for weeks on end, it was like winning the lottery.

After an overnight flight, I expected an eighty-three-year-old woman to be weary. When the sliding doors of the terminal opened, Julia charged out, her finger jabbing the air, demanding, *"Où SONT les chariots?!!"*

As we sped down the A6, she talked my ear off. She had a one-star restaurant picked out for lunch. By the time we got to Dijon, it was past one and Julia was hungry. We pulled up to the restaurant only to find it shuttered. She was utterly deflated.

But a few moments later, we settled on a small bar-café, packed with clusters of French teenagers who were smoking like a paper mill. Their heads turned in concert as Julia sat down. Look, their faces said, some old lady has plopped herself down in the middle of our hangout.

Julia, oblivious to it all, ordered *oeufs mayonnaise* and a beer. It wasn't exactly the menu I had dreamed up for my lunch alone with her, but I ordered the same. I fumbled with the blob of mayonnaise on my plate trying to figure out what to do with it, then copied Julia. She ate hers euphorically, spreading the mayonnaise on the eggs, the baguette, anything that could hold it, and lifting her head now and then to look around, smiling to the teens, who smiled sarcastically back. She was in France. She was at home.

Nowadays, I see Julia fairly often at food events.

Indeed, at a book party recently, Julia's producer asked if I had spoken to her lately.

When I said I hadn't, he said: "Well, why don't you write her now and then. She'd love it."

I sketched out a letter in my head.

Dear Julia,

Um . . . wassup?

I couldn't think of a single thing to say. And this began to bother me. By now I should have studied her recipes and dug up old tapes of her shows. Her books on French cooking are *the* reason for the food revolution in America. If she hadn't clued us in to what was going on abroad, we'd still be drowning in green-bean casserole.

But for my generation, she is more the bird-voiced cook maniacally wielding a butcher's knife than someone who has taught us how to cook. My friends vaguely wonder if she's still alive. I tell them, yes, very. But the truth is, I'm no closer to the real Julia Child than anyone else my age.

I was beginning to feel like a fraud. Mr. Latte soothed me with gentle words for a little while. Then he put an end to it. "Why don't we have a dinner party," he said, "and you can cook from her books?"

A dinner party was the perfect solution. Not only could I get closer to Julia, but I could also get closer to Mr. Latte. It would be our first dinner party.

I began paging through *Mastering the Art of French Cooking: Volume I* and was reminded that it came from a time when you could get to know the authors simply by reading the recipes. For instance, after two pages of very concise instructions on making fish quenelles, they wrote, "If by any chance your quenelle paste turns out to be too soft to poach as quenelles, it will taste every bit as good if you declare it to be a mousse." Who else would have the nerve?

The dinner party menu emerged from Volume I: Roquefort cheese balls, *daube de boeuf*, *charlotte Basque* and, of course, those fish quenelles with truffle.

I sent an e-mail to Paula, a friend I met while cooking in France. "I'll eat anything with the word *'daube'* in it," she replied. Mr. Latte, who was practically spoonfed since birth from Volumes I and II, invited some of his friends, too. The party was on a Saturday, and I had a typical week, which began with two days of solid cooking for an article, my computer crashing, a four-hour lunch at Ducasse, a deadline, then dinner downtown.

There wasn't much time for planning.

I managed a trip to the East Village to buy black truffles, where I was led to a home refrigerator in the back of the shop with a huge padlock rigged onto it. When the owner opened it up, it looked like a wall of coal, neatly packed in plastic pouches. I imagined Julia shopping for truffles at a charming outdoor market in France. "These are just $600 a pound," the proprietor said, pointing to a shelf of pouches. The rest was a blur of scales, calculators and cash.

On Saturday, the day of the party, I didn't begin cooking until four. By six, I was hating myself for starting so late. And by eight, I figured out why people don't cook this way anymore. You need eight pans for every dish.

When the buzzer rang, I dashed into my bedroom to change my shirt and douse myself with Chanel. As everyone filtered in, Mr. Latte poured kir royales and offered cheese balls. He scored major points for his hosting abilities.

Paula arrived with a premier cru Chablis, a favorite of mine. Then I recruited her to make quenelles. She made perfect little ovals and dropped them into fish stock, whereupon they immediately split open, puffed up and turned mushy—nothing to do with her technique, everything to do with my quenelle mixing. I had been greedy, adding extra fish and truffles to the recipe. What punishment! I kept whisking my béchamel sauce, hoping the situation would change.

The quenelles were served: knobby, white lumps swimming in a white sauce; the $8 million truffles were suffocated. Everyone politely oohed and aahed.

The daube, however, delivered in a big way. The beef, after four hours in the oven, had turned to butter, and the smoky lardons had permeated every slice of carrot and every drop of rich, winey broth. I gave them all a breather course with tiny heads of bibb lettuce simply split in half and drizzled with red wine vinaigrette.

Then the confessions began to flow like the wine. Everyone, as it turned out, had something to say about Julia and especially about their own mothers. Rachel's had snubbed the Julia years for twelve years of wok cuisine. John's got hold of a crockpot and never let go. My mother was a great cook but never considered Julia an option: she couldn't afford the books.

Later, I pulled out the *charlotte Basque* that I had thrown together in a panic about an hour before everyone arrived. It was supposed to chill overnight in the refrigerator. I had stuck it in the freezer and hoped for the best.

Unmolded, it looked like a big, slightly lopsided pastel fez. The ladyfinger layers were, like many of Julia's desserts, wonderfully boozy (thanks to a quick swim in orange liqueur), and in between the filling was a kind of fluffy chocolate mousse flecked with crunchy almonds.

By the time Mr. Latte and I cleaned up, it was three in the morning. I lay in bed deliberating over the quenelles. I should have declared them a mousse, as Julia had instructed. Or had the sense to call on another of Julia's brilliant tips: that's what parsley is for.

I realized as I fell asleep that now I had something I could write to Julia: a thank-you note.

A Julia Child feast

Oeufs Mayonnaise

This dish is really just an excuse to eat mayonnaise. I highly recommend it.

1 egg yolk
1 tablespoon Dijon mustard
1 tablespoon red-wine vinegar
Coarse sea salt
Freshly ground black pepper
3/4 cup peanut oil
4 eggs
2 handfuls Bibb or Boston lettuce leaves
2 handfuls red-leaf lettuce leaves, torn into pieces
1 tomato, sliced into wedges (if in season and beautifully ripe; otherwise skip)
6 small radishes, cleaned, stems and leaves left on if in good condition
Extra virgin olive oil
2 teaspoons chopped parsley

1. First make the mayonnaise: whisk together the egg yolk, mustard, vinegar and a little salt and pepper. Very slowly add the peanut oil, whisking and whisking, so that the oil is absorbed after each addition and the sauce thickens to a paste. Correct the seasoning.

2. Bring a small pan of water to a calm simmer. Carefully lower the eggs and cook for 8 1/2 minutes. Carry the pan to the sink and run cold water into it until the eggs are cool enough to touch. Peel the eggs and cut in half.

3. Arrange the lettuces on two serving plates. If tomatoes are in season, lay wedges over the lettuce. Place the radishes off to the side. Sprinkle with olive oil and season with salt and pepper. Set the warm eggs on the bed of lettuce. Sprinkle parsley on top. Drop a large spoonful of mayonnaise on the side of the plate—for dipping both the eggs and the radishes between bites of salad. Serve with a cold lager beer, poured into a chilled pilsner glass.

LUNCH FOR 2.

Kir Royales

The kir royale is like a security blanket to me. After a long day, it eases you with a little sweetness and chirps you up with fizz. It is best to err on the side of too little cassis. You can always add more, but if you start out with too much, it's like a cherry pop and spoils the palate.

3 tablespoons crème de cassis
1 bottle good Champagne
6 twists of lemon

1. Fill the bottom of 6 Champagne glasses with 1/2 tablespoon crème de cassis. Pop open a bottle of Champagne and divide among the glasses. The color of the drink will be a sunset pink. Garnish with lemon twists.

APÉRITIFS FOR 6.

Amuse-Gueules au Roquefort (Roquefort Cheese Balls)

Adapted from Mastering the Art of French Cooking: Volume I
by Julia Child, Louisette Bertholle and Simone Beck (Knopf, 1975)

Now that fancy cheeses from around the world have given us cause to be snobby about yet another food, cheese balls have gotten lost on the map. It's too bad. They're not what I'd call a light snack, but they can be good, with an element of surprise. You can roll them in bread crumbs, as Julia does, or use panko, or ground nuts like pistachios and hazelnuts. You may also vary the cheese. Goat cheese, a thick ricotta, Camembert and Chaource would all work nicely.

1/2 pound Roquefort or other good soft blue cheese
6 tablespoons softened unsalted butter (not quite room temperature; it
    should be waxy so you can mold the cheese balls)
1 1/2 tablespoons minced chives
2 tablespoons finely minced celery
Pinch of cayenne pepper
1/8 teaspoon freshly ground black pepper
2 teaspoons Cognac
1/2 cup fine stale white breadcrumbs
2 tablespoons very finely minced parsley

1. Crush the cheese in a bowl with 4 tablespoons of the butter and work it into a smooth paste. Beat in the chives, celery, seasonings and Cognac. If the mixture is very stiff, beat in more butter by fractions. Check seasoning carefully, adding salt if necessary (probably not). Using two teaspoons, shape into quenelles or roll into small balls about 1/2 inch in diameter.

2. Toss the crumbs and parsley in a wide shallow bowl. Roll the cheese balls in the mixture so they are well covered. Chill. Serve as is or pierced with a toothpick.

ABOUT 2 DOZEN CHEESE BALLS (PLENTY FOR A PARTY OF 8).

Daube de Boeuf

Adapted from Mastering the Art of French Cooking: Volume I

Like most stews, this gets better the next day. Don't be intimidated by the lengthy ingredient list. It's actually quite a simple recipe.

3 pounds rump pot roast or chuck pot roast, cut into 2 1/2 inch squares, 1 inch thick
1 1/2 cups dry white wine or dry white vermouth
1/4 cup brandy, *eau de vie* or gin
2 tablespoons olive oil
2 teaspoons sea salt
1/4 teaspoon freshly ground black pepper
2 tablespoons thyme leaves
1 bay leaf, crumbled
2 cloves garlic, peeled and mashed
2 cups thinly sliced onions
2 cups thinly sliced carrots
1/2 pound lean bacon, cut into strips 1/4-inch thick (or the thickest you can find) and 2 inches long, simmered in water for 10 minutes, drained and dried
1 1/2 cups sliced mushrooms
2 1/4 cups canned whole, peeled tomatoes, drained and chopped coarsely
1 cup sifted flour, on a plate
1 to 2 cups beef broth

1. In a large nonreactive bowl, combine the beef, wine, brandy, olive oil, salt, pepper, thyme, bay leaf, garlic, onions and carrots. Cover and marinate at least 3 hours, stirring up frequently.

2. Remove the beef from marinade and drain in a sieve. Preheat the oven to 325°F.

3. Line the bottom of a deep 6-quart casserole with 3 or 4 strips of bacon. Strew a handful of the marinade vegetables, mushrooms and tomatoes over them. Piece by piece, roll the beef in the flour and shake off excess. Place closely together in a layer over the vegetables. Cover with a few strips of bacon, and continue with the layers of vegetables, beef and bacon. End with a layer of vegetables and 2 or 3 strips of bacon.

4. Pour in the wine from the marinade and enough stock almost to cover the contents of the casserole. Bring to simmer on top of the stove, cover tightly and set in lower third of the oven. Regulate heat so liquid simmers slowly for 3 to 4 hours. The meat is done when a fork pierces it easily.

5. Before serving, skim off excess fat. Correct seasoning. The daube can be served with boiled baby white potatoes, lightly crushed and seasoned with melted butter, coarse salt and chopped parsley.

DAUBE FOR 6.

Charlotte Basque

Adapted from Mastering the Art of French Cooking: Volume I

1 cup sugar
8 egg yolks
2 teaspoons cornstarch
3 1/2 cups boiling milk
5 ounces semisweet chocolate, chopped
2 teaspoons vanilla extract
1/3 cup orange liqueur
1 1/2 packages (7 ounces) crisp Italian ladyfingers
1/2 pound unsalted butter
1 1/3 cups ground blanched almonds
1/2 teaspoon almond extract
2 to 3 tablespoons rum
1 cup lightly whipped cream, plus additional for serving

1. Make a crème anglaise: Beat the sugar and egg yolks until mixture is pale yellow and thick. Beat in the cornstarch. Gradually beat in the milk so the yolks are slowly warmed. Pour the mixture into a large saucepan and set over medium heat, stirring slowly and continuously with a wooden spoon.

Heat gently until the sauce thickens just enough to coat the spoon. Off the heat, beat the sauce for a minute to cool it. Strain through a fine sieve and beat in the chocolate and vanilla.

2. Line the bottom of a 3-quart charlotte or soufflé mold with parchment or wax paper. Line the sides with a strip of parchment or wax paper extending the paper about an inch higher than the edge. In a soup plate, combine the orange liqueur with 2/3 cup water. Quickly dip in the ladyfingers, one by one, and drain on a baking rack. Line the bottom and sides of the mold with ladyfingers. (You need to cut ones for the bottom so that they fit together like daisy petals.) Reserve the remaining dipped ladyfingers.

3. Cream the butter and almonds in a mixer. Beat in 4 cups of the cool crème anglaise, then the almond extract and rum and then 1 cup whipped cream. (Adding the cream here is my own notion; contrary to one's usual expectations of cream, it actually lightens the dessert.)

4. Turn a third of the almond cream into the mold. Arrange a layer of ladyfingers on top. Repeat with two more layers of almond cream and ladyfingers. Trim off any ladyfingers extending above edge of mold, and press the trimmed-off bits into the top of the cream. Cover mold with parchment or waxed paper, set a saucer over the paper and place a 1-pound weight on top. Refrigerate for 6 hours, or overnight. The butter must be chilled firm so the charlotte does not collapse when unmolded.

5. To serve, remove the paper. Invert the charlotte onto a chilled serving platter. Remove the paper from the sides and top. Slice and serve with whipped cream.

8 HEARTY SERVINGS.

Chapter 5

FOODIES' FACE-OFF

It had been a while since I'd been out with foodies, and I let my guard down.

We were convening at Craft, a new restaurant near Gramercy Park. It was the place all foodies were talking about. "Can you *believe* how expensive it is?" one shrieked.

"Those leather walls are horrid," griped another. "And, the menu—preposterous!"

That's how foodies talk about even the finest restaurants. No one is ever optimistic about a restaurant for fear of looking silly if the place tanks. Better to predict doom and then be smugly triumphant.

There's a reason for this. Foodies are competitive. It's not enough to just eat well and enjoy it. You must be able to whip off commentary about the amuse-bouche at Daniel, know the bodega in Red Hook that makes the best churros, and be able to recite the last five restaurants Wylie Dufresne has worked at.

Many foodies are also overfed, which makes them cranky and jaded. Eat out too often and you find yourself saying things like, "That foie gras was so flabby!" and pooh-poohing meals that are fewer than three courses.

Normally I don't like to go to restaurants until they've been open for a few months. It takes a restaurant time to figure out what it's doing, how to define itself, and how to deal with that fickle beast otherwise known as the New York diner. But my friend, and new foodie, Adam, was going to review Craft and insisted we go when it opened. He wanted a range of unvarnished opinions, so he invited another friend of mine, Ms. Foodie. Mr. Latte came as well.

When I arrived late, two scotches and a pear Champagne cocktail were being delivered to the table. I ordered a glass of Manzanilla. There was a quick group evaluation of the room. We liked the broad, satiny Mission-style wood tables. The overhead lighting was unflattering to the face, we agreed, casting that Bermuda Triangle over the nose.

When the menus arrived, a foodie ritual took place. Everyone stopped talking and attacked the page with their eyes. This is done to stock up ammunition for future conversations ("You won't believe it: there's NO tuna tartare!"). And also to get dibs on what you want to eat. Foodies do not allow order overlap. If you want the lobster, you'd better claim it quickly. Adam was scratching his head furiously as his eyes flickered down the page.

With Craft's menu, you got to assemble your meal. You could have, for instance, raw oysters, roasted cod or braised red snapper. And with it, you could order arugula salad, roasted Jerusalem artichokes or lamb chops, if you so desired. It seemed perfectly suited to New Yorkers, who love nothing more than calling the shots.

"This menu is stupid," chirped Ms. Foodie. Adam squinted hard. "It's like a goddamn IQ test," he mumbled. "I like it," I said, indignantly. They looked up, expressionless. "What is up with the food at Town?" Ms. Foodie said. "Haven't had it," I replied. "But we've been to Beppe. You?" I could feel Mr. Latte tensing up. He suffers it politely, but foodie chat makes his skin crawl.

I plotted out a meal of oxtail terrine followed by roasted langoustines, braised ramps and roasted beets. But then the waiter suggested that rather than just having the oxtail terrine, we could have an assortment of charcuterie for the table. That meant less oxtail, and what promised to be every part of the pig turned into some form of rich, salted meat.

When I go out to a restaurant, I do not like feeling as if I'm at a buffet. I like to construct my meal thoughtfully and then eat it. I don't want to pass plates and I don't want someone plopping a slab of his skate in my lamb jus. It's disrespectful to the chef, who tries to create dishes that entertain your palate from the first bite to the last. And it's greedy. If you must taste other things on the menu, come back another time.

But I was overruled on the charcuterie. Foodies always want the selection. Adam ordered as if it was his last meal. Ms. Foodie took care of the wine, a 1999 Domaine Tempier rosé.

A conversation about film abruptly ended when the first course arrived. It was set out family style. Plump, wet belon oysters. Prosciutto, duck ham and dried sausage stretched across a platter. Two slices of foie gras terrine were set next to thick, airy toasts nestled in a linen napkin. A rectangle of oxtail terrine sprinkled with salt loomed over a coin-sized sliver of aspic. Fat spears of white asparagus were stacked like logs. A tangled mound of marinated octopus was placed next to a plate carrying a strange and fragrant mushroom called the hen-of-the-woods.

"Check out these carrots!" said Ms. Foodie. "Can you *believe* them?" She held one up for all to see. The slices of carrot were cut into a flower shape, a style not seen in New York since the days of Pavillon. They were harmless and amusing—but the sort of thing that I, in another mood, might also mock.

Soon, I had a circus going on at my place setting. I took a little oxtail terrine and a piece of sausage. Adam wanted me to try his octopus, and when he wailed with pleasure about the mushrooms, I soon had a piece of one, too. I resisted the foie gras, but Ms. Foodie dropped an asparagus spear on my plate. Mr. Latte gave me an oyster. It was cool and tender with a marvelous, sweet, iodine flavor. I don't remember a thing about the terrine.

Mr. Latte caught on to what was happening and stayed his own course. He ate all of his oysters, quietly moaning with delight. When the entrées arrived, he pulled his plates close, barricading himself with his food. He lifted the best, crispest pieces of chicken onto his plate, spooned on the cranberry beans and roasted cipollini onions and got to work. He sampled the sweet, roasted beet I put on his plate, and nothing else.

Meanwhile, I was caught up in a terrible gastronomic eddy. Adam turned to me. "Taste this!" he demanded, waving at his roasted lobster. "What's the herb in there?" he asked. Without fail, if you dine with foodies, this will happen. Someone will ask what it is they're tasting in a dish. Sometimes it is genuine curiosity. Sometimes it is to test you. Sometimes it is to give the questioner an opportunity to display his superior palate. You rarely know which.

Adam was still far too new and innocent for such trickery. "Tarragon," said Ms. Foodie, doing me a favor. I wanted to get back to my languoustines, which were cooked so perfectly they burst in your mouth.

Things sped up. Adam passed his potatoes and skewered one of my langoustines. My ramps traveled out of reach. Ms. Foodie insisted I try her lamb. The rosé was suffering under the cloud of flavors. By the time dessert came, I had tasted 18 dishes, and we had discussed every new restaurant—Beppe, Olives, Town and Virot—in detail.

I ordered a grappa with the glum hope that it would settle my stomach, and my annoyance. I could no longer speak. "So what do we think of this place?" Adam asked. Everyone shrugged. Mr. Latte, well fed and content, got back to chatting about golf with Adam and sailed out of the room ahead of me.

As I staggered out, I was flagged down by Jeffrey Steingarten. "What's good?" he asked. I fantasized for a moment about the idea of getting to start over, then clicked into foodie mode and delivered a short list.

A few days later I sat next to a veteran foodie at a dinner party. He mentioned that he doesn't like eating with foodies.

"It's just so uninteresting," he said, dragging a piece of bread through the moss-green sauce on his plate. "It's just this obsession with ingredients, this obsession with the restaurants. There's a lot of oneupmanship."

He said he was going to a place called Craft on Thursday. I said I'd been.

"What *is* it?" he asked.

"It's Tom Colicchio's new restaurant," I said.

"Ugh!" he groaned. "What's this one? What's the concept?"

A sound meal at home

Component Stew

Here, rather than preparing eighteen dishes, I've created one—a balanced one-pot meal—blending many of the best flavors I had at Craft. There's duck, chicken, mushrooms, tarragon, beans, even a little Manzanilla, too. Somehow having it all in one dish makes it more manageable, and, to my mind, more easily enjoyed. Mr. Latte, who ate this with great enthusiasm, gave the dish its name.

The recipe is much easier than the ingredient list would make it seem. Everything is done in the same pan. I use a Le Creuset braiser, which disperses the heat well so nothing burns and has well-rounded sides on the pan and lid so that as the liquid turns to steam and rises, it clings to the lid for a few moments before dripping back down, mingling all the flavors and keeping the chicken moist. (By the way, it is a braised dish, not a stew, but "component braise" didn't have quite the right ring to it, and stew is not so far off.)

Chop all your vegetables and collect everything near the stove, then it's just a matter of adding things to the pan. First, you brown the sausage, then the mushrooms, cipollini, leeks and chicken. Each of these gets added back in due time, so that all the components finish cooking together, yet each maintains its character.

At the very end, there is a tiny trick: rather than serving the dish straight from the braiser, you spoon the many parts into a serving dish, then boil the cooking juices with a splash of sherry and a sprinkling of tarragon. When you spoon this sauce over the chicken, duck and beans, it brightens their flavors and gives the hearty dish a little snap.

Please do not get caught up in tracking down every last ingredient. If you can't get duck confit, use smoked duck breast. No sausage? Try pancetta or bacon. If you cannot find cipollini, the tiny disk-shaped onion, skip them. A one-pot meal is meant to simplify your life. It's for when you are fed up with foodie mode and just want to eat something good.

2 tablespoons olive oil

2/3 pound sweet Italian sausage, cut into 1 1/2-inch pieces

2 cups thickly sliced mushrooms (cremini, or any variety of flavorful
    mushroom like chanterelle, bluefoot, hen-of-the-wood)

3 thin leeks, halved, rinsed well and cut into 1-inch lengths

1 cup peeled cipollini

4 chicken thighs

Coarse sea salt or Kosher salt

Freshly ground black pepper

1 cup chicken broth

1 fresh bay leaf (optional)

1 confited duck leg, meat cut from the bone, trimmed of fat and slivered

1 15-ounce can cannellini, great northern or any kind of plump creamy
    bean, drained and rinsed (use cranberry beans when they're in season;
    shell 1 1/2 cups and blanch them until tender)

2 tablespoons Manzanilla or fino sherry

1 tablespoon chopped tarragon

4 thin slices country bread (ciabatta, if possible), lightly toasted

1. Pour 1 tablespoon olive oil into a large enameled cast-iron braiser, or similar pan (a thick sauté pan with a lid will work just fine). Place over medium-low heat. Drop in the sausage and let it sizzle away, rolling only when the sides turn color. Brown all over. If you have a splatter screen, this is the time to pull it out, as fat will be popping everywhere. Spoon the sausage onto a plate layered with paper towels.

2. Add the mushrooms to the pan and brown on both sides. Spoon into a bowl. The pan may be dry by now. You can drizzle in another tablespoon of oil. Scatter the leeks and cipollini around the pan and increase the heat to medium so they color a bit; there's no need to cook them through because they cook more later. Sauté for about 5 minutes, then spoon them into another. Take the pan off the heat.

3. Season the chicken on both sides with salt and pepper. Put the pan back over medium-high heat and add the chicken skin-side down. Brown well, then turn and brown the other side, about 8 minutes total. Put the chicken on a plate, then drain the grease from the braising pan.

4. Slip the chicken back into the braising pan and pour in the broth. The liquid should just cover the base of the pan. Add the bay leaf. Adjust the heat

to low and cover the pan. Monitor the heat so that the surface of the liquid is wobbly with bubbles like a glass of freshly poured champagne. You don't want it to boil.

5. After 20 minutes, spread the sausage, mushrooms, leeks and cipollini, slivered duck meat and beans (don't forget to rinse off those thick can juices) over the chicken. Use a wooden spoon to gently nudge the different parts down in between the chicken. The cooking juices should be pushing up the sides but not soaking the components. Cover again, and continue cooking until the chicken is cooked through and the cipollini are tender, about 15 to 20 minutes.

6. At this point you can shut off the heat, cool it down and serve it the next day. If you wish to serve it the same day, I'd let it cool for an hour or so. This little rest gives the flavors a chance to blend and the meats time to reabsorb the moisture, which has cooked out. When you're ready to sit down to dinner, heat it up over medium heat until it's bubbling, then use a slotted spoon to transfer everything but the cooking juices to a warm serving dish. Bring the juices to a boil. There should be about 1 cup (don't bother measuring); if not, add a little more broth. Taste and adjust seasoning. Stir in the sherry and let it cook for a minute, then swirl in the tarragon. Pour this into a pretty little bowl and pass it at the table, following the stew.

Everyone's place should be set with a shallow bowl. As the stew and gravy are passed, have each person set a piece of toast in his bowl. Spoon over the stew and then some of the fragrant juices.

A DINNER FOR FOUR THAT CAUSES NO CONFUSION.

Lemon Sablés

If you want dessert, I'd suggest one of a few simple options: an apple tart (you can prepare the peach tart on page 198 with sliced apples; add a little grated ginger or freshly grated nutmeg to the crumble topping), these delicate lemon cookies, or my personal favorite, a glass of good Armagnac.

You may also enjoy the Armagnac with these cookies. Sablés are meant to be buttery and sweet with a fine crumbly texture, like sand (thus the name). I like them to be a little salty, so I've added additional sea salt. If it's early winter and you find Meyer lemons in your store, try the recipe with them. The cookies will be twice as good. Either way, the lemon flavor takes time to emerge, so try to resist them for a few days before serving.

2 cups all-purpose flour
2 teaspoons baking powder
2 sticks unsalted butter, at room temperature
1/2 cup confectioner's sugar
1/2 cup sugar, plus more for dipping cookies
2 tablespoons grated lemon zest (from 2 or 3 lemons)
1 teaspoon coarse sea salt or Kosher salt
4 egg yolks

1. Stir the flour and baking powder together in a small bowl. Scrape the butter into your mixer and beat until creamy (use a paddle attachment, if you have one). Add the confectioner's sugar and beat for a minute. Then add the regular sugar and beat for a minute more. Flick in the lemon zest and salt and mix just briefly. Drop in the egg yolks one at a time, and again, mix for just a few moments to combine. With the mixer on low, gradually add the flour mixture, and blend just until the dough is formed. Use a spatula to do any last mixing.

2. Divide the dough between two 1-foot-long sheets of plastic wrap. The dough will be quite soft, don't worry. Shape it into a rough log, 1 1/2-inches round. Wrap the plastic around the dough and continue shaping and rolling to form a nice round log. Twist the ends and tuck them under the log. Refrigerate for at least 2 hours and up to a few days.

3. When you're ready to bake the cookies, preheat your oven to 350°F and set a rack in the middle of the oven. Line two baking sheets with parchment paper. Lay a third sheet on the counter and pour out a ridge of sugar, approximately the length of the logs, for dipping them in. Then do just that: lay a log on the ridge of sugar and roll it lightly to press some sugar into its sides. Completely coat the logs with sugar, then slice them into 1/4-inch-thick slices. A long thin carving knife works well for this. Lay the slices about 3 inches apart on the baking sheets.

4. Bake for 12 to 15 minutes (turning the sheets 180°F halfway through) until golden on the edges. Cool on baking racks. Store in a cookie tin. It's best if you can hold out for a day or two before eating—good luck.

ABOUT 40 COOKIES.

Chapter 6

THE ART OF DINING ALONE

It was a summer holiday and Mr. Latte was in San Francisco for work. I e-mailed my friend Paula to see if she was free, but she had to go to a barbeque.

I suddenly had an excuse to perform an old ritual. After a long day, I often used to reward myself with a good meal. Alone.

The first night Mr. Latte was away had been a bust. After starting the day on a farm in South Carolina lunching on iceberg lettuce salad, venison lasagne and sweet iced tea, I had the taxi from the airport take me directly to a bistro in Chelsea. I was relishing the idea of ending the day at a New York City restaurant with a good cocktail and a quiet, simple meal. I was exhausted.

I ordered a drink that I wanted to taste for a story. Over the phone, the bartender had told me that it was on their list. But it wasn't yet, so once I asked for it, my identity was revealed. I had barely settled into my banquette when a woman approached me asking, "Are you Amanda?" I'm a terrible liar, and one's name is almost impossible not to answer to. "Yes," I said. "*Why?*"

It is not that I mind a little friendly chitchat, but restaurants have a stake in being excessively nice to food writers. To her, I was merely prey. Before I knew it, the bar manager had plopped down next to me, the owner had visited and three cocktails and an order of rabbit ravioli with morels and peas had been delivered to the table. I was coerced into ordering things I didn't want and was "entertained" between courses. I was hungry for dessert, but was so irritated that I got up to leave. A manager chased after me with a Popsicle in hand. "The chef would like you to try this," he said. Weighted down by a suitcase and bag, I was trapped. I couldn't leave until I finished it, which I did, sullenly, like a child made to eat her broccoli. When I got home, I sat on my sofa with a bowl of Häagen-Dazs coffee mocha chip ice cream and savored every placid bite.

People believe that dining alone will mark them as a loser or a desperate soul, one who can't find a friend in all the world to eat with them. But the reality is that other diners hardly notice you. And if they do, they probably think you are from another country.

In the same way that you should get massages and take naps or meditate, you should, everyone should, make a point to eat out by yourself from time to time. You should be kind enough to yourself to lavish your appetite with good food without the interruptions of company.

When you are by yourself, you have the chance to read the entire menu, take in the décor, observe the theater of the place and, most important, pay attention to the food. You can concentrate on the interplay of flavors rather than having to make a mental note to do so in between delivering anecdotes about your vacation. (If the company is good, I often come home forgetting what wine we drank or what the spice was in the cake.) You may sit by yourself, but you are never lonely.

Which is why some of the best meals of my life have been solitary. In Europe, dining alone is much more common than it is here. When I turned twenty-three, I took myself to lunch at La Côte St. Jacques, then a three-star restaurant in Joigny, France. During the six-course menu dégustation, none of the army of waiters in tuxedos seemed to pity me. None of the other diners in the room expressed disapproval. The only person disturbed by the event was my mother, when she got the bill.

On this recent Fourth of July weekend, I had less ambitious plans. I finished work around eight, got dressed in a pink sweater, khaki shorts and my favorite orange Japanese slippers—something I would wear on a date—and took a train downtown. I walked jauntily down West 13th Street toward Fressen, and came upon a closed door with no sign of life inside.

I would not be discouraged. I had a list of potential spots in mind, and I pursued it.

I passed Pastis. Too packed with loud, beautiful people.

Then Inside. Closed.

John's Pizzeria. Pizza alone *is* sad.

Po. Closed.

Pearl Oyster Bar was illuminated, and I was so ecstatic that I tripped as I rushed toward it. It looked different. For the first time, its window was not fogged up with diners' warm breath. You could make out the tile floor, and even a few open seats in the tiny sliver of a room. I wanted to sit at the bar, so I ordered a large bottle of Chimay and waited by the door.

I knew what I wanted: salt-crusted shrimp and a Caesar salad. But I read through the menu anyway. Pearl's is like a poem that you return to again and again. It never changes, yet each time the words leap out at you with new vitality. While I waited for dinner, I read a little, but mostly I just watched oysters get shucked and listened to those around me. And when my meal was set down before me at the marble bar, everything else faded away. The shrimp were coated in a generous crust of salt and pepper. Fried with their shells on, they crackled under my teeth as the warm, salty juices washed over my tongue. I drank my beer, then worked my way through the salad. The tender romaine leaves sagged a little under a salty, tangy dressing and a cloud of garlic. Every few bites I got dabs of anchovy and tough little croutons.

I had a buzz of euphoria, that brief feeling that makes you sometimes want to talk to the bartender or waiter. But I kept to myself. I listened as the regulars who stole my seat begged the chef to let them eat at Mary's Fish Camp, which is owned by her former girlfriend. When they split, one kept Pearl, and the other, in one of the great defiant acts of New York restaurant life, opened a restaurant with nearly the same menu just blocks away.

The chef was not pleased with this idea. "Come on," said the regular. "We just want to check it out and report back." "For what?" cried the owner. "They do the same thing as we do, only here it's done *better*."

Meanwhile, a young British couple sat down next to me and was stumbling through the simple menu. I had to fight hard to resist telling them what to have. They asked what a lobster roll was and seemed bewildered by the waiter's response. Have it! I wanted to shout.

The man ordered it, and I was so relieved that when I left, I gave

them the rest of my beer. Outside, feeling light on my toes and rejuve-
nated, I decided on a destination for my next solo outing: Mary's Fish
Camp.

A solitary meal
All recipes adapted from Pearl Oyster Bar

Salt-Crusted Shrimp

My friend Paula introduced me to these shrimp. They were served in a
tangle, crisp and hot. I began peeling away the shells, burning the tips
of my fingers, when Paula nudged my arm and whispered, "You're supposed to
eat the shells and all." Indeed. The shells are coated with cracker meal and
salt, and they're nice and crunchy. If you peel them, you miss out on half the
pleasure.

Vegetable oil or peanut oil, for frying
1/2 cup flour
3 tablespoons cracker meal
12 medium-sized shrimp, shells left on
Coarse sea salt
Freshly ground black pepper

1. Fill a deep saucepan with 2 inches of oil and heat to 350°F. Combine
the flour and cracker meal in a bowl. Dredge the shrimp in the mixture. Shake
off excess and drop into the oil. Fry until shrimp is curled and crisp, and just
cooked through, about 2 minutes. Drain on paper towels and shower with salt
and pepper on both sides of the shrimp. Rebecca Charles, the chef, says "At
the restaurant we serve this with a little cold vegetable salad, tossed with a
light vinaigrette, and tartar sauce. Sometimes we serve a cucumber, tomato
and red onion with dill, other times haricot verts, red pepper and carrot with
tarragon. But you can make a little salad out of anything."

A WARM SNACK FOR 4.

Caesar Salad

Chef Rebecca Charles would give out Pearl's recipe only in vague terms. She promised her mother, whose recipe it is, not to give out the complete version. This one is still a dandy, but if you figure out Pearl's secret, do let me know.

2 eggs
2/3 cup extra virgin olive oil
2 large cloves of garlic, finely chopped
1 teaspoon dry mustard
3 tablespoons lemon juice
Coarse sea salt
Freshly ground black pepper
4 slices day-old bread, cut into 1/2-inch cubes
2 small heads romaine lettuce (a mixture of red and green, if available),
    trimmed, large leaves discarded
4 anchovies, rinsed, dried and minced
1/4 cup freshly grated Parmigiano-Reggiano cheese

1. Fill a small pan with water and bring it to a boil. Lower the eggs on a spoon into the water and coddle them for about 45 seconds. Remove from the water. In a bowl, whisk together the olive oil, garlic and dry mustard. Crack the eggs into the olive oil mixture and whisk. Add the lemon juice and season to taste with salt and pepper.

2. Preheat the oven to 300°F. Toast the bread cubes on a baking sheet in the oven for 15 to 20 minutes; they should dry, not brown. Rebecca says, "You can use almost any kind of bread; my mother uses, of all things, English muffins. When baked, they get rock hard and stand up beautifully to the dressing." Tear lettuce into a large bowl; at Pearl Oyster Bar, they use a mixture of red and green romaine. Add anchovies, Parmigiano-Reggiano, croutons and half the dressing. Toss until leaves are generously coated. Taste a leaf, and add more dressing, anchovies or salt if you like. Place a handful on each of four plates.

SALAD FOR 4.

Butterscotch Praline Parfait

What makes this dessert is the bitterness in the praline contrasted with the satiny ribbons of butterscotch.

1 1/4 cups packed light brown sugar
4 teaspoons unsalted butter
1 3/4 cups heavy cream
8 ounces unsalted pecans (pecan pieces are less expensive and fine for this recipe)
2 1/3 cups sugar
Vanilla ice cream

1. For the butterscotch: in a 5-quart saucepan, combine the brown sugar and 1/4 cup water. Place over high heat and cook until the mixture is thick and foamy, about 3 minutes. Take it off the heat and add the butter, swirling the pan until the butter is melted. Return the pan to high heat, add the heavy cream and bring to a boil. Reduce until slightly thickened, approximately 5 minutes. Pour into a stainless-steel container and refrigerate until serving. (The sauce may be used warm or at room temperature. It can be refrigerated for a week.)

2. For the praline: preheat your oven to 350°F. Pour the pecans onto a baking sheet and toast in the oven for 5 minutes. Shake the pan once or twice so the nuts don't burn. Remove the pan and set aside. In a large saucepan, combine the sugar and 1/2 cup water over medium-high heat. When the liquid starts to turn amber, gently swirl it occasionally. Don't take your eyes off the mixture: it will foam up and will be done in seconds. The sugar should be a mahogany color. Immediately pour over the pecans. Let the praline cool completely. Invert the pan and whack the bottom with something heavy to release it. Rebecca uses the butt of a chef's knife. Break into chunks. It stores best in large pieces, but for the dessert it needs to be broken into smaller bits. Leftovers can be stored at room temperature in an airtight container.

3. When you're ready to serve the parfaits, warm the butterscotch in a double boiler or water bath. Fill four tall glasses with scoops of vanilla ice cream. Drop spoonfuls of butterscotch over the ice cream and speckle with shards of praline. Serve right away with long thin spoons!

PARFAITS FOR 4 WITH CONDIMENTS TO SPARE.

Chapter 7

A TOUGH ACT TO FOLLOW

She had a look on her face that I recognized all too well. Pride and excitement mingled with anxiety.

It's the "Oh, my God, a food writer is coming to dinner" expression.

Mr. Latte and I were visiting his parents for the weekend. And his mother, Elizabeth, a woman with glittering eyes, a Katharine Hepburn voice and a lively sense of humor, announced that she was cooking dinner.

We arrived late on Friday and had a busy agenda (golf, a visit with friends and a tour of the town) scheduled for the next day. I had assumed we would go out to dinner on Saturday. But when she said she would be cooking, I got tense, too. She and I were curious about each other. She was stylish, opinionated, and the mother of the man I adored. She liked food, read my articles, and wanted to know who was spending all this time with her son. We were both eager to impress.

Cooking has become an anxiety for most people, even if they are good at it. And my profession was clearly not helping the situation. Friends assume that because I have trained as a cook, I never make mistakes, and that because I am a food writer, I have no tolerance for ordinary food. But one of my favorite things is toast, and I burn it all the time. I'm also good at less reparable gaffes.

Once, when making potato puree, I decided to take a shortcut and stick them in the food processor. If you have never done this, here is what happens: the blade in the food processor slices across billions of starch cells, which then pop like water balloons and flood the puree. In about three seconds, the soft buttery puree thickens to the texture of Silly Putty. Another time, I planned to make wilted spinach for ten. After spending what seemed like hours washing and trimming a mountain of spinach, it hit the pan and collapsed into a heap the size of a tennis ball. The diners were already at the table; I had to serve it. So I did, in a small bowl with a tablespoon. I also once tried to save myself a little money by buying dried morel mushrooms rather than fresh for a risotto. The resulting dish tasted like dirt.

But I wasn't yet comfortable enough with Elizabeth to let her in on these truths. Mostly, I was trying to answer her many questions without saying anything absurd.

Elizabeth had her apron on and was working quietly in the kitchen when we came home from playing golf. I thought offering to help out would only make matters worse, so I kept clear of the kitchen. I wasn't worried about the meal. I knew Mr. Latte's sensibility about food had to have come from somewhere. On occasion, he reminisced about the

Baptist cakes and oatmeal-molasses bread his grandparents' cook, BaBa, had made. But there had to be an influence closer to home.

And I had checked out her kitchen.

It had Julia Child's signature pegboard wall, dangling with pots, ladles, rolling pins and sieves. There was a well-edited array of equipment, all neatly arranged and in reach of the stove. She had rings and rings of tart pans, their fluted edges worn to a matte patina, a seasoned wood salad bowl, an old and sturdy Dutch oven, and plenty of Le Creuset. All of her dishes were stored in a tall, slim, open cabinet on precisely measured shelves. They held stacks of round Asian bowls, delicate plates and teapots. There was a long wood worktable and a pantry for dry goods and a second refrigerator.

It was the workshop of a true cook: simple, organized and without pretense. She had blue and yellow Portuguese tiles trimming the walls and a Kitchen Aid mixer, but an ordinary stove and dishwasher.

I've been in too many beautifully designed kitchens where you can tell water has never been boiled. Anyone who displays oils and vinegars above her Viking stove has probably never turned it on. If she had, the intense heat would destroy whatever is in the bottles, if not shatter the bottles themselves.

Before dinner, Mr. Latte, his mother, his father and I gathered in the living room. His father, Dorie, stirred together Red Lions, a whopper of a cocktail made with Pusser's rum, orange juice, coconut syrup and Grand Marnier. We nibbled on a little cheese.

Dinner was served buffet style. There were two ducks, so gently, slowly cooked that they lay almost flat on the carving board. Sprigs of watercress poked out from beneath them. There was rice and a shaved vegetable dish that looked something like a hash. Dorie carved the ducks, which almost fell apart at the touch of a knife. Always a good sign. The skin was deeply caramelized and crisp, and the meat was succulent, with a heady infusion of soy, sherry, ginger and onions. It had been simmered for hours the day before and then gently roasted. The rice glistened. Elizabeth had used the broth made from braising the duck to cook the rice. The long, plump grains had soaked up the fragrant broth and were glazed with duck fat.

She had also shredded carrots and parsnips into long thin strands and then steamed them with butter in a sauté pan and finished them with a sprinkling of chopped tarragon. The parsnips added sweetness and lovely contrast to the savory duck and sharp heat of the watercress.

I tried to temper my enthusiasm, for fear she would think I was being disingenuous. Everyone toasted and then, as at many of the memorable meals I've had, we pursued the real purpose of gathering at a table. We talked. About Mr. Latte's writing. About his father's trip to Indonesia. About his mother's painting.

His mother disappeared into the pantry to fetch dessert. Mr. Latte squeezed my knee under the table and smiled. He knew what was coming. It was an almond cake. A pale yellow disk, dusted with confectioners' sugar. It had a crust, fragile like a dry leaf, that led to a moist, downy layer of ground almonds and sugar.

It was a perfect dessert. And it punctuated one of the great meals of my life. We all seemed much closer than when we sat down, and Elizabeth looked at ease.

There was just one problem: how would I cook for her?

Elizabeth's superb supper

Dorie's Red Lion

"One part Grand Marnier; 2 parts Pusser's (British Navy) Rum, or one part only for Elizabeth, who gets easily anaesthetized; 4 parts orange juice ('lots of pulp'); 1/2 part coconut syrup (Torani's), but leave out coconut if playing to he-men or purists. Elizabeth and I fill a glass with crushed ice, and stir. Enjoy!"

Ginger Duck

Adapted from Margaret Dunn, a.k.a. BaBa

This recipe comes from BaBa, Elizabeth's parents' beloved housekeeper. BaBa lived with the family for more than sixty years, and her cooking has influenced everyone down to Mr. Latte's generation. I fear ever cooking Baptist cakes for him, because I know they will never match BaBa's!

When Mr. Latte and I visited a few months later, Elizabeth served spinach fettucine tossed in a creamy sauce with roasted turkey and mushrooms. It's not the kind of dish that you expect to be anything more than satisfying, but this was exceptional. The sauce, which had the depth of demiglace, infused the noodles, the turkey, the air in the kitchen. To make it, she first prepared a blond roux (3 tablespoons each flour and butter), then whisked in the leftover duck broth (1 cup) that she had frozen, and finished the sauce by stirring in cream (also 1 cup), sautéed mushrooms (1 cup) and slivers of leftover roasted turkey (2 cups). Once it was folded into the pasta, she sprinkled it with lots of Parmesan cheese.

1 duck (thawed overnight in the refrigerator), giblets removed
1 onion, peeled and cut in half, or 3 shallots, peeled
2 stalks celery, cut into 3-inch long pieces
2 teaspoons ground ginger
1/2 cup sugar
1/2 cup soy sauce
1 teaspoon sea salt
1/2 cup sherry
1 small bunch watercress, trimmed and washed

1. The day before, stuff the duck with the onion and celery. Place the duck, breast side up, in a large soup pot with enough water to half cover it. Add the ginger and bring to a boil. Cover and reduce the heat so that it simmers very gently (the bubbles should be lazy not fizzy) for 1 hour.

2. After 1 hour, turn the duck over. Add the sugar, soy sauce and salt. Continue simmering for another hour. Turn duck once again and simmer until tender and almost falling apart, about another hour. Turn off the heat and

when cool enough to handle, remove the duck carefully from the pot (it tends to fall apart after so much cooking) and place in a roasting pan. Cover and refrigerate until the next day.

3. Pour the broth from the soup pot into a container and chill overnight. A layer of fat will form on top. Scrape it off and discard it. What remains is delicious in rice (see recipe below) and soups and can be frozen for months.

4. Before serving, bring the duck to room temperature. Preheat your oven to 350°F. Add the sherry and 1 cup of the defatted duck broth to the roasting pan and place in the oven. Roast uncovered for 30 to 45 minutes, basting occasionally with the juices in the bottom of the pan. The duck is done when it is heated through and the skin is crisp and a dark chestnut brown. If the duck does not brown to your liking, place under the broiler for a few minutes to crisp the skin.

5. Transfer the duck to a serving platter and garnish with lots of watercress (disguising where legs and wings have fallen off, if they have).

DINNER FOR 4, WITH NO LEFTOVERS. RECIPE CAN BE DOUBLED; ELIZABETH USUALLY COOKS 2 DUCKS AT A TIME.

Rice Cooked in Ginger Duck Broth

Adapted from Elizabeth who adapted it from The New York Times Cookbook, *edited by Craig Claiborne (Harper & Brothers, 1961)*

4 tablespoons unsalted butter
l large onion, minced
1 clove garlic, minced
1 cup rice
2 cups defatted ginger duck broth (see recipe above)
Sea salt
Freshly ground black pepper

1. Melt the butter in a medium enameled iron (or other heavy material, which heats evenly) casserole over medium heat. When it foams, scrape in the onion and garlic and sauté until the onion is translucent. Pour in the rice and cook until the rice turns golden, adding more butter if necessary. Add the broth and cover with a tight lid. Bring to a boil, reduce the heat to as low as possible and simmer until the rice is tender, 16 to 20 minutes. Remove the lid to allow the rice to dry, and season with salt and pepper.

A SIDE DISH FOR 4.

Shredded Carrots and Parsnips

Adapted from Elizabeth who loosely adapted it from the
"Cuisinart Instruction Manual," 1984.

By shredding the carrots and parsnips, you release their sweetness and moisture. And the thin shreds feel miraculously light on the palate.

8 tablespoons unsalted butter
5 medium carrots, peeled and shredded (done most easily in a food
    processor with the grater attachment)
5 medium parsnips, peeled and shredded
Sea salt
Freshly ground black pepper
2 teaspoons chopped fresh tarragon

Melt the butter in a large sauté pan or skillet over medium heat. When the butter foams, add the carrots and parsnips and sprinkle with a little salt and pepper. Cover and cook over low heat, stirring occasionally, until just tender, about 15 to 20 minutes. They will wilt and may look lifeless, but they've got lots of flavor. Sprinkle over the tarragon and stir to incorporate it. Season to taste with salt and pepper.

VEGETABLES FOR 6.

Almond Cake

Adapted from Elizabeth

If you ever get in a Martha mood, bake this cake. It may be served plain, or with whipped cream, if you're feeling indulgent, and with berries in the summer time.

In this recipe, you may divide the batter so you get two flat 8-inch cakes, but Elizabeth bakes just one in a 9-inch springform pan. "You open the oven door," Elizabeth says, "and it looks great. And two minutes later, it's Grand Canyon department."

The center always sinks like a well, but it's okay.

Elizabeth says you can store the cake in a covered tin in or out of the fridge. It improves with age and can be made one to two weeks ahead.

2 sticks unsalted butter, softened, more for buttering pan
1 cup sour cream, at room temperature

1 teaspoon baking soda
2 cups sifted all-purpose flour (measured after sifting)
1/2 teaspoon sea salt
1 1/2 cups sugar
7-ounce tube almond paste, cut into small pieces
4 egg yolks, at room temperature
1 teaspoon almond extract
Confectioners' sugar, for sifting over cake

1. Preheat the oven to 350°F. Butter sides and bottoms of one 9-inch springform pan; line sides and bottoms with parchment paper. Butter the paper. (You may forego the parchment paper as long as you are generous with the butter on the pan itself.) Mix together the sour cream and baking soda in a small bowl. Sift the flour and salt into another bowl.

2. In the bowl of an electric mixer fitted with a paddle, cream the butter and sugar until fluffy. Add the almond paste, a little at a time, at medium speed, and beat for 8 minutes. Beat in the egg yolks one at a time, and mix until incorporated. It will look curdled; don't worry. Blend in the almond extract and sour cream mixture. Reduce mixer speed to low and gradually add the flour mixture, just until blended.

3. Pour the batter into the prepared pan and spread evenly. Bake about 1 hour. It is done when you press the top and it returns to its shape, and also shrinks from the sides of the pan. Remove from the oven and place on a baking rack to cool in the pan. When ready to serve, sift confectioners' sugar on top and slice like a pie.

ONE SUNKEN BUT DELICIOUS CAKE, SERVING 10.

Chapter 8

THE ROOFTOP PARTY

I hadn't spoken to Peter, a radio food critic, in ages. He called and left a solemn, rambling message, something about a six-month leave of absence, a death in his family, and his return, like a soldier from war, to the city.

We played a lengthy game of phone tag, and eventually, when we spoke, he suggested a quiet dinner. "I'd like to catch up," he said seriously. A few days later, he called to ask, "Can Billy come?" Sure. And later, "Billy can't come. But do you mind going to Tama's?" Not at all.

I didn't know any Tamas but one of the great pleasures of living in

New York is the opportunity to let its current carry you. Make friends with a friend of a friend and he or she will take you to new circles, and circles in New York are surprisingly small and insular. As the outsider, you get to swim around, observe and eavesdrop for a few hours and then leave, usually with a few business cards and offers to get together. You can come back, if you wish, if you try hard enough, or wait to be floated to the next circle. I tend toward the latter, preferring to hear new voices, see how others live, watch what they eat, and then return to my own pool of friends.

Tama, as it turned out, was the author Tama Janowitz. And she was having people over to her apartment in Brooklyn for the director James Ivory's birthday. This added intrigue, and anxiety. A couple of years ago, Ivory's partner, Ismail Merchant, asked me to lunch, hoping it would inspire an article. He is known for his skills in the kitchen, and has even written a few cookbooks. I believe he is a good cook, but was wary of the celebrity angle and the aggressive pitch. I ate, nodding here and there to be polite, and as he droned on about himself, I checked out the room, made a to-do list in my head and got swept up in every dreamy spoonful of a pistachio and coconut milk rice pudding I ordered for dessert. Then I went on my way. I wasn't eager to cross paths with him again, particularly as I hadn't seen either of his last two films.

Peter, my sponsor in this engagement, was a shining example of good social training. The night of the dinner party he was dressed like a French aristocrat, his plaid sports coat stuffed with a silk handkerchief. He wore delicate gold-rimmed glasses that occasionally slipped down his fine, thin nose.

He had a town car pick me up, and we swung by Jacques Torres's new chocolate factory in Dumbo to pick up a "golden bowl" he had commissioned for Mr. Ivory. It looked like a Roman wine goblet (made of chocolate), and was covered with a lavish daubing of gold leaf and filled with chocolate-covered macadamia nuts. I tried to conceal the $12 bottle of Lustau sherry I had brought behind my elbow.

We arrived at a building imprisoned by scaffolding, shuffled through its vast lobby, and ascended to the penthouse. I felt like we were in a midtown office building: most people I know do not live higher than the sixth floor. A pale, bald man opened the door and let us in, and we were soon introduced to Willow, Tama's playful, precocious daughter. She renamed me Apple and pulled me out onto the terrace, where there was an abundant table of hors d'oeuvres. One plate was covered with folds of bresaola, prosciutto and soppressata. There were fat asparagus spears, radishes with their tops, artichoke hearts and many kinds of olives, all glistening in the twilight.

Tama entered wearing long, slim, brightly patterned pants and a black shirt. Her black hair was big and chaotic with a ribbon of silver near to her scalp. She had on shiny blood red lipstick, and she radiated warmth and social unease. I liked her immediately.

She asked my name and took me by the arm to meet people. "I'm not very good at this hostessing thing," she said, "It's not what I do." She bobbed around the terrace, offering verbal captions to get things going. "This is Daisy. She does art stuff." "Do you know Jane? She has the best yard sale in the Hamptons."

A large, lively crowd poured in around nine. Bottles of wine emptied, the bresaola vanished. Willow flitted like a moth from group to group. Peter drifted from view. There were editors, writers, editors who quit to become writers, fashion people and the two filmmakers. The moon hung like a giant orange yolk just above the horizon, somewhere in Queens.

Dinner was served buffet style. As I picked up one of the mismatched plates and flatware, a man carrying a bright red suitcase dashed through the room, holding it above our heads, like someone running a bucket of water to a fire. He looked wild-eyed. "Oh that's Tim!" announced Tama, "That's my husband, the one who looks like a crazy person rushing around. He's leaving tonight. He's pretending we're not here!"

Everyone smiled after Tim. I spooned a little lasagne on my plate, aiming for a piece with the thickest, fluffiest looking layer of ricotta. I took some salad and a little garlic bread. People dispersed around the apartment, as guests will do. You don't need to have every detail plotted out. They will find the wine and pour it. They will find the bathroom and use it. They might even discover a stash of chocolates and eat them.

The woman with the outstanding yard sale asked me to sit with her at the main dining table, which was set with placemats decorated with a happy, dancing cat. The lasagne, prepared by Tama, was hearty with thick pieces of sausage and spinach tucked between layers of pasta and cheese. I drank my red wine greedily. I had avoided Mr. Merchant during the cocktail hour, but then he sat down at my table.

A calm overtook the room, with the gentle rise and fall of people's voices. Then Tama appeared, walking gingerly and singing "Happy Birthday" as she carried in a tall, plump layer cake showered with bright blue grated coconut. It glowed in the candlelight, like a tropical fish. People sang. Willow climbed on my lap and ate my cake, and then some macaroni. The golden bowl was set before Mr. Ivory. He sighed and smiled. "It's quite something," he said. People began passing the bowl around the table, and eating the macadamia nuts.

Then a small older woman sitting next to Mr. Merchant nudged him and whispered. "Yes, YES, I do know Amanda," he said, his voice gaining strength until it boomed across the table and heads turned, "We met and I wanted her to write about me, and she said NO!" I waved sheepishly, and took a deep interest in my cake crumbs.

Tama swooped in next to me. She wanted to talk about the food business. She had recently been to a foodie event. "I didn't realize there was so much glitz and glamour in the food world. It was like fashion or something," she said. "With better catering," I said, thinking that I've never considered figures like Bobby Flay or Sirio Macchioni glamorous, just savvy.

When Peter and I were leaving, Tama stood at her door like a schoolteacher saying goodbye to her students for the summer. She seemed like she would miss every one of us. Meanwhile, people were busy teaming up to share taxis and town cars, looking at their watches and thinking of the next event: sleep. I would probably never see any of them again.

Peter and I were back in the car and my little swim was coming to a close. "We'll have to do this again soon," Peter said, as we crossed the Brooklyn Bridge into Manhattan. "We didn't get much time to catch up."

Birthday cake for fresh faces

Coconut Layer Cake

Adapted from Maida Heatter's Book of Great Desserts *by Maida Heatter*
(Andrews McMeel, 1999)

This coconut cake looks like a fluffed-up feather bed. It's tender and a little saggy on the edges, drooping under the weight of the delicious coconut icing.

    2 1/2 cups sifted cake flour
    1 tablespoon baking powder
    1/4 teaspoon salt
    1 stick (8 tablespoons) unsalted butter
    1 teaspoon vanilla extract

1 1/2 cups sugar

2 eggs

1 cup milk

Finely grated zest of 1 large orange (or 2 small)

A few spoonfuls of melted and strained apricot preserves

For the fluffy icing

4 egg whites

1/4 cup light corn syrup

2 tablespoons water

2 1/2 cups confectioners' sugar

Pinch of salt

1 teaspoon vanilla extract

1/4 teaspoon almond extract

4 cups moist, finely grated coconut

1. Adjust rack to center of your oven and preheat oven to 375°F. Butter two 9-inch round layer cake pans. Line the bottoms with parchment paper, butter the paper, and then dust the pans lightly with flour. Set aside. Sift together the flour, baking powder and salt and set aside.

2. In the bowl of an electric mixer, beat the butter to soften a bit. Pour in the vanilla and sugar and beat for a few minutes. Drop in the eggs and beat until smooth. On lowest speed add the dry ingredients in three additions—alternately with the milk in two additions—scraping the bowl with a rubber spatula as necessary and beating only until smooth after each addition. Remove from mixer and stir in orange zest.

3. Divide batter between prepared pans. Tilt and shake pans gently to level batter. Bake until cakes come away from sides of pans and tops spring back when lightly touched, 25 to 30 minutes. Remove from oven and let stand for 5 minutes. Cover with baking racks and invert. Remove pans and papers. Cover with racks and invert again. When the layers have cooled completely, place one layer on a cake plate, upside down. Using a narrow metal spatula, spread with a thin layer of apricot preserves.

4. Now prepare the icing (you'll get back to the cake later): Mix the egg whites, corn syrup, water, confectioners' sugar and salt in the top of a large double boiler. Place over hot water on moderate heat. Beat with an electric mixer at high speed until mixture stands in peaks when beaters are lifted, about 5 minutes. Immediately transfer to a large bowl to stop the cooking.

Add the vanilla and almond extracts, and continue beating, scraping bowl often with a spatula, until very thick and smooth, about 5 minutes more. At this point, you may add a few drops of blue food coloring if you want your cake to be blue like Tama's.

5. Spread 1/3 of the icing on the bottom layer and sprinkle with 1/3 of the coconut. Place the second layer on top, right side up. Spread the top with the remaining preserves. Spread the remaining icing on the top and sides of the cake. With the palm of your hand, press another third of the coconut onto the sides and sprinkle the remaining coconut evenly over top.

ONE FLUFFY CAKE, ABOUT 10 SLICES.

Chapter 9

THE MAN WHO MADE ME EAT EVERYTHING

I met Jeffrey Steingarten, the food writer for *Vogue*, in 1997, shortly after I moved to New York from my home town near Scranton. A colleague invited me out for a restaurant review. She had asked Jeffrey and his wife to come as well.

I admired Jeffrey's work and was excited to meet him. Soon after the meal began, Jeffrey sized me up. He is an expert on bread baking, and he had discovered that I had worked at a pizza place in Rome. "So tell us," he began, "how hot is it exactly at the back of a pizza oven?"

I looked to my colleague and Jeffrey's wife for help, but they were waiting for my response. I thought it was 700 degrees, but I wasn't going to risk being wrong. So I firmly said, "Very."

Jeffrey's left eyebrow shot up, and he smiled. I smiled back. We would get along.

I would not categorize Jeffrey as a foodie. A bon vivant, perhaps. A gourmand. A gourmet too. He travels the world, writes ten times a year and may know more about food than any man alive.

Jeffrey is not a large man, but he eats like one. He seems always to be hungry, and always to have several hours set aside to linger over a meal. I sometimes wonder if he takes a break between lunch and dinner or simply gets up from one table and makes his way to the next. But despite a passion for eating, he is not easy to eat with. Over the course of a meal, he can be difficult, provocative, witty, amusing and, often, exhausting.

His problem is that he was born in the wrong century. He would have done much better at Versailles, where he could have supped for hours, begun and ended meals with oysters and discoursed with fellow courtiers on the finer points of the pea.

Instead, he must live in ruder times and dine with people like me.

That first dinner led to more dinners. One was with an editor from L.A. We went to Nobu, and Jeffrey did the ordering, which is always alarming. You have no idea what you will be having, how much you'll be having and when it will end. Asking would only invite mockery.

The courses rolled in one after the other, a blur of Kumamoto oysters, yellowtail, fluke and black cod. At the ninth course I stopped cleaning my plate. I wasn't sure how much more I could stand. Jeffrey took notice during the tenth and asked: "What's wrong with you? Are you watching your weight?" Our waitress, who was setting down more sake, butted in. "If I ever ate as much as she's had to eat, I think I would be dead," she said.

"Who asked you?" Jeffrey said.

But I continued dining with Jeffrey, often calling him to make a plan; we ate at Pearl Oyster Bar and Artisanal and Veritas. At first, his coarseness seemed part of a hazing process. Then I realized it was actually his personality. But he grew on me. When he picked on me for not knowing the pH level of ice wine, I picked on him back about his leisurely lifestyle. I think he liked such banter, seeing himself as a mentor and me as the poorly behaved protégée. I was fascinated by his insatiable appetite. And I liked that he was uncompromising.

One night recently, we started out at his apartment for apéritifs. We drank Scotch while Jeffrey reproduced an hors d'oeuvre he had had at Le Cirque 2000. It was toasted circles of brioche (which he had baked), topped with a quail's egg and a cluster of caviar, a clever riff on three eggs: chicken, quail and sturgeon. It was extremely tasty. He also served me blood sausage, which he had helped make during a pig butchering in France, then sneaked through Customs. He gets paid to do such things. No doubt, the journey also included a few three-star restaurants in Paris.

Our amuse-bouche was followed by dinner at La Lunchonette, a French bistro. It was winter, so we ordered rich, fatty foods like foie gras and venison in a wine sauce. During the venison course, my stomach began to make sharp, penetrating rumblings. Moments later, I was crouched over in my seat, like a basketball player on the bench. Jeffrey took no notice. I interrupted him midsentence to excuse myself. He shrugged and kept eating. In the bathroom, the first stages of food poisoning took hold. I made two more visits to the bathroom in the next half-hour. Jeffrey kept working on his venison. When I returned the third time, I said, "I'm sorry but I have to go home." I was as white as a sheet and sweating like a glass of beer on a hot day.

"You do?" he asked.

"Yes, *right now*," I said and staggered toward the door.

Jeffrey took a last bite, then hurried after me, waving a credit card in the air. He insisted on helping me get home. It took a few stops, including one in the center lane of West End Avenue. He directed traffic while I huddled by the taxi's back tire. He opened my apartment door for me, deposited me inside and called the next morning. My answering machine picked up. "Amanda, it's Jeffrey. Are you still alive?" he asked.

Though he probably gave me the worst case of food poisoning I've ever had, he also showed a never-seen soft, nurturing side. (And I revealed a side best kept to one's college friends.) We bonded, sort of.

What to eat when you've had too much

Chopped Salad of Romaine, Arugula, Dill and Lemon

You can make a meal of this salad, and I often have. I serve myself a tiny bowl of niçoise olives and pour a glass of Sancerre or Fino sherry. With the salad, I eat dark country bread and slices of feta or an aged goat cheese, sprinkled with olive oil and freshly ground black pepper.

    4 cups thinly sliced (1/4-inch) romaine leaves
    2 cups packed arugula leaves, chopped into 1/2-inch pieces
    1 1/2 tablespoons chopped dill
    1/3 cup thinly sliced scallions
    Sea salt
    Freshly ground black pepper
    1 tablespoon lemon juice
    1 tablespoon grated lemon zest
    1/4 cup excellent olive oil

In a nice big salad bowl, mix together the romaine, arugula, dill and scallions. Sprinkle with salt. Grind pepper on top. Sprinkle the lemon juice and zest over the leaves. Pour on the olive oil. Using a salad fork and spoon, mix the leaves together, folding them over again and again, until all the strips of lettuce are coated and the flavors are blended. Taste a leaf. Season again with salt, pepper, lemon juice or more oil, whatever is needed to make it taste balanced and good.

SALAD FOR 4; IF YOU HAVE THE OLIVES, BREAD AND CHEESE WITH IT, IT CAN SERVE AS A LIGHT MAIN COURSE.

Beet and Ginger Soup with Cucumber

1 1/2 pounds small beets, trimmed and scrubbed
3 tablespoons olive oil
Sea salt
1 small leek, trimmed and chopped
1 clove garlic, smashed
3 tablespoons chopped ginger
3 cups chicken broth
Juice of 1 lemon
1/2 English cucumber, peeled, seeded and chopped into 1/8-inch cubes

1. Preheat your oven to 325°F. Place the beets in a bowl and sprinkle with 1 tablespoon of oil and season with salt. Toss to coat. Place the beets on half of a large sheet of aluminum foil, and fold over to make a pouch. Seal tightly. Place in the oven and roast until a fork easily pierces the beets, about 1 hour and 15 minutes. Remove from the oven and let cool. While the beets are still slightly warm, remove the outer skin by rubbing them gently with a towel. Cut the beets into quarters.

2. In a large soup pot, warm the remaining olive oil over medium heat. Add the leek and cook until it begins to soften, stirring occasionally, about 5 minutes. Flick in the garlic and ginger; cook for 2 minutes more. Season lightly with salt. Add the beets, chicken broth and 3 cups of water. Bring to a simmer and cook for 10 minutes.

3. Transfer the soup in batches to a food processor and puree until smooth. Then return the soup to the pot and place over medium heat. Taste and adjust seasoning, adding more salt and lemon juice to taste and more ginger if you wish. Just before serving (the soup should not be served too hot; it could even be served chilled or at room temperature), add the cucumber to the soup and stir. Ladle into bowls. You may serve this with a dollop of crème fraîche.

SOUP FOR 4.

Chapter 10

LETTING GO

Friends often come to me with their food confessions.

"I didn't know what butter was until I went to college," a friend once told me. "I still hold it against my parents." (She should.) One friend cooks in her underwear. Another gets cravings for Lance's cheddar and peanut butter crackers.

I listen. I nod. I sometimes wish they hadn't told me. But the other day, one confession hit a nerve. I was having a drink with a friend, and we began talking about cooking. "I'm a kitchen nazi," she said. "Really?" I said calmly. Inside, I squirmed.

"I'm a terror," she said. "I boss people around. I have no patience for someone who doesn't know how to roast a chicken. I've even told one boyfriend's mother how to cook in her own kitchen." Oh, good, I thought. I'm not *that* crazy.

But I was pretty bad. Mr. Latte had broached the topic with me, and I had shut him out. I didn't want to hear it.

I have never been the type of cook who welcomes friends into my kitchen to make salad or to chat with me while I am cooking. I am not mentally coordinated enough to simultaneously sauté and tell a story. But more than that, I prefer the solitude of a kitchen; I like to hear the faint crackle as my knife slices into a fresh onion, to watch butter and sugar meld into milky fluff as I whisk. Sometimes I like to think: dream up travel plans, retrace my day or imagine an argument with my mother in which I win. I like to chop garlic, dice tomatoes, and carve chicken from its bones to relieve tension, just as someone else might go run a few miles.

My behavior comes partly from being trained in restaurant kitchens, where the work is solitary and intense. You work quickly and efficiently, following a set of classic techniques. If you need something, you ask in plain language and you get used to people barking back at you— "Your sauce is sloppy. Fix it!"

For the past four years, though, I have cooked alone. I have a small kitchen, with little room for another person. I spend more time in it than any other place in my apartment. It contains the objects I treasure most. A bone-handled fork my mother gave to me, copper pans I bought in Paris, plates my sister made, photos of my family on the refrigerator door. I keep bottles of my favorite oils in the refrigerator along with chocolates from France and often a good cheese. Many times, I've leaned on the sink, eating a mango or drinking a glass of wine, while staring at the water tower outside my window. I've spent hours at the tiny square of counter measuring flour, whisking eggs and sugar, pitting cherries. It is my sanctuary. I know how it runs, and I don't want anyone to disturb it.

The kitchen is an ecosystem. Vegetables, milk, fish, crackers, eggs move through it; fruits ripen and wilt. There are bottles of mayonnaise and horseradish that stay forever on the refrigerator shelves, while other foods like parsley, chicken and butter arrive and are soon transformed into something else. Plates, pots and utensils flow steadily from cabinet to stove to table to sink. And though it is meant to be a shared space, one person has to keep track of it all. This is why many people are territorial about their kitchens—and why as many issues get played out in them as do in the bedroom.

There are a few people—my sisters, my mother and a couple of friends—I have fun cooking with. I have grown used to the way they move, the kinds of foods they like to cook, the mix of conversation and silence. But these relationships took time to develop. Mr. Latte is still new and untested.

I haven't made it easy on him. I've sent him on far-off errands (Me: "Could you go to the wine store for a bottle of Riesling?" Him: "O.K., but you know you've already got five bottles, right?") and given him dull tasks like spinning lettuce, hoping he'd give up. But he has caught on to this, making it clear that when I ask him to do something, he does not want it to be presented as a chore and does not take well to requests unadorned with the magic word. I am apparently not very good at that either.

He does like to wash dishes. But this has only compounded the problem. Since I do not have a dishwasher, the dishes must be done by hand. We have different methods. Mr. Latte washes dishes in an empty sink with a soapy sponge, then rinses them. I, on the other hand, rinse the dishes, then fill the sink with very hot soapy water and scrub them with a dishcloth or coarse sponge before rinsing them again.

On the surface, it's a painfully trivial difference of opinion. We could easily come to a compromise. But it's not about washing dishes. The real issue is trust. Letting him feel at home would be letting go, letting him more deeply into my life. It is something I want, but I've been struggling with it.

Then a few weeks ago, Mr. Latte called to say that his college roommate, George, was in town. The last time I had seen George, he seemed doubtful about whether I could actually cook, so I felt obliged to set things straight.

When I got home from work, I had to come up with a menu. I set out slices of sopressata, a bowl of pistachios and a plate of radishes with sweet butter and coarse sea salt. For the main course, I had an idea of what I wanted—a light, brothy pasta with chicken stock, lemon zest, mint and ricotta salata—but I would have to figure it out as I went. I had some greens and asparagus, so with the pasta I decided on a busy salad of asparagus, haricots verts, fennel, tarragon and mixed peppery greens dressed with walnut oil vinaigrette.

Before dinner, I asked one too many favors of Mr. Latte. I called him twice asking him to pick up things I had forgotten. When he arrived, bags in hand, I was so preoccupied that I didn't offer him a kiss hello. I just took the bags and told him I needed him to run out for ice cream. He gave me a look, then went on his way. When he returned, he handed over the ice cream, then left the room.

Later, he came into the kitchen as I was frantically blanching the beans and chopping herbs and asked if there was anything else he could do. "It would be really great if you could light the candles," I said, wishing I could reverse time. It was too late. I had failed him again.

When George arrived late and tipsy, I was relieved. He was at ease, brimming with stories to tell. He seemed to like dinner and to believe that I had cooked it. His company cheered us up.

After he left, Mr. Latte offered to do the dishes. I put away the food. We rehashed the evening, resolving the crisis in George's love life, critiquing the meal, laughing with each other. Meanwhile, Mr. Latte busily piled heavy dishes on top of my crystal wine glasses and forgot to wipe the counters. For a moment, I wanted to pull my hair out.

Instead, I walked into my bedroom, took a deep breath and thought about how nice it was of him to help, then came back to keep him company. It was time to change.

Fresh flavors for a new way of thinking

Papardelle with Lemon, Herbs and Ricotta Salata

This pasta is best served with lots of the brothy sauce, so the noodles drink it up and the lemon comes through and then you have a nice little pool to soak up with bread. You can make the very same recipe, skipping the herbs and doubling or tripling the lemon zest, to taste. And you may want to do this if you choose to serve the papardelle with the salad, which is also flush with herbs.

2 cups low-sodium chicken broth
1 clove garlic, peeled and lightly smashed with the side of a knife
Grated zest of 1 lemon (use a Meyer if it's in season)
Juice of 1 lemon (ditto)
Sea salt
1 pound papardelle, broken into 2-inch pieces, or a small thin pasta like
     bowties or fusilli
3 tablespoons chopped mint
2 tablespoons chopped marjoram
1 tablespoon chopped fennel fronds, or tarragon or chervil
Extra virgin olive oil, for sprinkling
6 ounces ricotta salata, crumbled into almond-sized lumps (about 1 cup)
Coarsely ground black pepper

1. Fill a large pot with water and add enough salt so that you can taste it. Bring to a boil. Pour the chicken broth into a small saucepan, drop in the garlic and bring to a boil. Reduce by half. Remove the garlic and shut off the heat. Stir in the lemon zest and juice. Season and taste. It should be full flavored because this will be the sauce for the pasta. Keep warm.

2. When the water comes to a boil, add the pasta and cook until soft on the edges but still firm under the tooth. After a few minutes, ladle out about 1 cup of the cooking water and reserve. Drain the pasta, shake it lightly, then return it to the pot. Put it over low heat and pour in the chicken broth. Sprinkle in the mint, marjoram and fennel and a little olive oil. Stir vigorously. The pasta should be brothy and lemony. Add some of the reserved cooking water and more lemon juice, if needed. Season to taste with salt (keeping in mind that the cheese will add some salt).

3. Spoon into four warmed serving bowls, so that the pasta is lying in a bit of broth. Crumble the ricotta over it, sprinkle with a dash more oil and grind pepper over the top.

DINNER FOR 4.

Asparagus, Beans and Peppery Lettuces with Walnut Dressing

Sea salt
8 thin spears asparagus, woody ends snapped off or trimmed
1 handful haricots verts, stem ends trimmed off
2 teaspoons aged sherry vinegar
1 teaspoon cider vinegar
1/2 teaspoon Dijon mustard
Coarsely ground black pepper
2 tablespoons olive oil
2 tablespoons walnut oil
2 handfuls mixed greens
1 handful watercress or baby arugula
1/4 small bulb fennel, very thinly sliced
1 1/2 tablespoons chopped tarragon

1. Fill a pot with water, season with plenty of salt and bring to a boil. Drop in the asparagus and cook until tender but still firm, about 2 to 3 minutes. Transfer with a slotted spoon to a bowl of ice water to stop the cooking.

When the water comes back to a boil, cook and chill the haricots verts the same way. Drain the asparagus and beans and lay out on a towel to dry. Slice the asparagus into 1 1/2-inch-long pieces.

2. In a small bowl, whisk together the vinegars and mustard. Season with salt and pepper. Gradually whisk in the olive oil and walnut oil, until smooth and emulsified. Combine the lettuces, fennel, asparagus, beans and tarragon in a serving bowl. Pour over half the dressing and fold it into the vegetables until they are coated with a thin layer of dressing. Taste and add more dressing, or salt, if needed.

SALAD FOR 4.

Simple Dessert

Serve bowls of vanilla ice cream sprinkled with tiny cubes of pineapple (seasoned with salt, pepper and sugar), blueberries and torn pieces of mint.

Chapter 11

A SAFE PLACE

By the time I reached my grandmother's house on the Eastern Shore of the Chesapeake Bay, I was dizzy with hunger. I had firmly resisted a Snickers bar at a rest stop, knowing I would regret it if I showed up even partly full. And so I sped down the highway, and then the single-lane roads that dart through cornfields, hurrying to get there.

"It's about time you showed up!" my grandmother, Helen, cried through her kitchen window. "I need to eat!" I yelled back, scrambling from the car. "Well, let's see," she said; her skinny ankles and sneakers were all I could see as she bent into her refrigerator. "We've got waffles and ice cream, macaroni and cheese, dried beef gravy. I can cook you some rockfish. What would you like?"

I settled into my grandfather's old chair at the table, from which you can take in nearly the whole of the house—living room, kitchen, washer and dryer—as well as a sweeping view of the Bay. The house sits on a high bank, like a tiny throne.

I chose the macaroni and cheese, and it was just right. Sweet, pulpy tomatoes that my grandmother cans herself and thick slices of ham from local Mennonite farmers mingle with the noodles and cheese, and there is always a nicely browned, salty crust.

I was looking forward to this visit. As a child, I would spend weeks at my grandmother's house in the summer. Days were a tangle of fun and chores—shucking corn, fishing for perch (which mostly involved loosening the lures caught along the rocky shoreline), weeding the garden, swimming. But recently much had changed. My grandfather and my grandmother's sister, Betty, who lived next door, had died. Mrs. Kephardt, another neighbor, had also passed away. Betty's son, David, who lived down the street, had been having a tough time after his mother's bar was sold.

As I ate my lunch, I could see my brother, Dean, pull up in his S.U.V. He plowed through the door, tanned, in pressed shorts and a polo shirt, carrying a bushel of crabs. "Hey, you," he said. "What are you doing eating? I just got crabs and beer."

I headed for the porch, where Dean's wife, Leslie, and I spread newspapers over the table. My grandmother brought out the crackers, knives, mallets and the cutting boards my grandfather had fashioned from oak and walnut, which are hard enough to withstand the blue crab's steely shell.

The afternoon passed with us plucking the meat from crab after crab and watching ships and barges ease across the bay. We caught up on things, my grandmother slipping in her usual accounts of the surroundings. "The birds have been pretty quiet," she said. "They're shedding their feathers, I guess, getting ready to go south. Of course, that hummingbird is always coming to the window. He doesn't care. He never sheds a feather." As the light dimmed, the water slackened and shined like nickel. And when it was finally dark, we went inside.

The next day, I took a walk. The morning light revealed that the paint was peeling on the house and that the beach, where my siblings and I once built entire cities with pebbles and stones, had eroded. The people who moved into my aunt's house built a gazebo on a stretch of grass between the houses where my sisters and I used to do cartwheels. The garage was piled with Betty's remaining belongings. There were boxes labeled by my mother: "utensils," "curtains" and "ugly green lamp."

I went inside to the kitchen to seek refuge. My grandmother was there, skittering up and down the galley like a bird on a tree limb—opening the pantry, checking the stove, leaning into the fridge, just as she always has. She is not a gourmet cook but a good, sensible one.

I helped her make crab cakes with the extra meat we had picked the day before. We sifted through the meat for shells and picked out the dry pieces, making sure not to break up the moist lumps of meat. My grandmother grated breadcrumbs, holding a fistful of white bread like a baseball and rubbing it back and forth over a metal grater into the bowl of crab. I chopped parsley. She had me pour the dressing—Dijon mustard, Miracle Whip and egg—over the crab. "Now," she said, "there's a little secret that I discovered on my own one time when I didn't have parsley. I put a little bit of cilantro in there. Not a lot. Just a little bit. And I found it really brings out the flavor of the crab meat. It makes the cakes sweeter or something." I was pleased to know she was still so willing to try something new.

Her recipe box is piled high with clippings of recipes, any that interest her, whether from *Gourmet* or the back of a tapioca box. Lately when we've cooked together, I've gotten her to talk. I've discovered a smart, opinionated woman and a cook I admire.

"A lot of people put in Old Bay, but I think that spoils them," she continued, leaning over the bowl as I folded in the dressing. Then she interrupted: "You're mixing it too heavily. You have to lift and fluff it, or you'll end up with hockey pucks."

We were peeling shrimp for lunch—to sauté with corn and basil—when the phone rang. My grandmother answered, and when she hung up, she said she had to run down the street to find David. He hadn't shown up for work, and his phone line was, yet again, disconnected. Until recently, he had managed his mother's bar in a nearby fishing village. Crabbers and fishermen would come in from days at sea, and Betty would feed them while David poured them beer and whiskey. After she fell ill, things fell apart.

I kept peeling shrimp, while my grandmother dashed off. Why does an eighty-five-year-old woman have to watch after her nephew? I wondered, knowing that she invites it, that helping people keeps her happy. The phone rang again. This time, it was my cousin, Nicole, whom I feel I hardly know anymore. She and her boyfriend wanted my grandmother to give them a ride to a doctor's appointment. Usually she's asking for money. I took the message as if she were a telemarketer.

I stopped peeling the shrimp, went out to the garage for a bicycle and rode out the lane, pedaling as fast as I could. I kept my eyes fixed straight ahead, not wanting to take in David's crumbling shack or Mrs. Kephardt's home with its neglected fig tree, not wanting to see any more change. When I reached the first cornfield, I turned and glided down the hill to the marina.

When Dean and I were young, we would hike there with our

allowance, buying one hundred Swedish fish for a penny each at the marina shop. I paused there and tasted them in my mind, before slowly making my way back. My grandmother would need help with dinner. And I wanted to be with her in the kitchen, the place where everything remained intact.

A few of Helen's favorites

All recipes adapted from Helen Getz.

Macaroni and Cheese

My grandmother cooks the sauce and pasta in her Farberware pots and pans on an electric stove. She uses regular butter, cheese from the supermarket and she does not grind her own pepper. But she knows how to cook and she knows how people like to eat, and dishes like this macaroni and cheese make you want to weep with pleasure.

2 tablespoons butter, plus more for buttering dish
2 tablespoons flour
2 cups milk
1 1/2 cups grated Monterey Jack cheese, plus more for sprinkling
3 1/2 cups cooked elbow macaroni
1 cup small cubes roasted country ham
1 cup canned Italian plum tomatoes, drained (reserve the juice)
3/4 cup coarse breadcrumbs (made from stale bread cut into little cubes)
Freshly ground black pepper (or already ground, if you want it my grand-
    mother's way).

1. Preheat the oven to 350°F. Butter a casserole dish. In a saucepan, heat the 2 tablespoons butter until foamy. Sprinkle in the flour and whisk until it turns golden, then slowly pour in the milk, continuing to whisk. (The French call this béchamel; my grandmother calls it white sauce.) Bring to a simmer over medium heat and let it thicken. Stir in the cheese and remove from the heat. It should be a loose sauce. Fold in the macaroni, then ham. Add tomatoes by squeezing them between your fingers into small pieces. Taste and fix

accordingly. The mixture should be loose like a thin batter; if it's gluey and thick, add a little milk or drained tomato juice.

2. Pour into the casserole dish. Spread breadcrumbs over the surface and then sprinkle with about 1/4 cup cheese. Grind pepper over top (I like a coarse grind). Bake until browned on the top and bubbling, about 25 minutes.

LUNCH FOR 4.

Dried Beef Gravy

My grandmother buys her dried beef from a local market, run by Mennonites. It comes in dense, smooth slices. Although it is called dried beef, it should not be totally dry, or it will be tough, no matter how much white sauce you add.

It is important not to use salted butter, or all the flavors will be lost to saltiness. Over the years, my grandmother has taken to serving it with biscuits, but I find this too heavy. I prefer a plain white sandwich bread that's sturdy but not sour. The sauce needs its austerity.

3 tablespoons unsalted butter
1/4 pound dried beef, pulled apart into shreds (Knauss brand is good)
2 tablespoons flour
2 cups milk
4 slices sandwich bread, country bread or 4 buttermilk biscuits

In a skillet (preferably iron), heat the butter until foamy. Add the dried beef and fry over medium heat until edges are browned. Sprinkle with flour, stirring to coat beef with flour. Cook until the flour is just starting to color, then slowly add the milk, stirring to smooth any flour bits and thicken the sauce. Bring to a boil and cook until there is no longer any taste of flour. Meanwhile, toast the bread. Place the toast or warm biscuits on plates and spoon gravy on top.

A HEARTY BREAKFAST FOR 4.

Crab Cakes

1 pound crab meat, with yellow bits of fat
4 to 5 slices white bread, grated (my grandmother uses Pepperidge Farm)
1/2 tablespoon chopped parsley

1/2 tablespoon chopped cilantro
1/4 cup Miracle Whip
1 tablespoon Dijon mustard
1 egg
White pepper
1 cup very fine cracker crumbs (made from Saltines) or fine breadcrumbs
2 tablespoons unsalted butter
1 lemon, cut into wedges

1. Place the crab meat, bread, parsley and cilantro in a bowl. In another bowl, whisk together the Miracle Whip, mustard and egg. Season with white pepper. Slowly pour the dressing into the crab meat, using a fork to lift and fluff the texture. Add just enough so that it clings together.

2. Form the crab into cakes in the palm of your hand, about 3 inches in diameter and 3/4 inch high. Lay on a plate, cover with plastic wrap and refrigerate for at least 1 hour to set.

3. Before cooking, dip the crab cakes in cracker crumbs to coat. This prevents the crab meat edges from getting tough and chewy when sautéing. Heat the butter in a frying pan over medium heat until foamy. Add the crab cakes and let sauté until browned on the bottom. Turn them just once, and brown the other side. Arrange on a platter with wedges of lemon. My grandmother does not serve her crab cakes with any sauces. She likes them plain so you can taste the crab meat.

CRAB CAKES FOR 4.

Chapter 12

ABOUT TOWN WITH THE BON VIVANT

Jeffrey Steingarten had ignored my request for a dinner with Mr. Latte. They didn't exactly hit it off on the first try (something about Mr. Latte correcting him on the title of a book). So I thought to introduce him to my friend and peer in the world of food writing Jonathan Reynolds. Jonathan is gregarious and charming, a cultural omnivore. But he had never witnessed the likes of Jeffrey. And indeed, when I descended the stairs at Town, late as usual, I was pleased to spot their two white heads and suit coats, standing out like weeds in a field of blond and black.

Jeffrey has been writing a new book and claimed to be rising at dawn to work on it. So I was looking forward to a quicker than usual dinner. We would eat well, have a few laughs and go home.

"What kind of water would you like?" Jeffrey asked as I sat down. The waiter suggested a bottle of Hildon. Jonathan and I nodded. Jeffrey paused to look at us, then ordered tap water. "New York City water has almost no soluble compounds," he said, "so it's one of the closest to pure H_2O." Jonathan looked confounded.

"I find it sweet," I said.

"Oh, do you think God wouldn't have created something that is sweet?" Jeffrey asked.

Before I could respond, both he and Jonathan were transfixed by a woman in a flimsy low-cut dress sweeping by our table. "That's a nice back," Jonathan noted.

"Well, perhaps you should take a look at the back of the blond woman Bobby Flay just walked in with," Jeffrey said. Jonathan's eyes scanned the room. Then I turned to take a look. Bobby's eyes met mine. He waved, smirking.

Soon we were onto a discussion of yellowtail and toro (Jeffrey no longer orders "sushi grade" tuna, which he believes is rarely sushi grade) and then farmed fish (the next big health scare, Jeffrey predicted), mad cow (the overblown health scare, he declared), the best restaurant in the United States (which he would not reveal), camping (something Jeffrey claimed wide experience at; Jonathan and I exchanged looks of suspicion) and eventually back to women (Jeffrey thinks tables full of drinking women should be outlawed). Meanwhile, Jeffrey drank a glass of wine, ordered a bottle of Pouilly-Fumé and ate all of the bread, and most of the butter.

"You will have a drunk woman at your table if we don't order soon," I said. It was past nine.

Jeffrey waved down our waiter. "We'd like to order," he said.

"I was wondering," the waiter said. "You've been here for a while."

"I think we've been here since lunch," Jonathan said.

I had it in mind to order a salad of young lettuces, quietly. Foodies consider anyone who orders salad as a first course—whether it be asparagus, roasted beets and goat cheese, or a pile of greens—a hopeless amateur.

But a very good salad is as difficult to create as a translucent piece of sashimi. A good piece of fish must merely be sliced, whereas salad greens must be painstakingly selected and mixed and then dressed with a judicious blend of sweet, salty, bitter and sour flavors. I also do not feel the need to stuff myself with course after course of rich, heavy foods like foie gras and sweetbreads. I prefer a mix of cool, crisp textures with warm, creamy ones.

"You're going to order *that*?!" Jeffrey said. "Oh, O.K., so are you going to have chicken after? Skinless, nothing on it, sauce on the side?" I peered over at Jonathan for support. He was looking at me skeptically.

And so I caved, ordering the salad for the table and an appetizer of Taylor Bay scallops with a tarragon butter sauce. Roasted tuna with sea urchin sauce and wilted cucumbers would follow. Jonathan ordered quail and foie gras fritters and then veal tongue with artichokes. Jeffrey asked for the quail, too, and steamed mussels in a lemongrass broth.

The scallops were drowned in butter, the fritters were stiff, dry nuggets and the quail was underseasoned. The salad, however, was divine, with a snappy dressing and sprigs of chervil tumbled with delicate leaves of peppercress, red oak and mizuna.

Jeffrey, unfortunately, didn't seem to notice. As dinner whirred along, he kept happily chattering away to Jonathan about Thai food and salt, expense accounts and more on the secret restaurant—Bern's Steakhouse in Tampa. I told him my mother thinks Bern's is the pits. He pretended not to hear.

I tried to provoke him by telling him about my own secret—a pastry shop in Manhattan that could rival some of the best in Paris. He cocked his left eyebrow, then turned back to Jonathan, who seemed to be hypnotized by Jeffrey's relentless dissection of the world's foodstuffs.

Sometime after midnight, shortly after malt and caramel ice creams, cheeses, figs and chocolate beignets were set on our table, Jeffrey began describing to Jonathan how he had once achieved the requisite charring of a Neopolitan pizza on his home grill, even though he ended up melting the grill cover and several other important nozzles and buttons. The conversation was getting good. I reached for more of the goat cheese, lavishing it with shallot marmalade, a soft and tart tangle of shallots stained with crème de cassis.

"Charred?" Jonathan asked, worried that he had misheard Jeffrey.

"Well, not homogeneously," said Jeffrey, perking up. "But, yes, on the bottom it should be spotted with charring and moist on the top, but not all over. More like a slick of tomato. You know, canned ones just squeezed out with the hands. No salt. And the crust should have tiny bubbles in the center. Small little bubbles, one after the other, like that." He made tiny bubble shapes with his fingers. Jonathan looked exhausted to the point of stupefaction.

The next day, Jonathan sent me an e-mail thanking me for arranging the dinner. "I realized about 10 p.m.—just when the appetizers came—that this was going to last about the length of a plane ride to L.A. (or London), and lo and behold, when we split at 12:15, it almost had."

A meal to be enjoyed for hours and hours

All recipes adapted from Town

Mixed Greens with Herbed Vinegar Dressing

This is plainly a chef's recipe. A lot of work in little pans and jars goes into the dressing, but you will understand why when you take the first bite of salad.

1/4 cup balsamic vinegar
1/4 cup red wine vinegar
1/4 cup packed fresh herbs (a mixture of basil, parsley, thyme, rosemary
    and oregano; it's not necessary to use all of them)
About 1/4 cup peanut oil
2 shallots, thinly sliced
1/4 cup extra virgin olive oil
Sea salt
Freshly ground black pepper
5 handfuls young lettuces (a mixture of peppercress, arugula, frisée,
    mizuna, red oak or any other kinds you like)
1/4 cup chervil and tarragon leaves

1. Three days before, combine the vinegars with the herb mixture in a small jar. Seal and let infuse in the refrigerator for 3 days.

2. Strain the herbs from the vinegar and pour the vinegar into a saucepan. Place over high heat and reduce by half. Fill another saucepan with 1/4-inch of peanut oil. Heat the oil to 170°F, then add the shallots. Remove from the heat and cool. Strain. Place the vinegar in a small bowl, then gradually whisk in the shallot oil and then the olive oil until emulsified. Season to taste with salt and pepper.

3. In a large bowl, mix together the lettuces and the chervil and tarragon. Sprinkle with about 3 tablespoons of the dressing and toss gently and thoroughly, until all of the leaves are thinly coated. Add a little more dressing if necessary, but the delicate leaves should not be weighed down with it. Season with more salt and pepper if needed.

SALAD FOR 4, PLUS DRESSING FOR ANOTHER DAY.

Goat Cheese with Shallot-Cassis Marmalade

The next time you are throwing a dinner party, consider this for a course. It should not be served as an hors d'oeuvre, unless you want no one to be hungry for dinner—they will not leave leftovers. Instead, skip a first course, serve a main dish and then this before dessert.

2 tablespoons unsalted butter
3 cups thinly sliced shallots
1 teaspoon sea salt
5 sprigs thyme
2 tablespoons sherry vinegar
4 tablespoons crème de cassis
1/4 cup red currants, fresh or frozen, or 2 tablespoons red currant jam or jelly
1 round Chaource, brick of Lingot de Quercy or button of Chevrot (or any other goat or cow's milk cheese that has a soft rind and is still creamy inside)

1. Melt the butter in a large sauté pan and spread the shallots over the bottom. Sprinkle with salt. With the heat on low, allow the shallots to caramelize. It will take about 30 minutes, and you will need to stir from time to time so the shallots don't burn. In the meantime, pull the leaves from the thyme.

2. Stir the thyme into the shallots, then scrape the shallots into a bowl. Place the pan back on the stove, add the vinegar and over medium-high heat stir to deglaze the pan. Pour the contents of the pan over the shallots and stir to mix. Add the crème de cassis, a little at a time, to taste. Allow the shallots to cool, then stir in the currants (or currant jam). Refrigerate.

3. An hour before serving, set the cheese and shallots out to warm to room temperature. Slice a baguette or some country bread and serve the cheese with the bread and a large spoonful of the shallot marmalade on each plate.

A CHEESE COURSE FOR 4; WITH A SALAD, IT COULD BE LUNCH.

Caramel Ice Cream

While Mr. Latte says that I am biased toward all ice creams, I do think this one is exceptional. It's a touch salty, which makes it addictive, and not a bit flabby, thanks to the sternness of toasted sugar.

5 egg yolks, room temperature
1 1/4 cups sugar
1/4 cup light corn syrup
1 teaspoon coarse sea salt
4 cups half-and-half
1 teaspoon vanilla extract

1. The day before, make the ice cream base: in a medium bowl, whisk together the egg yolks, 1/4 cup sugar, corn syrup and salt, until pale and fluffy. Pour the remaining 1 cup sugar into a deep, heavy 3- to 5-quart saucepan. Place over medium heat and let heat until the sugar melts, then turns a caramel brown and all of the sugar granules have melted. As it gets near that point, have the half-and-half by the stove. When the sugar is a uniform caramel color, remove the pan from the heat and pour in the half-and-half in a swift fluid motion. It will spit and spatter; be careful.

2. Using a wooden spoon, stir the caramel mixture until all of the now-lumpy caramel has dissolved, about 5 minutes. Whisk about 1/2 cup of the caramel mixture into the eggs, then gradually whisk the egg mixture back into the caramel. Place over medium heat, whisking or stirring constantly in a figure eight pattern to keep the base of the pan clean, until the mixture thickens enough to coat the back of a spoon. Do not let it boil, or you will have scrambled eggs. Then remove from the heat, stir in the vanilla, and strain through a fine sieve into a bowl. Let cool, then chill overnight in the refrigerator. Pour the ice cream into an ice cream maker and follow manufacturer's instructions.

ABOUT 1 1/2 QUARTS ICE CREAM. PLENTY FOR 6.

Chapter 13

SHOW ME, DON'T TELL ME

Mr. Latte and I were not getting along as well as I had hoped. Over the months since we met, our contrasting opinions on food and dining had become combative. He ducked out of dinners, leaving me to dine alone too often, resisted any kind of food-related party, and sighed heavily whenever I suggested that we try some new places in our neighborhood.

These seemed like manageable conflicts until our differences began to infect other areas of our relationship. The more he wanted to go to the latest Hollywood film, the more I wanted to see an obscure foreign one. The more I wanted to walk to our destination, the more he wanted to take cabs. The more I wanted to play golf, the less I was invited. And he was making out better than I was. We were eating a lot of take-out, and after he endured three long hours of the Taiwanese film, *Yi-Yi*, I felt that I didn't have much cultural ammunition left.

The only thing we seemed to agree on was that we both liked to play pool. So there we were at the Amsterdam Billiards, drinking Budweiser with twenty-year-olds and venting our frustrations on the cue ball.

Many of our issues were small, but they raised a larger fear. Maybe Mr. Latte was set in his ways. He was only thirty-eight, but he had his social circle, his activities and the rhythms of his day down. He wasn't all that interested in changing them. I was younger (twenty-nine), but had had too many bad boyfriends, and I was hyper-vigilant. Even if Mr. Latte's intentions were good, I was quick to seek the flaw.

If the heart of the matter turned out to be that he didn't enjoy eating, it might be hopeless. I made occasional progress on the food front with the help of his friends. One night at Omen, a great old Japanese restaurant in SoHo, Mr. Latte brought up the latte issue with his friend Jessie, looking for an ally. "I don't understand why you can't have them after dinner," he said.

"You know," Jessie said, "no milk in any drink after eleven. Everyone knows that."

"A latte is a happy drink," he said, bewildered. "It's big and foamy. You can't tell me an espresso settles the stomach at bedtime. It's like a shot of battery acid."

"It's a digéstif," Jessie said firmly. "Europeans know what they're doing."

When another friend shrieked after he ordered a post-prandial latte, he began to register the issue. And when we ate at Ducasse, I couldn't help drawing his attention to the menu, which offers only espresso.

Without a word, he stopped ordering them as frequently. He also did away with the use of Equal. At least in my presence.

There are many parts of his approach to food that I didn't want to change. I like that he can get so wrapped up in a conversation that he won't notice his tie dangling in his Champagne. That he still orders the occasional beer at restaurants like Danube. And that he never seems happier than when a big, juicy hamburger is set down before him.

Plus I love Mr. Latte for so many other reasons. He is thoughtful and generous. He is a terrific storyteller and knows the most peculiar things: that Tanya Tucker sang "Delta Dawn" when she was thirteen; that hippopotamuses, though vegetarians, kill more people in Africa than the top five carnivores combined; that "strengths" is the longest word in English with only one vowel. Mr. Latte has an enormous number of friends and many of them confide their deepest troubles to him. He loves to travel and has read more than any person I know. He is trustworthy, sensitive and has an incredible talent for writing.

He brings food into conversation in his own way. "Eating meat is good for writing," he said one night as we were walking home from the pool hall. "Look at Salinger. After he went vegetarian, he didn't publish another word." Then he grew quiet, checking the soundness of his argument by riffling through his mental "Writer" file in search of notable vegetarians.

"How about Joyce Carol Oates?" I asked.

"Not sure," he said. "She certainly *writes* like a vegetarian."

I am charmed when he describes burnt toast as having the texture of petrified wood, a spicy salsa as indignant and a chocolate cream as placid. When I test recipes, he weighs in with useful, concise thoughts, and then finishes the food off "in the interest of science." And his palate has earned my respect. Once when we had dinner at Café Boulud, he made us do a blind tasting of twelve-year-old and twenty-five-year-old Armagnacs, guessing which was which. He won handily.

Mr. Latte has kept me in line, as well. On our last night of vacation in Seville, I couldn't decide where we should eat, and had us trudging from restaurant to restaurant, reading menus. When we reached the fifth one, he calmly said, "We're eating here."

For fun, we recently went back to Merchants, the site of our nearly catastrophic first date. We ordered a bottle of Moët & Chandon, chicken quesadillas and Cobb salads. Mr. Latte was annoyed with the woefully inattentive service and surprised at the youthfulness of the diners. Over lattes after the meal, he said, self-mockingly, "I think it's taken a turn for the worse."

Still, he sometimes hurried through meals, wolfing down his food like a college student. And when I asked him to go grocery shopping, he responded as if I had invited him to jump in boiling oil. Was Mr. Latte being so stubborn because he wasn't so sure about being with me? I tried to stifle the thought, but it nagged me for weeks.

Then one night he came over to visit while I was cooking. He lay on my crimson sofa with a thick book in his lap and the TV muted on golf, content as a dog lying in shade. Dinner was a long way off, so I asked if he wanted a snack. When he said yes, it occurred to me that I had never made anyone a snack before. I am so rarely home that I've never had anyone over just to hang out. Friends and former boyfriends have only come for planned dinners and parties.

I opened my refrigerator and searched for inspiration. I didn't want to miss my chance. I found a chunk of Parmigiano-Reggiano. I had some good country bread, a few days old, but no matter. I grated the cheese and placed it in a shaggy pile on top of a slice of bread. I ground some grains of paradise (a spice much like peppercorns, but better) on top, pressed the bread together and slipped it into a sauté pan foaming with butter. As it sizzled away, I stood over it, flattening the sandwich with a spatula. The heat coming up over the sides of the pan was soothing. I served him the grilled cheese with a glass of chilled Pineau de Charentes.

Mr. Latte crunched down on it, nodding and smiling at me. He drank his apéritif. "Mm," he said, between bites. "This is delicious. What is it? Is there more?"

I would have cooked until my refrigerator was empty. The light had finally turned on: I wasn't ever going to make him love dining, foreign films or anything else in my so-called world. We had to create our own world. And that wouldn't happen by me telling him to love food, goddamn it. I needed to be more generous, so he would be seduced by food in the same way I have been. Then everything else would fall into place. I hoped.

A number of weeks passed without any noticeable change. Mr. Latte came over for a late dinner on a Sunday. I was warming succotash in a pan, gently folding it so that the corn and beans heated through but were still noticeably crisp.

"Did you see the review of Craft?" he asked. I had and nodded, turning toward him as I stirred the corn. He continued, comparing his feelings about Craft to the reviewer's, and then reminded me that we needed to try Blue Hill.

I stopped stirring. Mr. Latte was talking about food.

Food for sharing

Succotash with Goat Cheese

You can add other beans, like cranberry beans, fava beans, navy beans or lima beans, if you like.

Coarse sea salt

2 ears corn

1 large handful haricots verts or green beans, stems trimmed

2 tablespoons extra virgin olive oil

1/2 tablespoon chopped thyme

1 tablespoon sliced chives

Freshly ground black pepper

2 ounces fresh goat cheese (no rind; should be soft), pulled into
  hazelnut-sized pieces

1. Fill a large pot with water. Season generously with salt, and bring to a boil. Add the corn and cook for 2 minutes. Remove from the water and let cool. Bring the water back to a boil and add the beans. Cook until tender but still quite crisp (they will cook more later), about 4 minutes. Drain the beans and tip them into a bowl of ice water to stop the cooking. Lay the beans out on a towel and pat them dry. Then cut them into 1/2-inch pieces. Cut the corn from the cobs, running the edge of your knife along the cob to extract as many juices as possible.

2. Pour the olive oil in a sauté pan and warm over medium heat. When the oil shimmers, add the corn and beans and stir to coat with the oil. When heated through, sprinkle over the thyme and chives and season with salt. Stir until fragrant. When the taste is to your liking, remove from the heat and grind over pepper, and stir. Spoon onto a shallow platter and dot with the lumps of cheese.

A FIRST COURSE OR SIDE DISH FOR 4.

Grilled Cheese

It may not seem like you're using enough cheese, but a little Parmigiano-Reggiano goes a long way. In this recipe, the pepper makes a statement, so you should use good peppercorns and grind them fresh. A mix of green, red and black peppercorns has a nice effect, but if you can get your hands on grains of paradise, which have a nutty, citrusy aroma, use them. They can be ordered from www.worldspice.com.

8 small thin slices country bread

1 cup finely grated Parmigiano-Reggiano cheese

Coarsely ground pepper, or grains of paradise

Unsalted butter

1. Cover slices of the bread with a fluffy layer of grated cheese. Grind pepper over top (in coarse flakes, if your peppermill does it; or grind with a mortar and pestle). Place the remaining slices of bread on top to make sandwiches.

2. Add enough butter to a large sauté pan so that it melts to a generous film (about 2 tablespoons should do it). Heat the butter over medium heat until foamy, then add the sandwiches, pressing them onto the pan. Sauté, regulating the heat, so that the cheese begins to melt as the bread toasts and browns, but the butter does not burn. Turn the sandwiches once, and press down with a spatula to compress. Brown the other side. Then transfer the toasts to a paper towel to drain. Cut in half diagonally, and serve with a glass of chilled Pineau de Charentes, or sherry.

4 SMALL SANDWICHES, BEST AS AN HORS D'OEUVRE OR SNACK.

Cobb Salad

2 small chicken breast halves
Coarse sea salt
Freshly ground black pepper
6 slices bacon
2 eggs
1 head romaine, large outer leaves discarded, torn into small pieces
1 ripe avocado, sliced like an apple into thick wedges
2/3 cup crumbled mild blue cheese, like Roquefort
2 tablespoons Dijon mustard
Pinch of sugar
1 tablespoon balsamic vinegar
1 tablespoon red wine vinegar
1/2 cup extra virgin olive oil

1. Fill a small saucepan with water (add a few sprigs of thyme or a clove of garlic, if you have some around). Season the water with salt, bring to a simmer, then add the chicken. Simmer until chicken is just cooked through, about 10 minutes. Remove from the water and let cool. Once cool, skin the chicken breast (if it's not skinned already), slice crosswise into thin slivers. Season with salt and pepper. Set aside.

2. Lay the bacon in a small frying pan, preferably cast iron, and place over medium low heat. Cook until nicely browned, turning once. Drain on paper

towels; when cool, break into small pieces. Fill a small pan with water and bring to a simmer. Add the eggs and cook for 9 to 9 1/2 minutes. Remove from the heat and run cold water into the pan to cool the eggs. Peel and slice into wedges.

3. In each of four large bowls (pasta bowls work well), place a large handful of romaine. On top arrange the chicken, bacon, eggs, avocado and cheese. I like to keep them separate, but you can mix them if you wish.

4. Whisk together the mustard, pinch of sugar and vinegars in a small bowl. Season with salt and pepper, then gradually whisk in the oil until smooth and emulsified. The dressing should be thick with a tartness that is balanced by sweetness. Adjust as needed. Serve the salads, passing the dressing in a pitcher so each person can dress and mix the salad on his own.

4 LARGE SALADS, EACH ENOUGH FOR A MEAL.

Chapter 14

DINNER WHEN NO ONE WANTED TO BE ALONE

In Raymond Carver's story "A Small, Good Thing" a baker feeds warm rolls and coffee to a couple who have just lost their only child. "You have to eat and keep going," he says. "Eating is a small, good thing at a time like this."

But after the terrorist attacks on September 11th, eating was the last thing on my mind. I had been working on a story about vanilla—the wonderful aromatic we often use but know very little about. Except that nothing felt wonderful, or even remotely okay. I sat at my computer screen, with a wrinkled vanilla bean in hand and a cold cup of coffee at my side, wondering what I was doing.

That evening, Mr. Latte and I went to some friends' house downtown for dinner. We had been making lots of dinner plans. We wanted to see friends.

"Dinner will be a little late," Tim said when we arrived. "I'm sorry. It happened the last time you were here, as well. Didn't it?"

It had, but this time dinner seemed irrelevant. There were about a dozen guests—some old friends who live nearby, others who were stranded in the city. Isabelle and Deirdre had been in New York for fashion week. Damien was here on business from Mexico City, Mitie was waiting for a plane back to Los Angeles. There were an English couple, a Bolivian friend and Maiken and Tim, the hosts. Tim's office at Lehman Brothers had been heavily damaged, and he had had to walk uptown out of the wreckage.

He was now home, a few blocks north on a calm street in Greenwich Village, wrestling with a grill that had all the power of a Bic lighter. The rest of us sat nearby in the cool air, drinking wine and smoking. Someone asked Damien about life in Mexico City. "What I like about it," he said, "is the unpredictability." There was a brief pause. "I mean," he said, "you never know if you're going to be able to get to work when you get up in the morning." The idea of it was suddenly too familiar.

As the time passed, each of us shared 9/11 stories we had heard, mostly stories of survival, close calls. Fear, sadness, anxiety, even exhilaration, all the emotions that are normally tucked away, enveloped us like heavy, humid air.

We sat down around 10:30, crowded around a long table, so that we had to cut our food with small pawing motions. It felt good to be so close to others. Mr. Latte sat at the other end of the table. The first time I ate with his friends, I hated to be separated from him. I liked having him next to me, a buffer against anyone who pried too much. Now I am just as happy to be able to look down the table at him. At his poker face gaze, which now and then turns down, his forehead wrinkled in thought, like ripples on a calm pool, or erupts into a wide, squinty smile.

Everyone was trying to talk about something besides terrorism. "So, A-man-da," began Charlie, seated next to me, each syllable like a separate word with his Colombian accent, "tell me, I want to hear the whole story, how you got into this food writing."

He was really asking another question: "Can I tell you why I love food?" Charlie is a solid, restless man with drowsy blue eyes. He and I had never really talked before. Food was easy, comfortable, a safe haven, and so I welcomed it. "I have always loved food," Charlie said. "I love to try new restaurants. I cook, you see."

"What I like is I like shopping," he continued, playing with a piece of bread. "And bringing the food home and arranging it all in my kitchen. And then you can look at it all and figure out what you will cook. And I love to cook for people. I want them to come into the kitchen and talk to me while I cook. But I do not want their help. I am a tyrant, Amanda. I am incapable of understanding how people can butcher a good piece of beef! It offends me. The way you touch a piece of food, it says a lot about you. If you are aggressive, or careful, or kind."

This made sense to me, but tonight my inner tyrant was laying low. "Don't you find many people are just timid?" I said. "Food is scary to people who don't cook much." I can remember the first few times I roasted a chicken. When I had that raw chicken on my cutting board, I touched it like it was a cold alien creature. Now I know all of the little bits of skin I like to trim off, I pluck any feathers, and I use my hands to rub salt on the inside. I truss it like a package and slip it into the oven without a worry.

As the meal got started, my hunger awakened. The lamb chops were pink in the center, not purplish-red, as is generally—and wrongly in my opinion—considered correct. (Why not just eat tartare?) The grill had caramelized the edges, and when it conked out, the slow dissolution of heat had kept the chops moist. The baby white potatoes, boiled in their skins and tossed with butter and herbs, had a sweetness that resonated with the sugars in the lamb. Green beans and tomatoes in vinaigrette were served cool. The beans were crisp, without tasting green, dripping with the tangy sauce, which bled into the juices from the lamb. I chased it around my plate with the potatoes, trying to mop it up. An already good meal was finally punctuated with a plate of cheeses.

Conversations were swirling around us; Deirdre and Tim were talking about their kids, others about terrorism. I was relieved to be talking about something other than tragedy. Please, more, I thought, as I nodded to Charlie.

Charlie is the kind of eater who does not stop. His hands are in continuous motion, reaching for bread or cheese or wine and leading it to his mouth. He does not seem to pay particular attention to the flavors as he continues to talk, though you know he does. It is probably intuitive, like his cooking.

Charlie had recently left a bank and was reeling over life decisions. He was thinking of moving to Madrid to open food stores and pastry shops, so that, he said, you could find a decent croissant. This awoke me from my pleasant daze. Croissants are for France, and so are baguettes. "Why would you want to do that?" I asked, feeling my blood rise.

"Madrid," he said, "has no good pastry or bread."

I hope it never will. I hope people in Spain continue to eat tortilla and pale bread with jam and drink that dense, milky coffee for another thousand years.

I noticed that the lamb chops had disappeared, and that there was no more salad. Everyone had eaten generously. Carver's baker was right.

I reached for some more cheese. It was a Reblochon, ripened so that the rind was like a waxy shell damming up the soft, runny interior. Its nutty aroma swarmed around my head. I was happy for its pleasure and was glad that Charlie and I were in disagreement, and that he had finally opened up to me. My skin was hot from wine and conversation.

It was a delightful evening that I hope never to repeat.

A dinner for when you need to be together

Lamb Chops

Have the butcher "French" the rib chops, which means trimming and scraping the top portions of the bones clean.

12 rib or loin lamb chops (about 2 1/2 pounds total)
1/4 cup coarsely chopped rosemary
4 cloves garlic, peeled and crushed with the side of a knife to release
  their juices
Extra virgin olive oil
Sea salt
Freshly ground black pepper

1. In the morning, get out a large bowl or dish. In it, combine the lamb chops with the rosemary and garlic. Sprinkle enough olive oil over the chops to coat them lightly. Toss to coat, then cover with plastic wrap and refrigerate giving them a stir every few hours.

2. An hour before serving, set out the chops to bring them to room temperature. Preheat a grill to medium high or a broiler. Shower the chops with salt and pepper. Grill for 2 to 3 minutes on each side, turning them just once, so that they are nicely browned on the edges but still quite pink inside. Pile onto a warm serving platter and set on the table.

LAMB CHOPS FOR 4, OR 3 PER PERSON (CAN EASILY BE DOUBLED OR TRIPLED)

Beans and Tomatoes with Vinaigrette

I f you make this salad ahead of time, the tomatoes will juice and the beans will marinate. This is the way I prefer it—with lots of vinaigrette, sweetened by the tomatoes, and soft, slippery beans.

Sea salt
1 pound green beans, trimmed
3 ripe tomatoes, cored and cut into 1-inch cubes
1 tablespoon Dijon mustard
1 tablespoon red wine vinegar
Pinch of sugar
1/4 cup best-quality olive oil
Freshly ground black pepper

1. Fill a medium saucepan with water. Season generously with salt. Bring to a rolling boil, and add the beans. Cook until tender on the edges but still quite crisp, about 4 minutes. Drain and rinse under cold water. Dry on a towel. Cut the beans in half, then combine in a large serving bowl with the tomatoes.

2. Whisk together the mustard and vinegar with a pinch of sugar and a pinch of sea salt. Gradually whisk in the oil, letting it thicken and emulsify as you go. Pour the dressing over the beans and tomatoes and toss to mix. It's okay if the dressing pools in the bottom of the bowl. Someone can later mop it up with bread or spoon it over their potatoes or lamb. Season generously with freshly ground black pepper and toss once more. Let sit for at least 15 minutes before serving.

SALAD FOR 4.

Chapter 15

SUNDAY RITUAL

"I feel like a 1940s housewife," Jennifer said over the phone, the sound of water running in a sink in the background.

"How so?" I asked.

"We're at war, I'm flipping out, I'm trying to guard my kid from the TV, I'm cooking dinner and I've got 1010 WINS on the radio."

It was a rainy Sunday afternoon. Going with Mr. Latte to Jennifer and Ed's house for dinner on Sunday has become a ritual, something I miss when the phone doesn't ring.

Jennifer and I became friends a few years ago when she introduced herself at work. "I hear you know a lot about cooking," she said one day over the wall of my cubicle. "We must talk." A month later, we threw a dinner party together.

Sometimes I'll get a frantic call from her at the grocery store early in the day. "The recipe says I need ten pounds of meat, and the butcher here is looking at me like I've got two heads. What do you think? What time are you coming over? Ooh! I just spotted some fabulous cheese. Let's have cheese! Fondue?!"

Or it may come later on, after she has done the work. "La soupe est prête!" she announced into my machine one day. Another time, when I was suffering a food hangover (the week had seen a cream-laden meal with two old-time foodies, a late dinner at Balthazar and a multi-course blowout to finish it, and me, off), she fed me a vegetable soup, a piece of bread and a slice of aged Manchego. She didn't push me to get seconds or seem insulted that I didn't ask for any.

The hours we spend together cooking these simple dinners have created an unusual bond. I see her in her home when it's not straightened up for guests, when there is no real plan, when she's reeling from stress. She sees me when I'm tired, blue, restless. Hannah, her two-year-old daughter, plays at our feet, and sad country music thumps from the other room. Jennifer has that real life that I sometimes long for when I'm at home in my subdued apartment.

Sometimes I take food there and cook for them. When Jennifer and Ed were both working around the clock reporting stories from ground zero after September 11th, I brought dinner. Ed greeted me and then, as he always does, quietly went about setting the table while I began chopping garlic and simmering chicken and celery root. When Jennifer got home, the click of the door was not followed by her cheerful voice. She said hello softly, and when she looked down at Hannah, she began to cry.

This Sunday, the timing couldn't have been better. "I'm thinking soup again," she said. "That carrot and fennel one. But we need something else."

I had just that something else in mind. Meatloaf. Something I had never made.

Jennifer seemed nonplussed, but I talked her into it. "How wrong can you go with meatloaf?" I said. "If it's not so great, it'll make a tasty sandwich later." (My mother's meatloaf was always better the next day.)

Jennifer is an ambitious cook with interests that stretch from bisteeya to layer cakes. But she has the rare qualities of a realist. She scoffs at Martha's obsessive detail (and yet, like many of us, uses her ideas), disdains recipes that call for more than three pieces of equipment and does not acknowledge garnishes. She will try any dish, but is never a slave to a recipe. Indeed, one reason her carrot and fennel soup is so good is that she can't be bothered cutting the carrots into thin slices. She slices them into large circles, cooks the soup a little longer and pulses it in a food processor. The soup has a fine balance of flavors, with sour cream softening the aroma of fennel, and fresh orange juice underlining the fruitiness of the carrots. Lumps of carrot bob around in the sweet, slightly viscous broth.

When Mr. Latte and I arrived, Hannah was visibly focused on eating enough of her chicken and green beans so that ice cream would follow. Mr. Latte opened a beer, and we sat down with her, while Jennifer dug around for a pan for the meatloaf. Jennifer, who is tiny, had on an NYPD T-shirt and faded jeans. She is the kind of woman who can put on such clothes and look chic. Hannah stared up at me as she extracted the sweet beans from the pod without damaging the pod and then hid the pods on her chair. It's quite a talent. Jennifer and I settled on a large iron skillet, which Ed had given her for her birthday. It was deep enough so that the meatloaf would be protected from drying out and heavy enough to cook it well on the bottom. If you were an extreme minimalist, you could live well with just an iron skillet and a good knife.

"What do we think about dessert wines?" Jennifer began, as I started preparing the meatloaf. "I just don't get them. They're cloying.

They're unpleasant. I mean, if there were three things in the world that I could get rid of, they'd be action films, snow in your boots and dessert wine."

"Don't sugarcoat it, Jen," Mr. Latte said. "Tell us what you really think."

"How finely do I chop the onions?" I asked.

"Oh, you know," she said. "Who has time to chop finely?" I settled on roughly half an inch, figuring they'd add a nice crunch in the mix. Her recipe, altered from www.Epicurious.com, blended white bread, egg, ground beef and chopped tomatoes from a can. It felt strange to be adding all of these savory ingredients to a single bowl. It was also distinctly satisfying. When you make something like this—a cake, a cocktail, a salad dressing—you are putting all of your trust in the recipe and putting distance between you and the flavor of a dish. You cannot take responsibility for a lack of salt or too much butter, because it tells you precisely how much. Which may explain why millions of American cooks latched on to meatloaf. It's easy, it's cheap and it's liberating.

I began mixing with a wooden spoon. "You want to use your hands," Jennifer said. "It's the only way." Yes, hands, squishing the meat and seasonings between your fingers, forcing the independent parts to coalesce. It is cold, oily, a bit like sticking your hand into a murky pond.

My mind drifted to the meatloaf of my youth, which was an odd pleasure. My Aunt Nora, who took care of my brother and sisters and me when my father was very ill, would make "mock lobster," a meatloaf in the shape of a lobster. The claws were striped with ketchup and slices of bacon lined up like ribs down the body of the lobster. It was back when lobster mattered, and having some was only a fantasy for us. Mock lobster cheered us up.

This meatloaf was much different. "You know what makes this good," Jennifer said as she stirred the basting sauce—cider vinegar, light brown sugar and mustard—"is the mustard. The ballpark mustard gives it a little sharpness, a little zing. I like it—it's kind of trashy in that American cooking way."

Mr. Latte and Ed sat in the kitchen with us while we cooked. "Next time you guys should do chicken-fried steak," said Ed, who is from Texas.

"I've never had it," I said, as I opened the oven to baste the meatloaf. The heat filled the room like a puff of smoke.

"Well, then," Ed said, "you haven't lived."

"His mom makes a very good one," Jennifer added.

"I know, you should watch her the next time we're there," Ed said.

"Yeah, you should both come," Jennifer said. "We'll go to a rodeo!"

The meatloaf was hearty and moist, and sharp and tangy where the sauce had soaked in. (Mock lobster, which has pork and veal in it, is richer, almost buttery, with salty swaths of bacon.) I was ashamed of the little salad I had brought. I had finely chopped curly green lettuce and arugula, and mixed them with toasted almonds, thinly sliced radishes and translucent slivers of pear. It seemed too fussy for our Sunday dinner.

After we ate, Mr. Latte read Hannah a bedtime story. We crowded around the television in their bedroom to watch Larry David. Then we gathered up my empty containers, loaded them in my little wheeled grocery cart, and Mr. Latte and I walked the few blocks home.

Dinner with friends

Carrot and Fennel Soup

Adapted from www.Epicurious.com

It is not unusual to find Jennifer barreling down Broadway, pushing Hannah in a stroller, talking to her editor on a cell phone while fishing something from her purse. She finished writing a story while in labor and was e-mailing editors just a few hours after delivery.

You wouldn't think that she would favor soups. Soups bring to mind a slow country life, a pot on the stove simmering at a snail's pace. But Jennifer is fanatical about them. This is because she has come to see, as many cooks do, that soups are one of the best accommodations to a busy lifestyle. There are usually just one or two main ingredients. You chop them up into pieces—as inexactly as you wish—add some seasoning and cover them with water, broth, milk, whichever you have around. Then you can go off and accomplish three million things while the soup simmers to life.

  2 tablespoons unsalted butter
  1 medium fennel bulb, stalks trimmed flush with bulb, and coarsely
    chopped; fronds reserved
  1 1/2 pounds carrots, peeled and thickly sliced (about 4 cups)
  1 large garlic clove, thinly sliced
  1 teaspoon sea salt, more to taste
  1/3 cup fresh orange juice
  1/4 cup sour cream
  Freshly ground black pepper

  1. Put the butter in a soup pot and heat until the butter is foamy. Add the chopped fennel and cook over medium heat, stirring, until softened and beginning to turn golden. Add the carrots and garlic and cook for another minute. Pour in enough water to just cover the vegetables (about 4 cups), season with salt and simmer, covered, until the carrots are very tender, about 20 minutes. (Add more water if the pot gets dry.)

  2. Ladle the soup into a food processor, and puree the mixture with orange juice, sour cream, and salt and pepper to taste. Jennifer just pulses it a few times, leaving the mixture very chunky. You may want to do this in batches, but do make sure that the feed tube is covered, or the hot soup will leap out like a geyser. Pour the chunky soup back into a pan. Heat the soup, stirring, just until heated through; do not let it boil. Taste it again. Pull the fennel fronds into pieces and drop them into the soup. Give it one last stir.
  SOUP FOR 6.

Aunt Nora's Mock Lobster

The original meatloaf recipe comes from 365 Ways to Cook Hamburger
by Doyne Nickerson (Doubleday & Company, Inc., 1958),
and has been substantially altered.

My aunt Nora is my mother's sister. They both use this recipe for meat-loaf. Aunt Nora never follows it, and she can never seem to bring her-self to shape it into a loaf. My mother, who is a few years older, follows it to a T. She shapes it into a perfect oval and spaces the pieces of bacon with a ruler. Well, not really, but it looks that way. There are infinite possibilities with any recipe. You can decide: should you be the rebellious sister, or the disciplinarian?

2 pounds mixed ground beef, veal and pork
2 eggs, lightly beaten
2 cups breadcrumbs
1 cup chopped onion
1/2 cup chopped green pepper
1/4 cup milk
1/4 cup horseradish
1 teaspoon dry mustard
2 teaspoons sea salt
1/8 teaspoon freshly ground pepper
1/4 cup ketchup, more for garnish
8 strips bacon

Preheat your oven to 350°F. Combine everything but the bacon in a large bowl. Mix, using your hands, until well blended. In a roasting pan or iron skil-let, shape the mixture into a plump lobster. With the ketchup, either rub a thin coating all over the lobster or make lines for visual appeal. Wrap the bacon slices across the body and tail, so everyone gets a little. Bake for 50 to 60 minutes, covering the claws with foil after 40 minutes so that they don't dry out. The meatloaf is done when a skewer inserted in the center comes out hot.

MOCK LOBSTER FOR 8.

Chapter 16

A VISITOR FROM INDIA

"Hello, is this Amanda?" said a strange voice on the phone.
"Yes," I said cautiously.

"I am Prakash, a friend of Claudia's," he said, "I am visiting New York, and she suggested I call you." I had not yet met Claudia, a friend of Mr. Latte's. And Mr. Latte was out of town.

"Where are you visiting from?" I asked.

"India."

"Oh, so you want restaurant recommendations?"

"No, not particularly," Prakash said.

"You want to know what to visit?"

"No. I thought maybe we could meet," he said.

Meet? The list of things I had to do over the next few days thundered through my brain. But I have so often been in his place, calling strangers in foreign places.

"Well, let's try for Thursday." I said. "In the meantime, do you like French food? If you want a real New York experience, I'd suggest Le Cirque. But if you want terrific food, then I'd say Jean Georges."

"Is Jean Georges very expensive?" he asked.

"Well, it's not cheap! Not bad at lunch, probably $100," I said.

"Amanda! I make the equivalent of $2 a day. I come from a third world country."

"Oh!" I said, blushing. "Hmm. Then how about Katz's Delicatessan?"

We decided to meet at six on Thursday evening, on the steps to the Metropolitan Museum of Art. I had suggested he go there even though it would be terribly expensive for him. If there was one splurge that was worth it, that was it. And I told him to keep in mind that the $12 "donation" is optional.

For our plan, I opted to go against the tourist grain, and take him places that New Yorkers went to for refuge and beauty.

It was a gorgeous summer day with glittering light. "Hello!" I waved, climbing the museum steps. "I thought we'd begin with a walk in Central Park."

"Oh great," Prakash said, "I love to walk." He was middle aged and trim with thick, shiny brown hair, and was dressed in a cream colored vest and loose trousers.

As we crossed the road that leads through the park, throngs of runners, walkers, and cyclists were bearing down on us. "This is a real American moment for you," I said.

"But you know, I notice there are so many people who are, well, large. How do you say, fat?"

"You see less of it in New York," I responded. "But I'm from a small town in Pennsylvania, and whenever I go home I'm surprised by how many people are overweight."

"Why is this? Do they eat too much?"

"Too much. The wrong things. We're not very good at feeding ourselves. We eat like children. Actually, worse than children."

We passed the Great Lawn where people were playing softball and throwing Frisbees. He stopped and gazed at The Dakota.

"What's that?" he asked.

"It's a fancy old apartment building, filled with lots of really rich, famous people," I said. He laughed.

"So what is it that you do?"

"I work for a newspaper," I said. "And I write about food."

"You write about food?" he said with another little laugh. "What does it mean to write about food?"

"Well, I once went to a watermelon farm in the south and wrote about how watermelons are grown and harvested and transported around the country. I have written about a chef in Spain, and I review cookbooks. I sometimes write about trends. Like if a bunch of restaurants all decide to start serving soup through straws or they begin wheeling you to your table on Herman Miller chairs."

"I see," he said, doubtfully. "You know, in India, we have many rituals when we cook and eat. It is very important. We say food is God."

We passed by the Boathouse, where he stopped to look at the patio bar, filled with overdressed people. "Young and not so young people come here to drink and pick each other up," I said. "And also just to look at each other."

"When we sit down to eat," Prakash continued, "we say the first bread of the day will be cooked for the stray dog, the second bread will go to a stray cow and then the rest of the bread will be cooked for the family. My mother will take a little piece of bread and put some ghee and whatever other things she cooked on it—she will put a little bit of everything—and throw it in the fire. The fire is the fire god. So we must thank the fire we are made of, which enables us to cook and gives the food the essence of life. Hunger is also called fire, so to calm down our fire of hunger we need the fire."

"You do this for every meal?" I asked.

"Yes."

We left the park and crossed to Madison Avenue, and Prakash stopped in front of Tod's, the shoe store. He stared quietly for a minute.

"Very nice," he said.

"Yes, I think so, too."

"You know, I have very little money, but I love high fashion," he said. I calculated how many days it would take him to earn enough money for a pair. Two hundred days.

I was beginning to see why so many people had volunteered to show me around in other countries. It was fascinating to see New York through Prakash's eyes. In Rajasthan where he lives, he farms wheat, millet, rapeseed, cotton, lentils, chickpeas and sorghum. And on the side he gives tours to English-speaking visitors, such as Mr. Latte's friend Claudia.

"We use millet a lot in our cooking," Prakash said, as he peered at a pair of persimmon-colored women's shoes. "We make a porridge of it in the evening. And with the leftover, we eat it for breakfast with fresh milk poured over. My mother says the millet I grow tastes terrible.

"She says the best millet comes from her town, Deshnok. The water there is better. She can actually distinguish between them. That is why I am trying to go back to organic. The irrigation and the fertilizer is not natural."

I hailed a cab and we headed downtown toward Union Square,

where I was taking him for a restaurant review. I thought it might be fun for him.

We were seated in the small, boisterous dining room at Via Emilia. I explained how the menu worked, with *antipasti* first, then *paste*, *secondi piatti*, etc., but he seemed alarmed at the amount of food I wanted to order. "Don't worry," I assured him. "I have to do this for my job. I have to taste many things, but we don't have to finish them."

"So do you have a family?" I asked, relieved to be off tour duty for a little while. Prakash was chatty, and I was ready to listen some more.

"Yes, now I do. My wife was found by my parents in the traditional way, through the musicians."

"The musicians?"

"Yes, they are traveling musicians, so they know everyone from town to town. And since I can't marry someone in my town, they would suggest women to my parents. I did not want to be married. There must have been one hundred women I refused. Finally I agreed, to please my mother."

"It always comes back to the mother," I said smiling. "So, do you love your wife?"

"Very much!"

"That's wonderful. You must feel lucky," I said. It seemed such a strange way to be paired up with the person you will spend your life with, but then, as I thought more about it, the way I met Mr. Latte was not all that different. Our friend Jennifer played the role of the musician and put us together on a blind date.

Our appetizers arrived. Prakash had ordered *cotechino* sausages with yellow lentils and a salsa verde. He seemed delighted to be eating lentils, something familiar to him, and had a hard time resisting eating with his hands. Every now and then he would scoop up some of the toasted corn, a side dish, with his fingertips and deftly pop it into his mouth.

When our main courses were served, he pulled out a picture of his wife. She was smiling shyly at the camera, and was much younger than Prakash. Their two young sons were clinging to her.

He stopped chewing for a moment and said: "Do you know that in India I cannot hold my wife's hand in public?"

"I didn't realize that."

"I have begun dancing with my wife at weddings and I take her to the movies. But if you and your boyfriend came to visit me, he could not speak to my wife. She would have to stay in the kitchen." It seemed a rather arbitrary system.

I gave him a tortelloni stuffed with spinach and ricotta from my plate. They were like feather pillows and flush with nutmeg.

"This, what do you call it?" Prakash asked

"Tortelloni," I said.

"We have a pasta like this, made from the flour of chickpeas."

"Do you cook?" I asked.

"I do, and I work with my laborers on the farm, even though they are a lower caste."

"You are a liberated man."

"Yes," he said with a gleam in his eye. "Yes, I am!"

Meanwhile, he savored his penne with fresh tomatoes and basil, one noodle at a time. Our waitress, in New York fashion, reached to clear his plate several times without checking to see if he was finished. By the third time, I considered slapping her hand.

When he finished, he took a long drink of Lambrusco, then said, "You have a wonderful job, don't you?"

"Well, yes," I said, caught off guard. "Yes."

Afterwards, we took a cab to the Brooklyn Bridge and walked across. At its highest point, Prakash stopped. He looked back at lower Manhattan, then up toward the Empire State Building.

"Beautiful place," he said, and drew breath as if he could inhale the entire city.

Eating well, the Modenese way
All recipes adapted from Via Emilia

Cotechino with Yellow Lentils and Salsa Verde

This dish can be prepared in stages and then assembled when you want to serve it, so it's a perfect dinner party dish. *Cotechino* can be difficult to find, but some specialty stores have begun to import it, or make their own. If you can't get it, then look for a large, fatty pork sausage that is gently spiced. D'Artagnan sells a French garlic sausage that works well; www.dartagnan.com or (800)327-8246.

The lentils are kept quite plain. "I don't really want to season it," William Mattiello, the chef and owner of Via Emilia, explained to me. "Just a little bit of salt, because the *cotechino* and *salsa verde* already have a lot of taste." He said that every family in Modena, where he's from, has their own *salsa verde* recipe. This is his family's version. It makes a large amount—about 2 cups—but it is a difficult recipe to prepare in smaller quantity. Give some away, or plan to slather it on grilled fish or roasted chicken the next day.

2 cotechino (or 1 pound), or other rich, fatty pork sausage (about 2 or 3 inches diameter)
Leaves from 1 bunch basil (about 1 cup packed)
Leaves from 1/2 bunch flat-leaf parsley (about 1/3 to 1/2 cup packed)
1/2 green pepper, chopped
1 carrot, peeled and chopped
1/4 white onion, chopped
2 small green tomatoes, chopped
3 anchovies
1 tablespoon capers
1 tablespoon balsamic vinegar
5 tablespoons best-quality olive oil
Sea salt

1 onion, finely chopped

1 1/2 cups tiny yellow or green lentils (preferably masoor dal, which start out a salmon color and turn yellow when cooked)

1. Prick the *cotechino* all over with a fork, then wrap in cheesecloth, tying the ends with string. Brush the cheesecloth with oil (just a little bit). Place the bundles in a pot, large enough to fit them across the bottom. Cover with cold water and set over medium high heat. When it begins to boil, lower the heat to a sluggish simmer and cook for 1 to 3 hours (this time will vary depending on the kind of *cotechino* or sausage you get; it is done when the fat has become soft and buttery and the sausage yields easily to a knife). Remove from the heat. (You may let it cool at this point, and serve it later; rewarm it by dipping it into simmering water for 10 minutes or so.)

2. In a blender, combine the basil, parsley, pepper, carrot, white onion, tomatoes, anchovies and capers. Sprinkle in the vinegar and half the olive oil. Pulse once or twice, then leave it on and add the rest of the oil in a thin stream. The sauce should be fine but coarse around the edges, and the consistency of pesto. Add more olive oil, if needed. Taste and season.

3. Cover the base of a medium saucepan with oil and place over medium heat. Wait a minute or two, then add the onion and sauté until translucent. Pour in the lentils and 3 cups water. Simmer until the lentils are tender and the mixture is like a loose puree. Season with just a pinch of salt.

4. To serve, cut the *cotechino* into 1/4-inch slices. Spread the lentils on a platter, arrange the *cotechino* on top, and dab a little sauce on the slices of *cotechino*.

A HEARTY FIRST COURSE FOR 4.

Hazelnut Ice Cream Doused with Espresso

I think of this as the Italian version of a float, only it leaves you with more of a buzz. You can make it with lots of flavors of ice cream—almond, vanilla, chocolate, even coconut.

1 cup sugar

A few drops of lemon juice

1/2 cup whole hazelnuts

Pinch of sea salt

4 cups milk
1 vanilla bean, split
6 egg yolks
1/3 cup toasted and chopped hazelnuts
1 cup heavy cream
1 cup hot espresso

1. The day before, butter a baking sheet. Place a small pan containing 1/2 cup sugar and a few drops of lemon juice over medium heat. Once the sugar is dissolved, add the 1/2 cup whole hazelnuts and a pinch of salt and stir until the hazelnuts are toasted and the syrup is dark. Pour this mixture onto the buttered baking sheet and let cool. Once cool, put it in a sturdy plastic bag and mash it to a paste using a meat tenderizer or rolling pin.

2. Scald the milk in a large saucepan, then remove from the heat and stir in the vanilla bean. Beat the remaining 1/2 cup sugar with the egg yolks until light and fluffy. Stir this into the milk and place over medium low heat, stirring constantly until lightly thickened. It is done when the mixture coats the back of a spoon. Remove from the heat and strain into a bowl. Stir in the hazelnut paste and remaining toasted hazelnuts, breaking up any large pieces of paste. Set the bowl in a bowl of ice and stir often until the mixture is cool. Stir in the cream and chill overnight.

3. The next day, remove the vanilla bean from the ice cream mixture, then process the ice cream in your ice cream maker.

4. To serve, prepare 1 cup of espresso. Scoop ice cream into 4 bowls and pour a little espresso over each. Serve right away!

DESSERT FOR 4, PLUS ICE CREAM FOR ANOTHER DAY.

Chapter 17

PEELING AWAY THE PAST

"Veal chops, one for each of us," I said over the phone. "The fatter osso buco kind, or the ones like a pork chop?" Sherry asked.

"The pork-chop cut," I said, "and make sure they have some fat around the edge."

My oldest friend Sherry and I were working out our shopping list. For the past two years, I've been teaching her how to cook. We do it whenever we feel like it, and rather than me intimidating her with a bunch of so-called classic recipes, we cook what she and her husband Mark are in the mood to eat. My hope was that this way she might pick up a few dishes that would stick. Normally, we start after work, shopping together, then preparing dinner. I wanted her to see that she could cook without it being a day-long ordeal.

I did the same thing for my sister-in-law a few years ago, and my guidance was so inspiring that she hasn't turned on her stove since. With Sherry, things were promising from the start. The night I taught her to make creamed spinach—blanching the spinach, then simmering it in cream, crème fraîche, freshly grated nutmeg, salt and pepper, all done in fifteen minutes—she said, "You're kidding me, right? I'm calling my mother. I cannot believe she used to buy this in a can!"

When we were kids, Sherry wouldn't eat dinner at my family's house. My mother made her own jams, baked bread and served fresh vegetables. For Sherry, this bordered on the bizarre. I would spend most of the day persuading her to stay for dinner, only to have her sit down with us and then cry until my mother made the call. "Joan, I think Sherry wants to come home a little early. She doesn't seem to like asparagus."

But in recent years, Sherry's appetite has finally blossomed. And when she said that she would like to learn to cook, I could barely contain myself. Teaching her to cook would be a great excuse to see her and also a chance to be generous with her, something I hadn't always been.

We met when we were three. We played house. We were in Little League. We played tennis. And I was bossy and a bad sport throughout. When we were seven, for fun on the schoolbus I would sometimes push her head to the floor and say, "Drink your milk, little kitty!"

When we started cooking, she had just gotten engaged, and we lived in the same neighborhood. Now, she is married and pregnant, living in New Jersey. Our friendship window has been sliding closed.

As Mr. Latte and I boarded the bus in Port Authority heading for

Montclair and veal chops, I could feel my heart fluttering. I couldn't wait to see her. Lights streamed over our heads as the bus rolled through the Lincoln Tunnel. The bus groaned in the rush hour traffic, as we passed neighborhood upon neighborhood of houses, laid out like game pieces on a board. Manhattan felt like a distant planet.

"It's all the way up," Sherry called down as we mounted the staircase of her apartment complex.

"We brought Champagne," I said, "Is that okay?"

"I'll forgive you this time," she said, popping it into the freezer.

"The beets look great," I said. For the first time, she had started a little of the cooking, roasting beets and Vidalia onions.

"You think?" she asked, then turning to Mr. Latte, "You want a beer?"

"If you insist."

The veal chops were laid out on a plate. She had let them sit out, so they warmed up a little before cooking and would cook more evenly. I couldn't recall telling her to do this. And that has been the strange part about cooking with Sherry. Anyone can learn to prepare food but only a few people take to it like it is an innate calling.

Sherry holds a knife with authority and flips a roast with confidence. In a few short months her cabinets and fridge filled up with staples like Dijon mustard, olive oil, sea salt, fresh thyme and good butter.

In the past, we've roasted root vegetables and chicken and pork loin (rolled in ground nutmeg, anise seed, coriander and pepper); made cheesecake; braised radishes with mint; and prepared hangar steak with mashed potatoes. This visit, we settled on a menu of sautéed veal chops with sage, polenta and a salad of roasted beets and onions.

"You roasted that label very nicely," I said, pointing to the onions, shrunken and browned from roasting, the labels still attached.

"It's a garnish," she said.

She couldn't find polenta in her store, but she had Arborio rice in the cabinet, a lemon in the fruit basket and crème fraîche in the refrigerator. Good staples can save any meal. "We'll wing it," I said.

I talked her through the salad, guiding her to peel off the outer layer of onion skin and trim the ends, which get tough in the oven. She slid the layers off a few at a time and sliced them neatly once more so they were narrow, soft strips. "You could have used any onion," I said, "but Vidalias are sweet and I think they're a nice complement to beets." Together we peeled the beets and cut them into wedges; then I folded them together as she sprinkled a little balsamic vinegar and ground sea salt and pepper over top. She tastes and decides; I am the assistant.

Next, we prepared the rice, an experiment for both of us. We toasted the rice in a slick of oil and butter, then began adding hot chicken broth a little at a time. Sherry stirred with a wooden spoon that was charred in several spots from being left too close to a flame. "It's an heirloom," she said, reading my mind. "It wouldn't be my family's spoon without being so tortured and misshapen, right?"

As I zested the lemon, her clear blue eyes widened. "That's zesting?" she said. "I thought it meant taking the whole peel off."

"Nope," I said, and I tossed the thin shreds into the rice, which was thickening and getting tender. "We'll add a little now, and then taste it later to see if we want more."

Standing over the stove was hot. I touched her swollen belly. "Do you think this heat is O.K.?" I asked.

"Yes," she said. "Pregnant women have cooked for thousands of years."

"So how have you been feeling?"

"Fine really," she said, "But I'm forgetting things like crazy. The other day I moved my laundry from the washer to the dryer, then put the money in the washer and started it."

When the rice was almost done, I had her stir in the remaining zest, a little Parmesan cheese and a few large lumps of crème fraîche. "Just so you know," I said, "if an Italian saw us doing this, he'd have us drawn and quartered. Italians don't put crème fraîche into risotto. But it's good. Fat is good for babies, right?"

She looked uneasy until she tasted it. "Ooh! It's lemony. Mark!" she said, yelling into the living room, where he and Mr. Latte were watching basketball. "Wait till you taste the rice!"

The veal chops we seasoned with salt and pepper. I had her put the sauté pan over high heat for a minute or two. Then I dropped in a nugget of butter and poured in olive oil. "Why butter and oil?" she asked.

"Because the oil allows you to sear at a higher heat without burning the butter," I explained. She tossed in a handful of sage leaves, and I showed her how to lay the meat in the pan, guiding it as it settles on the surface without splashing oil. I made sure to keep the heat on high, to show her it was okay—something that took me years to learn.

Mark set the table and Mr. Latte popped open the Champagne as we arranged platters of food on the table. "Beets," Mark said. "My favorite vegetable."

"No hiding them under your bread this time," I said.

"Oh, you caught that?"

For dessert, she had bought molasses-clove cookies and orange and cream sorbet. I couldn't think of a better choice. I was proud of her, but worried that, with their baby coming and their plans to move even farther away, our visits will become less frequent. That our renewed bond might weaken.

One night, several weeks later, I had a dream that Sherry was having her baby. The next day, a strange number came up on my caller ID at work. I clicked over from another call. It was Sherry.

"You had your baby, didn't you?" I said.

"How did you know?"

"I had a dream last night that you did."

"That's too weird," she said. "I gave birth around three in the morning—to Julia. You're going to love her!"

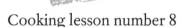

Cooking lesson number 8

Roasted Beet and Vidalia Onion Salad

The beets and onion are roasted to make them soft and concentrated. You slice them, and as you fold them together, the beets stain the onions a pretty pink. A little balsamic vinegar brightens the flavor and accentuates the sweetness. No extra oil is needed.

1 pound small beets, trimmed and scrubbed
2 Vidalia or Walla Walla onions, unpeeled and cut into quarters
Extra virgin olive oil
Sea salt
Freshly ground black pepper
1 tablespoon excellent balsamic vinegar (don't bother with supermarket brands)

1. Preheat your oven to 350°F. Place the beets on one half of a large piece of aluminum foil. Sprinkle with a little olive oil. Fold over the foil and seal the edges. Place the package on a baking sheet. Put the onions in a small roasting pan. Sprinkle with olive oil and turn to coat with the oil. Roast them both in the oven until they are tender. Turn the onions now and then. The onions should caramelize on the cut sides; they will probably finish first, in about 45 minutes. The beets will probably take an hour. Remove from the oven and let cool. Be careful when opening the foil; the steam will race out. While still warm, rub the beets in a towel (not your favorite one) to remove the skins.

2. Discard the outer skin and any tough ends from the onions, then slice in half lengthwise. Peel the beets and cut into 1/4-inch wedges. Scrape the onions and beets into a serving bowl (beets look great on white or cream).

Season with salt and pepper and sprinkle with the vinegar. Toss together gently, then taste, adding more salt, pepper or vinegar, as desired.

A LUSCIOUS SALAD FOR 4.

Creamy Risotto with Lemon

1 tablespoon butter
1 tablespoon olive oil
1 cup Arborio rice
5 cups chicken broth, simmering
Zest of 1 lemon
1/2 cup crème fraîche
1/4 cup freshly grated Parmigiano-Reggiano cheese
Sea salt

In a 4-quart pot, melt the butter and oil until foamy. Add the rice, and stir to coat. Cook for a few minutes, then begin adding the chicken broth a little at a time, just enough to loosen the rice without making it sloshy. Continue stirring. Pour in more broth when the previous ladleful has been absorbed. When half the broth has been added, stir in half the lemon zest. You will likely run out of broth before the rice is al dente. Add hot water; keep stirring! When the risotto is firm and not mushy, stir in the crème fraîche, Parmesan cheese and remaining lemon zest. Season with salt, if needed. It should be loose and creamy. (If you are making the veal chops, you will want to stop the rice before it is fully cooked so you can concentrate on the veal; add more liquid and reheat for a minute before serving.)

4 SERVINGS.

Veal Chops with Sage

If you are not in the mood for a big, hefty chop, pound the meat flat with a mallet, keeping the bone on, like they do with veal Milanese. It will cook more quickly. You may also substitute pork chops for the veal. If you do, get nice fatty ones (pork has gotten so dull and lean) and soak the chops in salted water for a few hours to brine them. It will keep them nice and moist and seasoned throughout.

4 veal chops, with fat on the outer edge, about 3/4-inch thick, at room temperature

Sea salt
Freshly ground black pepper, or grains of paradise
2 tablespoons unsalted butter
1 tablespoon olive oil or vegetable oil
12 large sage leaves

Season the veal chops on one side with a generous amount of salt and pepper. Place a sauté pan large enough to fit the chops in a single layer over high heat for a minute or two. Add the butter and oil and heat until the foam subsides. Lay the veal chops in the pan, seasoned-side down. Season the other side of the chops, and sprinkle over the sage leaves, pushing a few down into the base of the pan. Let the chops cook for 2 to 3 minutes, until browned, then turn and cook on the other side for 2 minutes. Regulate the heat so they don't burn. Pile them up on a thick rustic plate, if you have one.

VEAL CHOPS FOR 4.

Chapter 18

HARD THOUGHTS SOFTEN OVER DINNER

We arrived at Lupa in Greenwich Village late one Sunday afternoon. The sun was setting and a chill was sinking into the air like ink on paper. We had been walking for hours, and we were ready for a beer. The chairs at Lupa are hard, the tables small squares. It is spare but warm, like a ski lodge.

We drank Peronis and read our menus. When I looked up at Mr. Latte, he was studying his menu as if it were the op-ed page. Who knew that I'd see this day? He still orders pasta at French restaurants and duck at Italian ones, but he has proved to have the appetite and curiosity of a fine gourmand. He may devour sweetbreads like a grizzly bear tossing back fish, but he will be quite discerning about them, without the inhibitions of a foodie. At Ducasse, for instance, he announced that his foie gras ravioli "smells like minestrone." (It did.)

He still needed some reform, but he was no longer my bumbling dining muse. "Mr. Latte" didn't really fit him anymore. He was just Tad. Tad Friend—his likable and fitting given name.

I went back to my menu. My eyes bounced from fried pork to zucchini with almonds to testa (head cheese). "I'd like one of everything," I said.

"It is a tempting menu," Tad agreed. "I think I like Italian food best."

"What would be second? American?"

"Probably," he said. "I know it should be French, but French food just doesn't convince me. It's either too fussy and pristine, or too smeared in heavy sauces. I never feel good after eating it." I smiled. It reminded me of something a Roman restaurateur once told me: "People like French food because the flavors capture your attention, but you have to sleep at night, and this is not so easy."

Tad was heading for an issue that had long been rumbling beneath our relationship. We both enjoy good food, but I adore dining, and my profession calls for me to take an interest in all levels of food, all the time. It is not the same for him. And he was still weighing in too heavily. We needed a course correction.

"I think it's something else," I said. "I think that if you saw dining in a different way you might enjoy French restaurants, and French food, more. Before we met, you dined to see friends and feed yourself, rather than as a form of entertainment or pleasure."

"That's true," Tad said, nodding. Like many people, he feels trapped in fancy restaurants. He worries that he is at the mercy of the waiters, who might inflict a four-hour meal on him, so he'd rather go back again and again to the same three cozy neighborhood places.

We dipped bread in freshly pressed green olive oil and drank our beers. The first course arrived: *bavette cacio e pepe* and *bucatini alla amatriciana*.

"What's the difference between this and lamb chops served at Jean Georges?" Tad asked, as he swirled the bavette. "Why is that supposedly better?" The *bavette*, a long thin pasta, had been folded together with grated sheep's milk and cow's milk cheeses, fresh cracked pepper, butter and terrific olive oil. The noodles had a silky coating of sauce; it was creamy and peppery and you could taste the earth in the cheeses. It was a beautiful dish.

"Both can be delicious," I said. "It's just that there may be more to preparing the lamb chops than you might see, and this is simpler and less precise."

"So why do people want to eat food of equal pleasure but have six waiters fluttering around them, giving them a new napkin every five minutes?" Our only waiter cleared away our dishes.

"Some people like to be pampered or need to feel special," I said. "Or they feel that the food demands such formality, and they see it as entertainment. What do you think?"

"I think it's silly."

On some level he was right. A recent dining experience was still haunting me. I had been the guest of a restaurant critic who takes free meals. He ordered up a Roman banquet, and grew more glassy-eyed and jolly as each course rolled out. Five hours passed, during which I had about thirty minutes-worth of topics to talk to him about. At one in the morning, as we parted on the curb, I couldn't hold back my frustration. "Thank you for inviting me," I said, "I'm impressed by your dining stamina. I've never done well at long meals like that. I can't keep track of everything."

"Really?" the man said, looking drugged by foie gras. "I love them. I love to just let the flavors wash over me."

So I knew exactly what Tad meant. But I couldn't concede his point entirely, or we'd be eating pizza every night.

So, as our desserts arrived, I said: "I think it's just that you find it insincere."

"Yeah, I like real human interaction. Ducasse's waiters are smiling zombies. You could say to them, 'There is a tarantula crawling up your neck,' and they'd bow."

He took a sip of his beer while I sunk my spoon into a spiced date. They had shed their skins while simmering in red wine, and now lay in a pool of wine sauce, fragrant with honey, clove, peppercorns and orange zest. Next to them was a dab of mascarpone. As I finished each one, I was left with a long, smooth brown seed—something that would never be the case at a fine French restaurant. But I was beginning to regret what I had said about the imprecision of this kind of cooking. At its best, it was precise and the flavors were clear.

"So, you don't like the theater of dining," I said. "I understand that." And I do. I used to be more in awe of the restaurant experience. Now, I am just as interested in how well the restaurant allows me to enjoy the people I'm with. A restaurant that is welcoming does not have to have flawless food to be likable.

"But the way food is presented, the palette of colors used, the lighting in the room, the thickness of the plate all affect the enjoyment of it," I continued. "And if you're interested in more than just feeding your hunger, there should be room to appreciate those things."

"Maybe," Tad said. "But restaurants started as a way to feed people, right?" I nodded, reaching for more of the dates. "Then they were feeding and pleasing, and that's fine. But I don't need feeding and pleasing and stupefying. The further an activity moves from its original purpose, the closer it comes to decadence." I agreed. There were a lot of decadent restaurants in New York in the late 1990s.

We sat in silence for a while, the noise of the diners burbling around us.

"Maybe we should think of it in terms of writing," I said, trying another tack. "Some of the writers you admire most appear to write quite simply. Their sentences are clear, concise."

"Right, and it seems effortless."

"Yes, but not all readers appreciate the effort, or the effect," I said, "and I think that's the way it is with the best cooking these days."

"Yeah, but what about writers like Proust, who craft incredibly complicated prose?"

"But very few writers can pull that off, right?"

"Right."

"Well, it's the same way with chefs."

Tad reached for my hand and smiled. We had been eating, and talking, for a long time. Nearly four hours.

The best kind of food for dining

Both recipes adapted from Lupa.

Bavette Cacio e Pepe

One is tempted to add more cheese, butter and oil to this recipe. Resist this impulse. There should be just enough butter and oil to coat the pasta like a salad dressing, and just enough cheese to season it. If you add too much, the pasta will get oily and the cheese will make it loathsomely heavy. When done just right, it's an elegant dish with compact flavor.

Sea salt
1/4 cup finely grated Parmigiano-Reggiano cheese
1/4 cup finely grated pecorino Romano cheese
1/2 pound DeCecco linguini fini
2 tablespoons unsalted butter, chilled
2 tablespoons extra virgin olive oil
1 tablespoon very coarse, freshly ground black pepper

1. Bring a large pot of water to a boil. Sprinkle in enough sea salt so that it tastes seasoned. Meanwhile, mix the cheeses together in a small bowl. When the water boils, add the linguini and cook it for 6 minutes, stirring occasionally. Near the end of cooking, scoop out about 1/2 cup of cooking water and reserve.

2. Drain the pasta and return it to the pot. Drop in the butter, oil and 1/2 tablespoon pepper and stir with tongs or a large fork, lifting and folding the pasta together. Add about 1/4 cup of the pasta water to the pot and place it over medium-high heat. Cook for a minute, stirring to emulsify the sauce. Test a noodle to see if it's done. It should still be a bit firm in the center, though not as stiff as licorice. Remove from the heat and sprinkle half the cheese over the pasta. Blend once more, then divide the pasta among four warm bowls. Pass the rest of the cheese and pepper at the table.

PASTA FOR 4, AS A FIRST COURSE.

Apician Spiced Dates

When Tad and I ate at Lupa, the dates were served whole with the seeds in them. But when I asked for the recipe, it had been altered so that the dates were stuffed with almonds. I loved the plain version, but this is even better. The crunch of the almonds gives you relief from the rich, sticky dates, and they add a quiet background flavor.

1 bottle light-bodied red wine, like Beaujolais
8 medjool dates
16 whole almonds, skin left on, lightly toasted
1/4 cup honey
1 tablespoon whole black peppercorns
1 tablespoon cloves
1 tablespoon dried or fresh grated orange zest

4 whole allspice berries
2 2-inch cinnamon sticks
1 dried bay leaf
1/4 cup mascarpone cheese, at room temperature
Coarse sea salt

1. Pour the wine into a saucepan and bring to a simmer. Add the dates and poach them until the skins blister, about 5 minutes. Using a slotted spoon, lift out the dates and, while they're still warm, take off the skins (taking care not to burn your hands). Discard the skins. Cut open the dates on one long side, remove the pits and place two almonds in the center of each date. Fold closed.

2. Add the honey, peppercorns, cloves, orange zest, allspice, cinnamon sticks and bay leaf to the wine and continue simmering until the wine is reduced by half, about 20 minutes. Strain the wine. (The dessert may be prepared to this point up to 2 days ahead, then stored in the refrigerator.) When ready to serve, pour the wine into a saucepan. Add the dates to the wine and heat gently, over medium low heat, until warmed through, but not hot. Place a dollop of mascarpone in the center of each of four plates. Spoon 2 dates and a little wine sauce on each plate, then sprinkle lightly with sea salt.

DESSERT FOR 4.

Chapter 19

WHEN IN ROME, EAT OXTAIL STEW!

I held my grandmother's hand as the plane took off from New York. "Your hands are cold!" she said. "These hands are made for pastry. Don't you like to fly? You must not. I do. I think it's fun!"

"Grandmom," I said, "You may be the only person in America who feels that way right now."

After her first trip out of the country the year before, my grandmother said there was one more place she would like to go: Rome.

For more than a decade, she had been the host at an elegant Italian-American restaurant in Hatboro, Pennsylvania. This was her chance to see, and taste, the real thing. My mother, my sister Rhonda, and I had planned carefully, arranging a trip that was a mix of Roman ruins, the food market, churches and street life. I was in charge of making sure we ate well.

Once there, we would meet Rhonda, her husband Paul and their eighteen-month-old son Luke. I plotted a good trattoria each day for lunch. We decided, having Luke along, that lunch should be our big meal and that trattorias would be the most accommodating. It was an easy compromise. In most of Italy, and in Rome in particular, that's where the best food is.

Our first night, my mother, grandmother and I went to a restaurant called Perilli, in Testaccio, a neighborhood known for its butchers and for its restaurants, which serve classic Roman dishes like *pajata* (calves' intestines on pasta), *involtini* (thin pieces of veal or beef rolled around fillings like prosciutto, chard, nuts, raisins and basil), and rabbit cacciatore.

We arrived at eight, just as the restaurant was opening, and were immediately pegged as tourists. I stumbled through the menu, translating as best I could and distinguishing between the classic and new dishes. My mother pinched her face at the various offerings of liver, tripe and pork jowl, and ordered *penne alla arrabiata*, which has a simple, spicy red sauce. My grandmother, to my delight, ordered *rigatoni con sugo di coda*, or rigatoni with oxtail sauce.

"What would you like after?" the waiter asked us. I explained to my mother and grandmother that in Rome, people usually begin with pasta and then have meat or fish as a main course. "Oh, no, that will be plenty," my grandmother said. "Do they have salad?" my mother asked. The waiter pressed his lips together and shifted his weight.

"That will be fine, thank you," I said to him.

My grandmother nibbled her pasta as she always eats, with her eyes on her plate and her arms held closely, like a mouse, until there wasn't a speck of sauce left in the bowl. When she finally looked up, she lamented that there hadn't been more meat in the sauce. The rigatoni had been coated in a rich, velvety jus with a single oxtail nestled among the noodles.

"They serve it that way," I said, excited for her to understand, "because that kind of dish was something poor people ate. You only got a single oxtail, because meat was scarce. The pasta helped make a meal out of it." She shrugged.

Things didn't improve much. Every morning at our hotel's pleasant but standard buffet breakfast, she would feast, and no gentle nudging would stop her. She might have a piece of lemon crostata or cereal, then move on to a plate of cured meats. There were good, crisp rosetta rolls, and she ate them too.

By the time we reached our lunch destination, she was barely hungry. She would order soup, or a pasta, or perhaps a salad, a dish Romans consider no more than an accessory to the main course. As much as I tried to persuade her, she never dined in courses. And yet, even when she said she wasn't all that hungry, she would clean her plate.

It is not that I wanted her to gorge herself like a goose destined for foie gras, but that she was missing the chance to understand how another culture eats. She would go home thinking Italians eat just the same as we pretend they do here.

My grandmother did, however, choose well from menus. And so after a deliriously good meal of braised oxtails for me and rabbit cacciatore (braised, with a simple sauce of vinegar, cooking juices and rosemary) for her, I tried once more to explain how Italians dine.

"I wouldn't be able to finish it all," she said, after I made my case.

"You don't have to," I said. "It's more about the variety and rhythm of the meal."

"Well, I just wasn't raised that way."

"I know," I said, "but it's the difference between eating for sustenance and dining. People eat in restaurants because they have money to pay someone to make and serve their meal. So the food isn't so scarce or precious. You should taste everything you want to taste. Plus the dollar is incredibly good right now."

"But all of the starving people in the world."

"You're not saving them by finishing your plate at a trattoria in Rome!" I said sharply, regretting the words as they tumbled from my mouth. I had always talked back, and I was still doing it now.

"When I was young," she said firmly, "Pop and I, on our way to the market, would stop at the bar. If you bought a beer, you'd get a free sandwich. So he'd go in, order a beer and eat his sandwich. Then he'd order another beer and bring the sandwich out to me. That was lunch and that was dining out."

My mother leapt in to mend the situation. "It's all right, Judy," my grandmother said to her, "she's young yet. She's got a lot to learn." I thought I might self-combust.

O.K., I thought, she had found a way to live that made sense to her and made her happy. But now I needed to do the same for myself.

And so I ordered braised lamb and roasted porcini. I devoured Roman artichokes, braised with pennyroyal, and leggy *puntarelle*, a chicory served with a garlicky anchovy dressing. I savored *stracciatelle*, the egg-drop soup, which, as the name suggests, looks like "rags," and *bucatini alla amatriciana*, a spaghetti-like pasta served with *guanciale* (cured pig jowl or cheek), tomato, cheese and onion. I drank wine at lunch and ate dessert alone. I loved Rome more than ever, and I wanted to swallow it up with me.

Some of my favorite things—in Rome, at least

Stracciatelle, a.k.a. "Little Rags" Soup

This is not the kind of soup you will see on magazine covers. But it compensates for its homeliness with exceptional flavor.

5 cups chicken broth, preferably homemade
1 clove garlic
6 egg yolks
3 egg whites
3/4 cup freshly grated Parmigiano-Reggiano cheese

Bring the broth to a simmer in a deep, narrow pan. Drop in the garlic and cook for 5 minutes. Meanwhile, whisk together the eggs and cheese. Take the pan off the heat, tilt in the egg mixture and gently swirl the pan a few times (swirling keeps the egg intact, stirring would ruin this), just until the egg lightens in color and collects in fluffy lumps. (You may also do this in the serving bowls: pour the hot broth into deep bowls, tip a little egg in each one and then swirl or very gently stir.) Carefully ladle the broth into four warm bowls.

SOUP FOR 4; PERHAPS AS A FIRST COURSE—IT'S NOT VERY FILLING.

Coda alla Vaccinara (Oxtails Braised with Tomato and Celery)

Oxtail often gets lumped with offal in people's minds. It's not; it's exactly what the name suggests. What is so unseemly about a tail, when we happily eat the hind legs? Oxtail is powerfully flavored (as opposed to something dull and expensive like the fillet) and has lots of gelatin, which means it makes great stews and terrines.

After I returned from Rome, I called a few chefs to ask how they prepare and serve oxtail. A number of them said they now deboned the meat and arranged it on the plate, because diners didn't want to deal with the bones. Attacking the bone is half the pleasure of eating this cut of meat, so encourage your guests, or family, to enjoy it.

If you have leftovers, you may stretch them by cooking pasta (rigatoni or penne) and folding it into the reheated sauce and oxtails.

1/4 pound pancetta, cut into 1/4-inch dice

1 carrot, peeled and finely diced

1 small onion, finely diced

4 inner stalks celery, 1 finely diced, 3 sliced into 3-inch-long pieces

Extra virgin olive oil

3 pounds good meaty oxtail (trimmed weight), severed at each joint into
     pieces about 3 inches long

Sea salt

Freshly ground black pepper

1 1/2 tablespoons tomato paste

2 cups white wine

3 sprigs marjoram or 1 1/2 teaspoons dried leaves

1/4 teaspoon ground cloves

1/4 teaspoon ground cinnamon

1 28-ounce can peeled San Marzano tomatoes, drained

1. Preheat your oven to 325°F. Find a deep, heavy casserole or pot that can fit all of the oxtails in one layer. (Don't put them in yet!) In the pot, put the pancetta, carrot, onion, and diced celery, and enough olive oil to cover the bottom of the pot with a thin film. Place over medium heat and cook until the pancetta renders its fat, about 15 minutes. Season the oxtails on all sides with salt and pepper, add them to the pot and brown well on all sides, turning them only after they've browned. Remove the oxtails to a bowl, spoon off any excess fat, then put the pot back on the heat.

2. Add the tomato paste to the vegetables and stir so that it comes in contact with the bottom. Cook and caramelize it a little, about 2 minutes. Stir in the wine and bring to a boil for a few minutes. Toss in the marjoram, cloves and cinnamon, then the tomatoes, squishing them between your fingers as they fall into the pan. Give it a stir.

3. Return the oxtails to the pot, nestling them in the vegetables. The liquid must be as high as one-third of the ingredients. If it's not, add a little water. Bring the liquid to a boil, cover the pot and slip it into the oven. Braise for 1 1/2 hours, turning the oxtails now and then. Add the remaining celery pieces, then continue cooking until the meat is tender and falling off the bone, about 30 to 60 minutes longer.

4. Remove the pot from the oven and let sit for 15 minutes. Skim off excess fat. Season with salt and pepper. Serve on a large platter or in shallow bowls, making sure everyone gets a bit of the pulpy sauce and some celery.

DINNER FOR 6.

Puntarelle with Anchovy Dressing

This dressing may remind you of Caesar dressing with its pungency, but it is less apologetic. The anchovies are not mellowed with egg, so they cry out before you even put them in your mouth. The puntarelle greens are crisp and bitter, the salt is pronounced. It is one of the great salads of the world yet is barely known here.

This salad is not meant to be served as lunch. You cannot eat a lot of it. Serve it only as a change of pace in a meal. There are many dishes—like the braised oxtail, tripe stew, roasted chicken or lamb cacciatore—that beg for its candid relief.

    4 handfuls puntarelle, torn into small pieces (puntarelle is tough to find
        on this side of the Atlantic—try a farmers' market; frisée is a good
        substitute)
    1 head Belgian endive, cut into long, thin strips
    1 large clove garlic
    4 plump oil-packed anchovy fillets, rinsed
    2 tablespoons red wine vinegar
    Extra virgin olive oil
    Freshly ground black pepper

1. Fill a large bowl with water and ice. Add the puntarelle and endive and chill for half an hour or so.

2. Rinse the anchovies. In a mortar and pestle, mash together the garlic and anchovies until a smooth paste forms. Stir in the vinegar and let stand for a few minutes.

3. When ready to serve, drain and dry the greens in a salad spinner and place in a large bowl. Pour a tablespoon or two of olive oil over the greens and season with pepper. Toss until lightly coated. Divide among four shallow bowls. Serve each with a spoonful of the anchovy dressing dolloped on top, or simply leave the dressing in the spoon and set it on top of the salad. Each person should mix his or her own salad, using a fork and spoon.

4 SALADS DESIGNED TO ACCOMPANY A RICH MEAL.

Chapter 20

HEIDI SAVES THE DAY

Before my family left for Rome, I did the math. Given eleven days of lunches and light dinners, each of us could taste approximately fifty-five dishes. We could compare *carciofi alla romana* among restaurants, squeeze in a few visits to Giolitti, the famous gelateria, and stop in for *pizza bianca* at the Antico Forno in Campo dei Fiori.

But to my surprise, my family members had their own interests. They wanted to see the Forum and wade among the throngs in the Sistine Chapel. The more I pressed my case, the more disapproval among my family grew against me.

My nephew, Luke, who is one-and-a-half, was my only ally. In restaurants, he lived it up. He has blond curls all over his head and big hazel eyes. Waiters doted on him; they served him cold milk, extra-milky coffee (he likes coffee), gnocchi with butter and freshly grated pecorino Romano cheese, artichokes and tiny bits of prosciutto. And he ate heartily.

With Luke on my side, I ate so many artichokes that I thought my skin might turn green. I dragged everyone to Giolitti (alas, only once) and the bakery in Campo dei Fiori, and even managed a trip to a small dairy shop that sells slices of fresh-baked ricotta. The exterior of the cheese chars in the heat of the oven, rendering it crisp and salty, while the inside is like a warm, creamy custard.

My popularity continued to plummet until Heidi Da Empoli, an old friend, came into the picture. She had offered to come by to meet my family and to take us on a driving tour of the city. I hadn't seen her in almost a decade. Now sixty, she is still striking, with fine bones, porcelain skin and thick dark brown hair. Heidi grew up in Switzerland. When she was a young woman, she fell in love with a Roman and has lived in Rome ever since. I met her and her son, Giuliano, on a train in Switzerland when I was in college.

When she arrived at our hotel, we squeezed into her pale blue 1973 Fiat coup, and headed out, breezing by the Santa Maria Maggiore, pausing at the pyramid near the city wall. She wanted to show us the Appian Way, but at its entrance a police officer signaled for us to turn around. Heidi stuck her head out the window and called the guard over, deluging him with words and pointing down the road, then at us in the car. We sat tight. Her Italian, with its remnants of Swiss German, swoops high and low in thrilling musical notes, like an excited bird. Finally, he waved us by.

"Wow," Paul said. "That was great. How did you do that?"

"Oh, I told a very big lie," she said, shifting gears along the lumpy road. "I told him you were staying in one of the villas and I was taking you home." Paul nudged me and smiled. I knew they would like her.

The next evening, we were invited for dinner at her home. When Heidi opened the door to her apartment, we shuffled in quietly and sat down on sofas draped with tapestries in the living room. Heidi disappeared for a moment, and while she was gone I could feel the tension among my family fading. They were travel weary; being in someone's home was good medicine. Heidi returned carrying a bottle of Champagne. Everyone perked up. "Who can open these things?" she asked. "I am not so coordinated!" Paul took the bottle, while she sat down among us like a nurturing queen at court.

Giuliano, who is my age, arrived, in Italian fashion, very late. The last time I saw him, he had been a shy college student. Now he was confident and witty. He dressed in a suit and was handsome, with dark curly hair and long sideburns. In the years that have passed, our interests have oddly merged. Giuliano has published a number of books on culture and is a political columnist for *Il Sole 24 Ore*, Italy's main financial newspaper. He has also become a serious gourmet. After his father died suddenly a few years ago, he lived in Paris and became obsessed with dining, methodically visiting all of the city's great restaurants.

Heidi disappeared again behind a door into what was formerly a maid's hallway leading to the kitchen, isolated so that no sounds of cooking could be heard. My family and Giuliano were discussing the Disney aspect of the Vatican—"They're hauling in the dinero," Paul was saying, then Rhonda: "Yes, but for the cost of admission, I'd like to see the Pope in that Pyrex-cube mobile he's got"—when Heidi called us to the table. It was set with delicate white linen and silver. Heidi carried a large ceramic tureen, serving rigatoni with a white Bolognese, a meat sauce made without tomato, a variation you rarely see in America. Its sweet, beefy aroma curled up from the dish in ribbons of steam, dissolving into the air. "How much would you like, Judy?" Heidi asked as she served my mother. "There will be another course after this." Aha! They would be forced to eat a proper Italian meal.

Across the table, Rhonda had warmed to Giuliano, who was pouring wine. "Heidi," she said, trying to look serious, "just so you know, Giuliano dripped on your tablecloth. That wasn't me!"

"Rhonda, you have such fine manners," he said. "Amanda, I thought you told me your family was properly brought up."

When we tasted the rigatoni, Rhonda and I looked at each other with a mixture of shock and delight, that feeling you have when you taste something that will stay with you forever. The tubes of pasta were swathed with the rich, sticky juices. Without the acidity of a classic Bolognese, it seemed more aromatic, as if tomatoes masked the flavors of the meat and other vegetables. There were tiny bits of carrot and porcini among the silky lumps of beef and pork.

Heidi went into the kitchen once more while Giuliano told us stories of summers spent in Switzerland, where he was once pulled over by the police for riding his bicycle with no hands. "I am telling you," he said, "cow bells and neutrality create a good image. But the Swiss are a very peculiar species."

"You are still half Swiss, you know, Giuliano," Heidi said, as she brought in a plate of crisp fried potatoes and veal scallopine, which were sealed in by a thick layer of eggs and Parmesan cheese. When Heidi sautéed them, the eggs had fluffed up around the veal, creating a crust that was like a soufflé, gently flavored with cheese. It was an Italian dish with her Swiss influence.

"My mother, she does not always cook this way," Giuliano said to me. "I normally get soup from a can."

"Oh, do not listen to him!" Heidi said, laughing, brushing her hand in the air toward him. "I can have ambition, you know!"

Seeing them was a joy. It reinforced an old friendship that, with luck, will last for life. To my delight, the evening also put me back in favor with my family and changed the tenor of our vacation.

A few nights later, our last in Rome, I ordered a grappa after dessert.

"Hm, what's that?" my grandmother asked as the waiter set the glass down before me.

"It's grappa," I said, "Would you like a sip?"

"I suppose I'll give it a try."

I handed her the tall glass with the clear fiery liquid, saying nothing more. She tilted her head back and took a mouthful. Her eyes scrunched up, her lips squeezed together in a thin line and she shook all over. Then she began laughing, and said, "That's awful!!"

She still talks about that grappa, and the dinner Heidi made. But I haven't heard a word about the breakfast at the hotel.

Heidi Da Empoli's rejuvenating dinner

Rigatoni with White Bolognese

Two days after we returned from Rome, I got an e-mail from Rhonda, who lives in England, announcing the results of her experiments with the rigatoni and various other treats that we tasted on our trip. The race was on. Our e-mails flew back and forth as we both refined our versions of this dish. In the end, stubborn as we are, we stuck to our own recipes. Rhonda uses less carrot, more wine and twice the bouillon; she also adds the mushroom broth and bouillon at the same time. Play around and see which way you prefer it. Rhonda also had an excellent tip. "I saved the pasta cooking water," she wrote, "and added some of it to the leftovers when I put them away—it helped keep them moist when reheated."

Extra virgin olive oil
1/2 sweet onion, finely chopped
2 medium carrots, peeled and finely chopped

1 stalk celery, finely chopped
Sea salt
Freshly ground black pepper
1 pound mild Italian pork sausage meat, removed from casings
1 pound ground beef (not lean; you want fat in it)
1 1/2 cups dry Italian white wine
1 cube beef bouillon dissolved in 2 cups simmering water
1 1/2 ounces dried porcini mushrooms rehydrated in 3 cups lukewarm
    water
1/3 cup heavy cream
1 pound rigatoni
3/4 cup freshly grated Parmigiano-Reggiano cheese

1. Add enough oil to a very large, deep sauté pan to coat the bottom with
a thin film and place over medium high heat. When the oil shimmers, add the
onion, carrots and celery and sauté, stirring to coat with oil, until glassy and
just tender, about 5 minutes. Season lightly as they cook. (If the pan does
not have much room for the meat, pour vegetables into a bowl near the stove,
and return the pan to the heat; otherwise, leave them in the pan.) Add the
sausage and beef to the pan, breaking them into walnut-size pieces. Brown
the meat well, adjusting the heat so the meat does not stew.

2. Pour in the wine and keep at a rapid simmer until the pan is almost dry.
Then pour in 1 1/2 cups beef bouillon and lower the heat to medium. Simmer
gently, uncovered, until the bouillon is nearly gone. Stir now and then. Meanwhile, chop the rehydrated porcini into small pieces, reserving the mushroom
broth. Bring a large pot of salted water to a boil.

3. Stir the chopped porcini along with enough mushroom broth into the
simmering sauce to cover the meat halfway (about 1 cup) and continue simmering another 10 minutes. The sauce should be quite loose, but not soupy.
Taste and adjust seasoning. It should be highly seasoned. When you think it's
the right consistency, pour over the cream and fold to mix, then shut off the
heat and cover.

4. When the pasta water is at a full boil, add the rigatoni and cook until
still firm, but not hard, in the center. When the pasta is almost done, scoop
out 1 cup of pasta water and keep it near the stove. Drain the pasta and add
it back to the pot. Pour the sauce on top and fold it in with a wooden spoon.
The pasta should not be dry. Add a little mushroom broth or pasta water to

loosen it. (It will continue to soak up sauce on the way to the table.) Present the pasta on a deep platter or in a tureen. Pass the cheese at the table.

PASTA FOR 4.

Veal Scaloppine With Fluffy Parmesan

The one difficult part of this recipe is flipping the veal without squishing the nice fluffy browned coating. Use a long and very thin spatula (not one of those plastic ones with vents) and use a fork to steady the meat on the spatula. Hold the veal close to the pan, so it doesn't flop into it, and with the fork—piercing the meat if necessary—carefully turn the veal and lay it back in the pan. You can also do this off the heat, so it doesn't seem so pressured.

4 eggs
1 cup freshly grated Parmigiano-Reggiano and pecorino Romano cheeses
    (1/2 cup each)
Flour
4 veal cutlets (about 1 pound total), pounded very thin (like lemon peel)
Extra virgin olive oil

1. In a wide, shallow bowl, lightly whisk the eggs and stir in the cheese. Cover a large plate with a thin layer of flour. Put the bowl, plate and veal near to the stove. Place a large nonstick sauté pan over medium-high heat. Add enough oil to the pan to thinly coat the base.

2. As it heats, dip a veal cutlet in the flour, pressing lightly, then flipping it to coat the other side. Lift the cutlet and shake off any excess flour (I hold it pinched between my fingers and flick it with my other hand), then lay in the egg mixture, turning to coat, and making sure the cheese clings to it. Lay the cutlet in the sauté pan, and repeat with the other cutlets, filling the base of the pan. Let sauté until lightly browned, about 1 minute. Then, using a thin spatula and a fork to guide the cutlet, turn and brown the other side, another minute. If it sits, it will lose its fluff, so remove the veal from the pan and serve right away.

VEAL CUTLETS FOR 4.

Chapter 21

A REASON TO COOK

I consider it normal to go to bed thinking of Dover sole and to wake up pondering beets. But lately my food fantasies had reached a feverish pitch. While I was on the subway, I dreamed about shaving truffles over pasta. As I pushed my cart around Fairway, I assembled a pear tart in my head. As my editor talked to me gravely about my expenses, I imagined a *croque monsieur* bubbling away under a broiler.

My desire to cook has always depended on my mood. When I am blue, I make tea and cook simple, spare dishes. A soft boiled egg. Chickpeas with a cumin dressing. When things are going well, my kitchen becomes crowded with food. There will be ice cream in the freezer, a good sherry in the refrigerator door, persimmons or figs on my fruit plate.

Since I've known Tad, my refrigerator has been near to bursting. But even so, I had stopped inviting people over for dinner. My small apartment had become cluttered with books, wine bottles, suitcases and bags of dried beans. I was tired of borrowing chairs from my neighbor and asking guests to keep the same fork all night, from duck through the apple tart.

Now, though, I wanted to cook and I wanted friends to come over again, to share my bounty.

So I asked our friends John and Aleksandra to dinner. I was fixated on a meal that Tad and I order from a nearby Italian restaurant. Each time, we scour the menu, then surrender to the same dish: pappardelle with veal ragù. I felt a pang of guilt every time we ordered it. Why didn't I just make it?

I finally did. I went to my butcher and asked for the fattiest ground veal he had (it came from the shoulder) and some pork and fennel sausages. I browned the meats, and then sautéed celery, garlic and a little carrot, deglazing the pan with red wine, and cooking it all down in milk and beef broth with a few sage leaves and a handful of canned San Marzano tomatoes. It tasted good—although it was nothing like the takeout veal sauce.

Normally, I don't invite people to help in the kitchen, and I don't like to express my worries about the meal. Guests don't need to feel nervous about what their host is cooking. But I asked John, who spends a fair amount of time in Italy, to teach me to cook pasta correctly, standing by the stove with me as we tested the noodles. Unless it is in soup or is baked, Italians eat their pasta quite firm. Al dente means you should feel your teeth cutting through it. Pasta goes from hard to mushy quite quickly, and I've always had a tough time believing that it will continue cooking out of the water, so I take it out too late and by the time it reaches the table, it's gummy.

"Here, taste this!" I said, fetching a piece of fusilli for each of us. It was like biting into a new piece of gum. "Oh, hurry, it's done," he said, leaping in and dumping the pasta into the colander in my sink.

I rarely serve pasta for guests, but I've since decided to change this policy. You can make a sauce ahead of time, it's easy to serve, and it's the kind of food that is enjoyable to watch people eat. They twirl the noodles, lifting and working to capture bits of sauce. And people always go back for more. Aleksandra, who eats slowly and daintily, had two helpings.

For dessert, I turned to an old favorite, Marcella Hazan's walnut cake (in *Essentials of Classic Italian Cooking* and on page 30 in this book), which I altered by doubling the lemon zest and adding whole walnuts to the batter. Its flavor was robust and buttery with the tang of lemon in the background. But because I had ground the nuts before they were completely cool, they had become pasty and gave the cake all the delicacy of a dry sponge. (It is quite delicious if you behave and follow the original recipe.)

Gulping water between every bite, John and Aleksandra insisted it was fine. But I shrugged it off. I was happier than I had been in years, and it was righting things long out of balance. I am sure that cake will be outdone by other disasters and, in the future, perhaps even redeemed by something exquisite. They'd be back for dinner again.

I invited more friends over, this time Mark and Sherry. And that is where the Dover sole and beets came in. I went to the grocery store and stared like a zombie at the fish display, waiting for something to catch my eye. I wanted a sweet, oily fish to pair with parsnips and some small potatoes I had at home. How exactly they would configure themselves was still unclear. Beets, I thought, would marry well with a sweet fish and could be dressed with something also a little sweet but tangy. I left the store with Chilean sea bass, beets and chives.

I dropped off my groceries at the café where Tad was reading the paper and then went for a walk in the park. Often, a menu will take the entire day to shape itself in my head. Ideas float in and out like daydreams. As runners fluttered by me, I decided to roast the fish and serve it on a very loose, almost saucelike puree of the parsnips and potatoes. We would begin with Prosecco and a few simple hors d'oeuvres— olives and slices of baguette, some with butter, thin slices of radish and coarse salt, others rubbed with *anchoiade* and a little radish on top (an idea from a man at the grocery store).

Tad and I went to a revival house that afternoon. Buster Keaton was tumbling out a window when it hit me: chive oil would give the dish the snap I wanted. I looked over at Tad, who was so focused on the movie he seemed to be in a trance.

That night, folding napkins and setting glasses on the table, I remembered how I had gone on a baking frenzy the first few weeks that Tad and I were dating. I dragged him to an apple orchard and made him an apple galette with our pickings. I baked him a peach tart as an excuse to drop by his apartment and packed an elaborate picnic with chocolate chip cookies for a field trip to Storm King.

For his birthday, I made him the chocolate cake my mother had made for family birthdays. "You're a lucky man," his friend Michael announced across the table after tasting the cake. It was a lovely compliment. At the time, I felt I was the lucky one—I feel it even more so now.

I began slicing the beets into small cubes for a salad. They glistened in the light of my kitchen. The potatoes and parsnips were simmering, the bubbles wiggling up to the surface before flattening out. I was running behind and for once was at ease about it. I've known Sherry for most of my life and Mark for several years. They would understand.

Things had changed for me at a wedding in Amagansett a few weeks ago. Tad and I had stayed over at his family's house nearby. The old house was deserted, and we slept in the one heated room upstairs, looking out over a pond and the ocean beyond. It was quiet and dark; we slept deeply. In the morning, I made us coffee in the kitchen before we put on our dress clothes.

The outdoor ceremony was shrouded in a dense fog, except for a single shaft of sunlight that pushed through the clouds just as the bride and groom took their vows. Tad and I got to the reception early, then drifted apart in the gathering crowd. When he reappeared to check up on me, I was consoling a couple who argue about cooking. "Want to take a look around?" Tad asked. "Sure," I said, knowing this was our cue to search for hors d'oeuvres.

He headed for a dim and drafty passage that led to the kitchen, hoping, I supposed, he could catch the servers coming out with full trays. But just then he turned to me. "I've been thinking," he said, "and I think we should get married." I smiled encouragingly, feeling nervous and ecstatic. I was aware that this was a moment that will stand alone in our history together, a moment when one door shuts and another opens. I wanted it to last as long as it could. "And, so, um," he paused, his normally steady composure out of reach, "I'm proposing to you."

My normally poor composure was, for once, in my power. "Well, I think that's a great idea," I said. "I am so happy you want to spend the rest of your life with me!"

"Is that a yes?" he asked.

"Yes!"

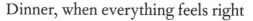

Dinner, when everything feels right

Roasted Chilean Sea Bass with Chive Oil

At the time of this publication (2003), Chilean sea bass has been over-fished and is now on the endangered list. But there are plenty of other delicious fish, like cod and halibut, that may be substituted for it.

This chive oil is very handy. You can drizzle it over salads, on tuna and over white bean soup. Or blend it right into mashed potatoes.

1/4 cup sliced chives (1-inch long pieces)
1/3 cup extra virgin olive oil, plus more for sprinkling on the fish
Coarse sea salt
Freshly ground black pepper
2 pounds Chilean sea bass (or any other firm white fish, like cod or halibut), cut from the thickest part of the fillet, at room temperature

1. Preheat the oven to 400°F. Place the chives in a food processor. Turn it on and add the olive oil through the feed tube in a thin steady stream. Season with salt and pepper. Stop to taste, then adjust, adding more oil, chives, salt or pepper, as desired. It should have a crisp, pointed flavor. Strain through a fine sieve into a bowl, pressing the chive pulp with the back of a spoon to get out every last bit of oil.

2. Place the sea bass in a sauté pan or roasting pan just large enough to fit the fillets. Sprinkle with olive oil and season with salt and pepper. Place in the oven and roast until the fish is just barely cooked in the center. It will continue to cook once it is removed from the oven. (It should take about 9 minutes per inch of thickness.) If you are serving it with the puree (below), lay each fillet on top of a large dollop of puree, and dapple with the chive oil. Otherwise, just serve it with the oil.

WITH THE PARSNIP POTATO SAUCE BELOW, AN ELEGANT DINNER FOR 4.

Parsnip and Potato Sauce

This is a mild sauce that can be used in a thousand ways—with a roasted leg of lamb seasoned with lots of thyme, under pieces of roasted chicken, with roasted rib eye, letting its juices pool around the puree, and in a tiny casserole served next to duck confit.

1 small white potato (about 5 ounces), peeled and cut into 1/4-inch dice
1 parsnip (about 5 ounces), peeled and cut into 1/4-inch dice
1/4 cup milk
Coarse sea salt
1 tablespoon unsalted butter

1. Put the potatoes and parsnips in a saucepan, pour over the milk and enough water to barely cover the vegetables. Season with salt, cover and heat to simmering. Cook until the vegetables are very soft, about 15 minutes.

2. Pour the vegetables and cooking broth into a blender or food processor and puree until smooth, adding more water or milk until you have the consistency of a vanilla sauce. (You can do this by hand with a potato masher, but you won't get the same silky texture.) Taste and adjust the seasoning; make sure you season it well, or it will seem bland. Pulse in the butter.

ABOUT 2 CUPS, WHICH IS ENOUGH SAUCE FOR THE SEA BASS (PLACE A SPOONFUL OF SAUCE ON EACH PLATE, AND THE FISH AND CHIVE OIL ON TOP.)

Beets, Apples and Ginger with a Clementine Vinaigrette

I've cooked beets many ways: boiling them, roasting them in an open pan with oil and roasting them dry. This method—roasting them, wrapped in foil pouches—is by far the most effective. The beets cook through while maintaining their structure. You get firm, silky, intensely flavored beets, slicked with great olive oil. And the skins slip off like a glove. You will find this technique in many excellent cookbooks, including James Peterson's *Vegetables* and Mario Batali's *The Babbo Cookbook*. I learned it from Tom Colicchio, the chef at Craft and Gramercy Tavern.

6 beets, rinsed
3 tablespoons excellent olive oil, more for beets
2 small apples (Fuji, Braeburn, or Gala), peeled, cored and cut into very
    thin wedges
1/2 cup quartered ripe cherry tomatoes (optional)
1 tablespoon chopped ginger
1 1/2 tablespoons red wine vinegar
Juice of 2 clementines

1 tablespoon Dijon mustard
Coarse sea salt
Freshly ground black pepper

1. Preheat the oven to 350°F. Place the beets on one half of a large piece of aluminum foil. Sprinkle with a little olive oil. Fold over the foil and seal the edges. Place the package on a baking sheet and roast in the oven until the beets are just tender, about 1 hour. Be careful when opening the foil; the steam will race out. While still warm, rub the beets in a towel to remove the skins. Cut into 1/2-inch dice.

2. Combine the beets, apples, tomatoes and ginger in a pretty serving bowl. In a separate bowl, whisk together the vinegar, clementine juice, mustard, salt and pepper. Place the bowl on a wet towel to hold it still and whisk vigorously as you add 3 tablespoons olive oil, one at a time, until the mixture is smooth. Pour half the dressing over the beet mixture and stir gently until all the ingredients have a light coating. Add more if needed. Cover and let sit, stirring every now and then, for at least 2 hours.

SALAD FOR 4.

Chapter 22

COMMITMENT ISSUES

A few months ago, when visiting Tad's parents, I noticed one of his mother's cookbooks lying on the kitchen counter. It was open to a recipe for slow-roasted turkey. The book was old, the pages a dull yellow. In the margins were notes, some in pencil, some in faded ink. Over the years, Elizabeth had kept a record of her efforts to refine the recipe: "1977," one note read, "12 lb. turkey took 4 hours including 1/2 hour browning." Another read, "Make a tent of foil over all." She had originally followed the recipe and spread shortening on the bird, then substituted margarine in the 1980s. Now she uses butter.

I mentioned this to Tad. "I hope someday I'll have recipes like that," I said. "You know, ones that I'll want to return to for years and years."

Tad nodded. "It's a good idea. You don't really seem to have a repertoire."

He was right. Although I have a few favorite dishes, I rarely make them. My job keeps me on the chase. So if I spot an unfamiliar ingredient in the grocery store, I try it. If I'm having a dinner party and I want to serve a cheese course, I buy something I've never tasted. I am always experimenting on guests, and although I feel more or less assured that dinner will be edible, there is something impersonal about following a recipe or winging something for the first time. When you make a dish again and again, altering it to your liking, it becomes an expression of your aesthetic, of your palate, of who you are. And when you serve that dish to guests, they come to understand you a little better.

Thus my mother, who is very practical, generous and a perfectionist, makes a superb roasted chicken with herbs tucked under the skin and lemons and onions neatly packed into its cavity, and crisp almond biscotti that look as if the nuts were arranged one by one. My sister Rhonda is indulgent and has a good sense of humor. One of her specialties is spaghetti with fried eggs.

People used to learn to cook by making dishes in their mother's or grandmother's repertoire. But now that cooking is no longer a necessity, very few people do this, which is probably why many young people may never cook. Without a handful of recipes to start you off, cooking seems overwhelming. There are too many choices. Why begin with roasted chicken when you could make chicken satay or chicken curry? Why make chocolate pudding when you're used to the molten chocolate soufflés that you get in restaurants?

But if you learn six or eight dishes, things you will want to eat week after week, cooking won't seem such a labor. And other cuisines will no longer feel so out of reach. You don't need to learn everything. A few timeless dishes that you love is enough. Any additional ones you pick up become accessories, like a beaded clutch, that you can trot out for special occasions.

Having your own stash of recipes also allows you to travel anywhere and cook in anyone's kitchen. If you can roast a chicken, make a salad and bake a simple cake, you will always be a prized guest. Even Tad, who, as far as I can tell, only cooks one full meal per millennium, has a few favorites. He makes a sensible vinaigrette and can roast fish. He can also prepare a very good watercress-and-pea puree.

I know all of this, and yet I lack such a tidy set of recipes. My mother and grandmother have taught me a number of their favorites, and I have picked up a few things from my sisters and friends, but I have never taken the time to organize them all or integrate them into my everyday cooking. And I haven't had the chance to achieve the kind of cooking rhythm established by my mother, who prepared dinner every night for a family of six. If I make a lamb stew, I'm either eating it all week long or pushing it on my neighbors.

But for someone who has little tolerance for people who don't cook, these are feeble excuses. What I've really resisted is being a mature adult with a clear identity. (That's what my shrink says, at least.) I'd always worried that once friends count on you for your macaroni and cheese, they'd never see your potential to prepare a delicate soufflé.

Now I am marrying into a family that has been cooking the same recipes since 1642. When Tad's father was a college president, his mother entertained nearly every day. She would keep records of who attended dinners, who sat next to whom and what was served, so that a guest could have a new experience each time. She has done the same with my visits. Each of the dozen meals we've shared has been carefully designed, without any menu being repeated. With the broth from braised duck (page 68) and the leftovers of that slow-roasted turkey, she once made turkey Tetrazzini. There has been baked local shad served with Julia Child's labor-intensive and highly rewarding ratatouille. Julia's steak sautéed in butter also showed up once at dinner with a creamy potato gratin. A fallen chocolate soufflé cake came after butterflied lamb. There were no hors d'oeuvres or garnishes, which people often feel pressured to do in order to make the meal memorable. These dinners were just a main course and dessert, all well prepared. They've all made a lasting imprint while giving me a better sense of her own history, of her style.

Elizabeth told me that she thinks of a cooking repertoire as a way to stay connected to all who are important in her life. She uses recipes from friends and family, as well as her own. It also eases the anxiety of having guests come for the weekend; she doesn't get flustered because she knows she can serve them a tested staple. She experiments when she's just cooking for herself. "Your generation," she said, "you're more likely to go out to some fabulous restaurant. And it's just not going to work that way. You're not going to have this arsenal."

"You're probably right," I said before going back to New York, eating at the latest restaurant and forgetting all about my little repertoire project.

But then Tad and I were invited to our friends Rachel and John's for dinner. They have two children and were leaving for a long vacation early the next day—not the easiest circumstances under which to have a dinner party for a large group. I admired their bravery. We happily ambled in, hungry and thirsty as ever.

Rachel, who I never knew to be a serious cook, was a bit tense, as any host is, but quite convivial. She and John lingered over cocktails and then went to the kitchen for a short time before dinner. We began the meal with a robust beet soup, served at room temperature. Rachel had added Champagne vinegar, which made it spritzy and tangy, and chopped red onion, which were like tiny crunchy beads. She was indeed a serious cook.

Then John emerged from the kitchen carrying a platter of poached striped bass on a feathery bed of dill and lemon slices. It was arresting and stylish. Rachel had poached it and swirled together a green sauce, heady with garlic. As bowls of green beans with dill and tiny red potatoes tossed with olive oil and parsley made their way around the table, I remembered that Elizabeth makes a poached fish. She serves hers with a tangy herbed cream sauce. I also recalled how I once poached fish for a story, then never made it again.

I was beginning to tense up about my shilly-shallying in the kitchen, just as someone at the table asked Rachel how she came up with all of these good things. "I couldn't figure out what to make," she said, at ease now with a glass of wine in her hand, "so I called my mother and talked to her. We decided I should make things I knew well."

It was such a simple explanation. And about time I took it seriously.

Rachel Urquhart's repertoire

Cold Beet Soup

The original recipe for this soup is from *The New York Times Cook Book* by Craig Claiborne. Over the years, Rachel has made it her own. She has replaced the yellow onion with red onion and has blanched it to mellow it; she has added a splash of orange juice and substituted the sour cream with Greek yogurt. In other words, she has lightened it and softened it, making a coarse soup seem elegant.

1/2 small red onion, chopped and blanched in boiling water for a minute
1 tablespoon Champagne vinegar

1 cup sliced cooked beets (2 medium), cooked yourself or the vacuum-
      packed variety from Europe
2 tablespoons lemon juice
1 medium potato, boiled and peeled
1 teaspoon sea salt
1/4 teaspoon freshly ground black pepper
1 cup chicken broth
1 cup Greek yogurt, or regular whole-milk yogurt or sour cream
1 cup cracked ice
Splash of orange juice or pink grapefruit juice
Snipped fresh dill

1. Place the blanched onions in a small bowl. Sprinkle with the vinegar
and let sit for 5 minutes.

2. Put the beets, lemon juice, potato, and the onions with the vinegar in
a food processor. Sprinkle in a dash of salt and pepper. Pulse a few times to
coarsely chop the vegetables, then, with the motor running, pour in the
chicken broth and yogurt. Add the cracked ice and splash of juice and blend
briefly. It should be viscous but not slushy. The ice will melt and add a little
more liquid, so keep that in mind. Add more seasoning as desired. Chill for an
hour or two, and serve with dill sprinkled across the surface.

REFRESHING, CHILLED SOUP FOR 6.

Poached Fish

Poaching is one of the least stressful ways to prepare fish. Even if you
season the poaching water with nothing but a little salt, it will be good.
The only way you can go wrong is to boil it to death. But if you're nervous
about cooking it, this will never happen because you'll probably be staring
over the edge of the pot the entire time.

All you need is a long narrow pan. Fill it with just enough water so that
once the fish goes in, it will be covered. You can test it out, then remove the
fish. Bring the water to a simmer, season it with salt, then lower the fish
(whole or fillets) into it. The water temperature will drop, so heat it up again,
then adjust the flame so that bubbles rise lazily around the edges. Simmer
with the cover askew until the fish is almost done, about 8 minutes for each
inch of thickness. Then shut off the heat and carefully lift the fish from the
liquid. Pat it dry. Peel back the skin, fillet and bone the fish if you like, or if
it's whole, serve it as is on a platter, and give it to someone to carve.

Rachel shared a number of great tips with me: "I got the basics for poaching fish—buying a fillet from the middle of the fish to avoid skinny ends, timing the cooking, getting the skin off, etc.—from Mark Bittman (*How to Cook Everything*), but I think I may have combined his mechanics for poaching a large piece of salmon with my own idea of doing it in a fish broth with onions, carrots, celery, lemon rind and a ton of dill laid over the fish as it cooked. I also laid the fillets on a large piece of cheesecloth as they soaked in the broth, so that I could remove them more easily without the flesh breaking up. Messy, but ultimately effective. One thing I was a little surprised by was the slight scum that accumulates on the fish after it's been poached. Doesn't look great, so you have to gently wipe it off. Also, I found it much prettier to serve the fish in pieces, garnished with sprigs of fresh dill and slices of lemon, rather than trying to lay it out whole, like a piece of wedding salmon."

Thomas's Green Sauce for Poached or Grilled Fish

This recipe is from Rachel's brother, Thomas Canfield. He said that he likes to serve it on the side, rather than over the fish. "This can be a powerful sauce," he writes in his recipe, "and people's enthusiasm varies." It would also be delicious with poached chicken.

    1/2 medium onion, coarsely chopped
    2 cloves garlic, coarsely chopped (use less if the garlic seems strong)
    1 good-size bunch Italian parsley, large stems removed (about 2 to 2 1/2
        cups)
    2 tablespoons capers
    1/3 cup best-quality olive oil, and perhaps a little more
    Small pinch of dried red pepper flakes
    A few drops of lemon juice
    Sea salt

Scrape the onion and garlic into a food processor. Drop in the parsley, capers, olive oil, pepper flakes, and lemon juice. Process in bursts, stirring occasionally and adding more oil if the sauce is too dry. Do not overblend; it should not be too fine. Season with salt. If the garlic is overpowering, you can tame the sauce, as Rachel did the night I was over, by adding a little bread soaked in milk.

ABOUT 3/4 TO 1 CUP SAUCE; PLENTY FOR 4.

Rachel's Green Beans with Dill

Sea salt

4 large handfuls haricots verts or green beans, tops trimmed but not the
   tails

2 tablespoons unsalted butter

2 to 3 tablespoons chopped dill

Coarsely ground black pepper

Fill a large pot with water and season it with enough salt so that you can taste it. Bring to a boil. Plunge the beans into the water and cook until just tender, but still quite firm, 2 to 3 minutes. If you're using green beans, it will take a minute or so longer. Drain and return the beans to the pot. Drop in the butter and 2 tablespoons dill and grind pepper (coarse grind) over top. Stir the beans with the pot over low heat, until the butter is melted. Taste a bean, and season with more salt, pepper or dill, until the beans taste delicious.

BEANS FOR 4 (VERY EASY TO DOUBLE FOR A BIG PARTY).

Chapter 23

DROPPING BY

It had been more than three years. I picked up the phone, eager to talk to my old friends, and worried they might have written me off.

"I'll be passing through Boston," I told Nan. "Can I come visit?"

"Of course you can, Amanda!" Nan said. As if we had just talked the day before, she added, "Now, we're happy to eat at home, but there must be some new restaurant you'd like to try."

"Let's stay home so we can talk and hear each other!" Tony, her husband, hollered in the background.

I wanted to have dinner at their house, too. Nan is an extraordinary cook, and they are the best hosts I know. They welcome you as if you are the most important person on Earth, lavish you with good food and wine, and even if the most exciting thing you've done lately is clean out your closets, they always want to hear all about it.

"We want to hear ALL about Mr. Latte!" Nan said.

I came by train to Boston from Maine, where I had been out on frigid waters, interviewing oyster divers, and took the Red Line to Harvard Square. Tony, who wears round glasses and favors bow ties, picked me up in their Camry. We looped around to their simple blue clapboard house. I hadn't been there in five years, but it all looked the same. Large glass doors framed the kitchen, making it seem like a lifesize diorama. Nan met us in the garage. "Amanda!" she said, throwing a high pitch on the second "a" in my name, "You must still be thawing."

"Yes," I said, "And I smell like a fishing boat."

"Well, we don't mind. The cats may follow you around. Have you met Cal?" she asked, referring to the abandoned tabby they took in.

"Yes," I said, "it must have been when you just got him, in Berkeley."

I had visited them in California one Halloween. Tony, who is an economist and a professor at Harvard, was working for a semester at Berkeley. They took me to all their favorite spots—Peet's Coffee, Café Fanny, the farmers' market—before stopping off at Kermit Lynch to buy a bottle of wine. We had dinner at Chez Panisse and the French Laundry. In between meals, I worked on a story about Emeril Lagasse, and tested his potato gratin recipe, which consisted mostly of garlic and cheese. Nan hung around the kitchen, a few feet from where I was working, unable to conceal her distaste for Lagasse's concoction.

Even though she comes from a small town, near the small town I grew up in, Nan is as close to being French as any American I have met. Her mother sent her to a private school in Gstaad, and the lifestyle flowed into her veins. When she used to smoke, she held her cigarette with her one arm bent closely toward the shoulder and her hand curled inward like a swan's neck, so the smoke would lift off the tip of the cigarette at the top of her head. She is petite and dresses in lush, expensive fabrics. A charcoal grey cashmere sweater. Perfectly fitted wool slacks. Driving loafers.

Nan eats like a Parisian woman, too. During the day, she drinks coffee and has a light lunch. In the evening, she eats a serious dinner, never before eight. When dining out, she does not order salad. She will begin with foie gras or sardines and move on to things like braised rabbit, lamb and pheasant. When she shops for groceries, she buys her cheeses, olives and wines from the Wine and Cheese Cask on the corner of Washington and Kirkland, bread from Hi-Rise, and her meats from a butcher. Nan understands that it is all right to buy a good pâté for an appetizer, and that one perfect croissant is better than five good muffins. She is a dedicated minimalist who knows how to be generous.

I have been aware of Nan since I was twelve, when my mother took me to her clothing boutique in Scranton. For years, Nan dressed my mother, my sisters and me. But it wasn't until she moved to Boston, after marrying Tony, that I really got to know her. While I was in college, I babysat their cats when they traveled and they would occasionally invite me to dinner. As must be apparent by now, I long wished to model my life after hers.

Back then she introduced me to Patricia Wells's *Bistro Cooking*, and later to James Beard. She cooks and Tony bakes. He is the only man I know—and surely the only Harvard professor—who owns a professional cake-decorating kit.

"Now, we want to hear everything," Tony said, as he poured me a glass of pinot blanc. "How is work? How did you meet Tad? When are you getting married?"

I sipped my wine, and while slicing mushrooms into slivers, began telling them first about the oystermen. "O.K., Amanda," Nan said, "Are you ready for another job?" I came around her stove, which is a full professional—not a home version—stove, set into a black granite island. Thelma, one of the cats, slinked out of the way, her tail fluttering every time it neared a pilot light. The rest of Nan's kitchen is white with a wall of high glass cabinets and a long counter, on which sit two wooden wine bins, converted to cat beds.

"I'm trying something new," she said. "Do you know this book, *Simple Italian Food*?" I did, but hadn't cooked much from it—mostly, I'm afraid, because I couldn't stand the book's typeface. "It's this little salad with scallops and balsamic vinegar and frisée. I want you to cook the scallops for me. Do you know how to sauté them?"

"I think so," I said. I turned on the heat, which was like a roar compared to the peep I am used to. I added the scallops a few at a time, trying not to splash the hot oil. Scallops should seize up as if inhaling and their edges, saturated with sugars, should stick in a rigid circle. I stood over the pan with a spatula in my hand.

"Now, don't touch them!" Nan said. At this point in my life, having gone to cooking school and worked in restaurants, I don't make too many rookie mistakes. But cooks trust no one. If Nan had Jean-Georges Vongerichten helping her sauté scallops, she'd be bossing him around, too.

She had good reason. The enemy of sautéing, the fastest cooking method, is, ironically, impatience. You must wait for the meat or vegetable to properly sear before moving it. Otherwise, the meat may stick to the pan, and tear when you try to move it. Also, it may stew rather than stay dry and brown. But most home cooks, hungry for dinner and staring down at the raw side of a piece of meat, simply cannot resist the temptation.

"So, Tad and I met on a blind date," I told them. "My friend Jennifer set us up. She told me that he was really smart, was nice to her daughter, and that he had bright red hair and was remote."

"Ack!" Tony said, standing to the side, petting Thelma. Nan was stirring a Moroccan lamb and beef stew. I could smell the cinnamon.

"Don't worry," I said, "He's got brown hair and he's totally in touch."

I have probably told these stories a thousand times by now—how I did a Google search and found an image of a bald, sweaty man listed (incorrectly) under Tad's name, how at the end of our first date, Tad suggested we get together again, and sure that he was just being polite, I merely shrugged. (It took Jennifer to put us back on track.)

But now, especially, the story felt pleasing, sturdy. After I had seen Nan and Tony that last time in Berkeley, I had dropped out of touch, retreating—as I did from many friendships over the past few years—to my hollow trench, unwilling to let anyone know just how hollow it was.

Nan had sent me postcards from her travels. An alley in a small French town. A temple in Thailand. A market in India. I saved them, but couldn't bring myself to respond. Where would I begin? How would I catch up with them without it seeming generic, a veil over the truth? I was tired of telling them about a new boyfriend who would soon be an ex-. Or about my new life in New York, which felt untethered and chaotic. I had nothing really but my work. I was failing at having a life as assured and elegant as Nan's. And I was embarrassed.

Nan and I sautéed the mushrooms and made a syrupy pan sauce with balsamic vinegar and shallots. The frisée was added at the last minute to wilt in the sauce. Meanwhile, Tony pulled out a black binder.

"What should we drink with dinner, Nan?" he asked. "Oh, how about that Vega Sicilia?" He turned to me. "Do you know it?"

I didn't, although I should have. The wine, an '89, was from Ribero del Duero, Tony explained, and was made by one of Spain's top producers. I was touched that they'd pull out such a nice bottle for my visit. Their wine collection has grown so vast that they now catalog it in the binder.

"You're so organized," I said.

"Well, it looks that way, but—" Tony said.

Nan interrupted "—I'm always in trouble with Tony for not scratching the wines that we drink off the list."

While he disappeared to the basement, I told Nan about the apartment we are buying. "So are you living together now?" Nan asked.

"No," I said, "Our apartments are way too small. He's got about a million books. Books on his dining room table. Books on his coffee table. Books on his stereo."

"Just like Tony," she said.

"Yes, and look around, do you see any?" Tony asked as he emerged from the basement.

Nan laughed. "I made him take them all to his office. He's probably the only professor without a single book in his house."

"Nan's aesthetic is damaging my reputation," Tony said.

The wine was taut at first, then relaxed, revealing earth and spices. We sat down in their dining room, with its smoky gray walls and Windsor chairs around a modern lacquer table. The scallops, thankfully, were cooked just right, opaque in the middle, crisp on the edges. It was a sweet, salty, robust combination. Tony served the main course, couscous topped with the fragrant lamb and beef. The meat was in small pieces the size of almonds in the shell and was surrounded with soft carrots, apricots, prunes and broth.

I was on my second helping, when from the kitchen, a high hiss could be heard, followed up by a desperate, whining "Meow!" Cal was swatting at Thelma.

"They're like siblings!" I said.

"Yeah," Tony said, getting up to separate the cats. "But you know what? You don't have to send them to college."

After dinner we moved back to the kitchen where they had two small stools and two mahogany chairs set up near a round glass table. It is their den. We drank chamomile tea and had thin slices of vanilla pound cake from Hi-Rise bakery. It had heft and that pebbly texture you find in the French pound cakes called "*quatre-quarts*" (pronounced CAT-carr).

Nan and I talked late into the evening, until our eyes could no longer bear the weight of their lids. Their guest room had a low bed that fits into a wide dormer in the pitched roof. And in Nan's discreet way, it was made luxurious. The bed had a feather mattress cover and comforter and feather pillows, all wrapped in fine white sheets. It felt like sleeping in a bowl of whipped cream.

The next morning, they drove me to the train station. I never apologized for being out of touch, and if they minded, they never said. I was really looking forward to introducing them to Tad.

A good dinner for catching up

Sautéed Scallops with Wild Mushrooms and Frisée

Adapted from Simple Italian Food *by Mario Batali*
(Clarkson N. Potter, 1998)

12 large sea scallops (about 1 pound), or the equivalent in Nantucket bay
     scallops
Freshly ground black pepper
1/2 cup good olive oil
4 shallots, thinly sliced
8 ounces mixed mushrooms, sliced 1/4-inch thick
3 tablespoons best-quality balsamic vinegar
3 heads frisée, or mixed baby lettuce (about 6 cups)
Sea salt

1. Season the scallops with pepper. In a large nonstick skillet, heat 2 tablespoons of the olive oil until smoking. Lay 6 scallops in the pan and cook without moving them until crisp and golden brown, 5 to 6 minutes (less time for smaller scallops); Mario Batali, and Nan, emphasize NOT to turn the scallops if you want one side crisp and the other silky. Remove to a plate and repeat with the remaining 6 scallops. (If you're using a smaller scallop, you may be able to do it in a single batch.)

2. In a large sauté pan, heat 2 tablespoons olive oil until smoking. Drop in the shallots and sauté until softened, 3 to 4 minutes. Add the mushrooms and cook 3 to 4 minutes, stirring and folding them until softened. Stir in the vinegar and then add the frisée. Toss quickly, season with salt and pepper, and divide among four plates. Arrange 3 scallops on each salad, browned side up, and dapple with the remaining olive oil.

SERVES 4 AS A FIRST COURSE.

Kadjemoula (North African Lamb and Beef Stew)

Adapted from The New James Beard *by James Andrews Beard*
(Knopf, 1981)

James Beard suggests serving the stew with quince paste or quince preserves. Nan skipped both, and the stew was perfectly delicious without them. Tony spooned it on top of couscous, which soaked up its rich, sweet juices and let the excess run around the plate.

    2 pounds lamb shoulder, cut into 1 1/2-inch cubes
    2 pounds beef chuck, cut into 1 1/2-inch cubes
    1/2 cup flour, more if needed
    2 tablespoons butter
    2 tablespoons olive oil, more if needed
    1 teaspoon sea salt
    1/4 teaspoon ground cinnamon
    1/4 teaspoon ground ginger
    1/2 teaspoon freshly ground black pepper
    2 medium onions, sliced
    4 carrots, peeled and quartered
    2 medium turnips, peeled and diced
    3 cloves garlic, chopped
    2/3 cup dried apricots

2/3 cup prunes, pitted (prunes from Agen, if possible; they're delicious)
3 to 4 cups beef broth

1. Trim all the fat from the lamb and beef cubes. Put the flour in a plastic bag and add the meat one handful at a time. Shake the bag to thinly coat the meat, then shake the pieces as you lift them from the bag. Heat the butter and oil in a braising pan over medium high heat. Add the meat cubes, a few at a time, and brown them quickly on all sides. Remove them as they cook to a plate.

2. Put all the browned meat back in the pan and sprinkle it with the salt, cinnamon, ginger and pepper. Add the onions, carrots, turnips, garlic, apricots and prunes. Pour in enough broth to barely cover the meat and bring to a boil. Lower the heat so the bubbles are sparse and languid; cover and simmer gently for 2 hours, or until tender. The vegetables and fruits should have blended into a thin but flavorful sauce. Remove the stew to a hot platter and surround it with mounds of rice pilaf, couscous or cracked wheat. Place slices of quince paste or quince preserves around the edges.

STEW FOR 6.

Vanilla Bean Loaves

Adapted from Hi-Rise Bread Company in Cambridge, Massachusetts

There are three forms of vanilla in the batter and two vanilla beans in the syrup and still Rene Becker, the owner of Hi-Rise, told me, "You should use as many vanilla beans as you can afford to." He knows what he is talking about. This is the most splendid vanilla cake that I have ever tasted. And it has a crumbly, pebbly texture that reminds me of Parisian pound cakes, a distant cousin to our fluffy, cottony ones.

After the cakes are baked, they are brushed several times with vanilla syrup. At Hi-Rise they simply dip the whole cake into a pot of syrup—a fun job, indeed. "I think that contributes to its graininess and to the texture in general," Rene said. He's a big fan of the cake himself. "I must admit," he said, "around four o'clock in the afternoon when the spirit is flagging and you've got half the day left, it's tempting.

"We also slice it down and people always ask for an inside slice. Me, I like the end because it's got all the vanilla syrup."

With this recipe, you have four ends to dole out as you wish!

3 sticks unsalted butter, at room temperature
2 1/2 cups vanilla sugar (1 split vanilla bean stirred into 1 pound of
    sugar; let sit for a few days)
1 vanilla bean
1 tablespoon vanilla extract
8 large eggs, at room temperature
3 cups unbleached all-purpose flour
1 1/2 teaspoons baking powder
1/2 teaspoon salt

For the syrup
1 3/4 cups sugar
2 vanilla beans, split and seeds scraped

1. Heavily butter two 8×4×3-inch (or similarly sized) loaf pans, and pre-heat your oven to 325°F. Using a paddle attachment in your mixer, cream the butter and vanilla sugar until the mixture is pale and fluffy. Scrape the vanilla bean and flick its seeds into the mixer, along with the vanilla extract and eggs. Beat to mix.

2. Sift the flour, baking powder and salt into a bowl. Add this to the batter and mix just until smooth—a few turns of the paddle should do it. Take the bowl off the mixer and use a spatula to scrape the bottom and fold the mixture a few times, to make sure everything is blended. Divide the batter between the buttered pans. Bake for 30 minutes, then turn the pans around, and bake until a cake tester or skewer comes out almost clean, another 25 to 40 minutes.

3. While the loaves bake, prepare the syrup: in a small pan, dissolve the sugar in 1 cup of water over medium heat. Add the vanilla beans and stir a little so their seeds and fragrance disperse. Take the pan off the heat.

4. When the loaves are done, cool for 10 minutes on baking racks, then turn them out of their pans and set back on the racks. Place the racks over parchment paper or a baking sheet and brush generously all over—bottoms, tops and sides—with the syrup. Brush a couple of more times as they cool. These cakes store well. They may be wrapped and frozen, although I can't imagine not eating one of them right away.

2 FRAGRANT CAKES.

Chapter 24

A FEW OR A DOZEN FAVORITES

As a Christmas present last year, Timmie, Tad's sister, gave me six of her favorite recipes: among them, tabbouleh, corn chowder and her beloved raspberry-almond vacherin. She must have read my mind. For months, with Tad's gentle encouragement, I had been trying to distill the mass of recipes in my head down to a manageable stable of favorites, a repertoire that I could rely on and that friends and family, and Tad in particular, would look forward to.

I wanted it to contain recipes that represent who I am, what I find pleasurable, how I live. It should express my true sensibilities as a cook, not my ambition. And all of the dishes should be simple enough that I could make them on a moment's notice.

There were a few natural choices. A couple of years ago, my mother taught me to make her dense but moist chocolate birthday cake. She calls it "dump-it cake" because you mix all of the ingredients in a pot over medium heat, then dump the batter into a cake pan to bake. For the icing, you melt Nestlé's semi-sweet chocolate chips and swirl them together with sour cream. It sounds like it's straight from the Pillsbury Bake-Off, but it tastes like it's straight from Payard. Everyone loves it.

I have also adopted one of her peach tart recipes, which has a crust moistened with olive oil and scented with almond extract, made right in the pan. You layer it with sliced peaches and sprinkle it with chilled bits of butter, flour and sugar. The crust becomes crisp and pebbly, and the juice from the peaches thickens around the fruit. (With it, and many desserts, I serve crème fraîche lightened with whipped cream. I learned this from Nancy Silverton, the owner of La Brea Bakery. She whisks heavy cream with just a dash of sugar and stops whipping it when it holds a loose, droopy peak. Then she folds in crème fraîche.)

Other recipes I've happened upon. While reviewing *The Glorious Foods of Greece* by Diane Kochilas for the newspaper last year, I made her tagliatelle served with sheep's milk yogurt, grated sheep's milk cheese and caramelized onions. The warm pasta, slippery with yogurt, lies in a tangle as you bury it under a heap of onions and grated hard cheese, creating a splendid web of mild, tangy, earthy flavors. Tad liked it so much that he hugged me. Any dish that elicits a hug automatically gets included.

Some favorites have entered our lives more recently. A few weeks ago, when we went to our friends Jacob and Deborah's for dinner, they served linguine with Parmesan cheese, crème fraîche, arugula and Meyer lemon. While we talked and they took turns putting their kids to bed, they shaved the cheese into a big serving bowl and grated the lemons, the lacy flakes of zest falling on top. The whole tag-team production was probably stressful for them, but it was aromatherapy to us, as we inhaled the perfume of ingredients floating under our noses. We sipped Champagne as Jacob tipped the pasta into the bowl. Deborah added crème fraîche, a tiny bit of the cooking water and some lemon juice, and mixed it as she talked, passing strands to us to taste. We were in love with the dish before we sat down to eat it.

A few days later, I made it myself and added it to my mental list, which included pork braised in milk and cream, Corby Kummer's almond biscotti, saltimbocca, my mother's oven-fried chicken, vitello tonnato, potatoes fried in goose fat, *revueltos* (Spanish scrambled eggs), braised artichokes, and tarragon mayonnaise. Pretty soon, my new collection was getting out of control. It is painful to whittle—my mind swirls with foods that I love. I wondered if streamlining was just futile. The only way to break in a repertoire, I realized, was to test it out.

So when we were invited to a dinner party recently, and I was asked to bring an hors d'oeuvre, I knew immediately what it would be, a recipe that I was once served at a dinner: foie gras mousse and a tart berry jam spread on soft bread. I cut off the crusts and sliced the sandwiches into triangles. They looked like peanut-butter-and-jelly sandwiches, but they were good enough to excuse that hint of cuteness.

At the party, our friends lapped them up. Tad squeezed my hand, as if to congratulate me. When Maya, the hosts' three-year-old daughter wandered in, she went right for them, picking one up and taking a large bite. "Look!" said Deb, one of the guests, "even Maya likes them." Everyone turned to see. At that moment, Maya stopped chewing and looked very alarmed. Then she opened her mouth up wide so as not to chew any more of the offensive substance and started to sob.

I may need a separate repertoire for children.

Recipes to hold onto

"PBJ's"

Adapted from Bernadette Cura

In Bernadette's version, the foie gras mousse was homemade and the berry jam was prepared by simmering fresh cranberries with sugar until they reduced to a thin sticky jam. She used brioche rather than sandwich bread, which you may want to try. Hers were delicious.

8 slices white sandwich bread (which should be soft and buttery, not dry)
8 tablespoons foie gras mousse, at room temperature
Coarse sea salt
4 tablespoons berry jam (preferably tart berries, like cranberries, blackberries and currants)

1. Lay the slices of bread on a breadboard. Spread the foie gras mousse on four of the slices. Sprinkle with coarse sea salt. Spread the jam on the other 4 slices of bread. Join the jam slices with the foie gras slices to make 4 sandwiches.

2. Using a bread knife, cut off the crusts with gentle sawing motions, then cut the sandwiches diagonally into quarters, so you end up with triangles. Stack on a serving platter and march them out to the party.

HORS D'OEUVRES FOR 4 PEOPLE, AGES 12 AND OLDER.

Timmie's Raspberry Almond Vacherin

When Timmie was in her twenties, she studied to be a pastry chef and worked at some of San Francisco's best restaurants, including Rubicon in its heyday. In the end, the grueling hours of kitchen life were not for her. But they have served her well. She makes a dacquoise that Tad describes as pure bliss and oatmeal-chocolate-chunk-pecan cookies that make your heart swell. This vacherin is her summer specialty.

Timmie uses almonds with their skins on because, she says, it gives the meringue a deeper flavor. And she bakes the meringue until it has a toasty golden hue. This summer Timmie showed me how to make individual vacherins, by piping 4-inch circles on parchment (don't bother drawing circles—this is like making cookies). In addition to raspberries, I added blue-berries and sliced peaches and tossed them with a tablespoon of sugar so they would began juicing before I spooned them on the dessert.

4 ounces almonds, skins on
1 1/2 cups sugar
6 egg whites, at room temperature
1 cup heavy cream
1 tablespoon confectioners' sugar, more for dusting
1 1/2 cups raspberries (or a mix of blackberries, blueberries, peaches, plums and any other summer fruit)

1. Preheat your oven to 350°F. Place the almonds on a baking sheet and toast until golden and you can smell them when you open the oven door, 5–8 minutes. Remove from the oven and let cool completely. Put them in a food processor with a few tablespoons of the sugar, and grind them finely. Timmie does this because the traction from the sugar helps work the almonds more finely.

2. Lower the oven to 250°F. Line two baking sheets with parchment paper. Draw an 8-inch circle in the center of each sheet.

3. Slip the egg whites into a mixer and beat on high until they are stiff but not dry. Lower the speed and beat in half the remaining sugar, adding it 1 tablespoon at a time. Shut off the mixer and fold in the rest of the sugar with the ground almonds. Divide the meringue between the two circles on the parchment. Spread evenly, so the circles are about 3/4 inch thick. Bake in the oven until meringue is dry, about 1 hour. Monitor the heat so that the meringues dry without coloring too quickly. (You may want to turn the baking sheet, so the meringue bakes evenly.) Check after 40 minutes. The meringues are done when they feel crisp and are no longer springy. Remove from the oven and let cool.

4. Meanwhile, beat the cream for a minute, then add 1 tablespoon confectioners' sugar and keep beating until it holds a soft peak. Lay a meringue on a serving dish or cake plate. Spread the whipped cream on top. Sprinkle with half the raspberries. Set the other meringue on top. Scatter the remaining berries on top and dust with confectioners' sugar.

ENOUGH FOR 4 DESSERT LOVERS, OR 6 DISCIPLINED GUESTS.

COOKING FOR MR. LATTE 195

Chocolate Dump-It Cake

Adapted from Judith Hesser

My mother did all of her baking late at night, after we were in bed. Around one in the morning, the aroma of this cake would begin wafting up to our bedrooms. We'd watch her frost it while we ate breakfast.

2 cups sugar

4 ounces unsweetened chocolate

1/4 pound unsalted butter (1 stick), plus more for greasing the pan

2 cups all-purpose flour, plus more for dusting the pan

2 teaspoons baking soda

1 teaspoon baking powder

1 teaspoon sea salt

1 cup milk

1 teaspoon cider vinegar

2 eggs

1 teaspoon vanilla extract

1 1/2 cups Nestlé semi-sweet chocolate chips

1 1/2 cups sour cream, at room temperature.

1. Preheat the oven to 375°F, and place a baking sheet on the lowest rack, to catch any drips when the cake bakes. Put the sugar, unsweetened chocolate, butter and 1 cup of water in a saucepan. Place over medium heat and stir occasionally until all of the ingredients are melted and blended. Remove from the heat and let cool slightly, 15 to 20 minutes.

2. Meanwhile, sift together the flour, baking soda, baking powder and salt. In a small bowl, stir together the milk and vinegar. Grease and flour a 9-inch tube pan. (If you prefer, you can grease it, line it with parchment and then grease and flour it. This is not necessary, but parchment does make getting the cake out easier.)

3. When the chocolate in the pan has cooled a bit, whisk in the milk mixture and eggs. In several additions and without overmixing, whisk in the dry ingredients. When the mixture is smooth, add the vanilla and whisk once or twice, to blend. Dump the batter into the tube pan and bake on the middle rack until a skewer inserted in the center comes out clean, about 30 to 35 minutes. Let the cake cool for 10 minutes, then remove from the pan and cool on a rack. (This can be tricky, so if someone is around, enlist him to help.

Place a ring of wax paper on top of the cake so you have something to grab onto when turning it out.) Let cool completely.

4. Meanwhile, melt the chocolate chips in a double boiler, then let cool to room temperature. It is very important that the chocolate and sour cream be the same temperature, otherwise the icing will be lumpy or grainy. (Test it by stirring a little of the sour cream and chocolate together in a bowl; if it mixes smoothly, it's ready.) Stir in the sour cream, 1/4 cup at a time, until the mixture is smooth. Taste some! It's good.

5. When the cake is cool, you may frost it as is or cut it in half so that you have two layers (when I do this, I use 2 cups chocolate chips and 2 cups sour cream). My mother uses any leftover icing to make flowers: she dabs small rosettes, or buttons, on top, then uses toasted almond slices as the petals, pushing them in around the base of the rosette.

10 SERVINGS. (MY MOTHER KEPT IT IN THE FRIDGE, AND IT IS SUB-LIME EVEN WHEN COLD.)

Linguine with Meyer Lemon Zest, Crème Fraîche and Parmesan Cheese

Adapted from Deborah Needleman and Jacob Weisberg, who got the idea from Lora Zarubin, a friend of theirs who is an editor at House & Garden

"We're winging this," Deborah said as she was cooking. "I saw Meyer lemons in the store and I couldn't resist them." It was the first time I had met her. It was all I needed to know to like her. It is brave to be inspired by an ingredient and let it lead the way. Tad and I were willing subjects, particularly as crème fraîche and Meyer lemons, if you haven't already noticed, are two of our favorite ingredients.

While she and Jacob cooked, they served Tad, me and their three-year-old daughter Lily blinis with caviar. Lily licked off the caviar and crème fraîche and then ate the blini. "Lily," Tad said, "That's like an Oreo for you, isn't it?" It was tempting to mimic her way.

We began with this pasta, then moved on to a more chaste main course: pan roasted sea bass with fennel simmered in orange juice. It was a stimulating intermezzo. For dessert, I had brought the "gooey chocolate stack" from Nigella Lawson's *Domestic Goddess*. It consists of layers of chocolate mousse interrupted by layers of chocolate meringue. Made a few hours before, the meringue had softened and become chewy, so the layers blended and it was just a giant, but divine, chocolate bomb. The virtue of the fish course was long gone.

Sea salt
1 pound linguine
Parmigiano-Reggiano cheese (a wedge for grating)
2 Meyer lemons
3 handfuls arugula, roughly chopped
1/2 cup crème fraîche
Freshly ground black pepper

1. Fill a large pot with water and season with lots of salt so that you can taste it. Bring to a boil. Add the linguine and cook until al dente, so that it's still firm, and not quite cooked through. While it cooks, finely grate a handful of cheese into a large serving bowl. Zest the lemons into the bowl, then add the arugula. Scoop out about 1 cup of the pasta water and reserve. Juice one of the lemons and reserve.

2. When the pasta is cooked, drain it and tip it into the serving bowl with the cheese and lemon. Working quickly, sprinkle over the lemon juice and a little pasta water. Add the crème fraîche, then begin to fold all of the ingredients together. Fold over and over again until the pasta is slicked with sauce, the cheese is melted, the arugula wilted and the flavors harmonized. Season with pepper. Taste a strand of pasta. Add more lemon juice, salt, pepper, and crème fraîche, as desired. If the sauce is too sticky, add a little more pasta water and mix again.

PASTA FOR 4, OR 6 AS A FIRST COURSE.

Pasta With Yogurt and Caramelized Onions
Adapted from The Glorious Foods of Greece *by Diane Kochilas*
(William Morrow, 2001)

Although this principle should apply to everything you cook, it is especially important to use the best ingredients you can find for this dish. There are very few of them, so each is vital. Use full-fat yogurt and excellent olive oil from a recent harvest. Buy sea salt if all you have is kosher, and grate the cheese yourself. Your labors will be repaid.

2 cups sheep's milk yogurt
5 tablespoons extra virgin olive oil
6 cups coarsely chopped onions
Sea salt

1 pound tagliatelle

1 cup coarsely grated kefalotyri cheese, or pecorino Romano

1. Line a colander with cheesecloth and set over a bowl or in the sink. Add the yogurt, and let drain for 2 hours.

2. Heat the olive oil in a large nonstick skillet over medium-high heat and add the onions. Reduce the heat to medium-low and cook, stirring frequently, until the onions are soft and golden brown, 20 to 30 minutes.

3. Meanwhile, fill a large pot with water and bring to a boil. As the water heats, add enough salt so that you can taste it. Drop in the pasta and cook until soft, not al dente. Combine the drained yogurt with 1/2 cup pasta water and mix well. Drain the pasta, and toss with the yogurt mixture.

4. Divide the pasta among four warm bowls. Sprinkle generously with cheese, and spoon over the caramelized onions and their juices.

PASTA FOR 4.

Peach Tart

Adapted from Judith Hesser

This is a recipe I travel with because you don't need a rolling pin, food processor or even a good pan. All you need is ripe fruit. So steer clear of peaches unless it's July or August. In the fall and winter, you can use apples or pears, and in the early summer months, there are apricots and plums (leave the skins on). During spring, make something else and look forward to apricot season.

I have made this many times, and as with any fruit dessert, it varies every time. If the peaches are juicy, you may want to add another tablespoon of flour to the crumble mixture so that it helps the juices thicken and prevents a soggy crust. I have taken to adding a pinch more salt to both the crust and the topping, because I like a little extra salt in my desserts. My mother never uses olive oil; that is another adjustment I made. The olive oil makes a richer dough; vegetable oil makes a flakier one.

I've done it in square pans, as in the recipe, but also 9-inch round tart pans and even a large sheet pan for a crowd. For this, I tripled the dough recipe. No matter what size you are making, you simply want to cover the base with slices of fruit that are as thick as the sides of the pastry are high.

1 1/2 cups plus 2 tablespoons all-purpose flour (measured using the dip and sweep method)

3/4 teaspoon medium-coarse sea salt or kosher salt
3/4 cup plus 1 teaspoon sugar
1/2 cup olive oil or vegetable oil
2 tablespoons milk
1/2 teaspoon almond extract
2 tablespoons cold unsalted butter
5 ripe peaches, peeled, pitted and thickly sliced (about 6 slices per peach)

1. Preheat oven to 425°F. In an 8-inch square (or similarly sized) pan, stir together 1 1/2 cups flour, 1/2 teaspoon salt and 1 teaspoon sugar. Stirring enables the salt and sugar to sift the flour, so you don't need to sift it in advance. In a small bowl, whisk together the oil, milk and almond extract. Pour this mixture into the flour mixture and mix gently with a fork, just enough to dampen; do not overwork it. Then, use your hands to pat out the dough so it covers the bottom of the pan, pushing it up the sides to a height of about 3/4 inch. This will be easy if you pat firmly and confidently, but not if you curl your fingertips into the dough. It should be about 1/8-inch thick all around; trim and discard excess dough.

2. In a bowl, combine 3/4 cup sugar, 2 tablespoons flour, 1/4 teaspoon salt and the butter. (If the fruit is especially juicy, add a little extra flour.) Using your fingers, pinch the butter into the dry ingredients until crumbly, with a mixture of fine granules and tiny pebbles.

3. Arrange the peaches in rows over the pastry; they should fit snugly. Sprinkle the pebbly butter mixture over top (it will seem like a lot). Bake for 35 to 45 minutes, until shiny, thick bubbles begin enveloping the fruit and the crust is a nut brown. Cool on a rack. Serve warm or room temperature, preferably with generous dollops of crème fraîche whipped cream (below).

ONE 8-INCH TART, TO SERVE 6, WITH A LITTLE LEFTOVER FOR BREAKFAST.

Crème Fraîche Whipped Cream

Adapted from Nancy Silverton, La Brea Bakery

Make this to your taste. If you like it tangier, add more crème fraîche. If you want it less sweet, cut back on the sugar.

1 cup heavy cream
2 tablespoons confectioners' sugar
1/2 cup crème fraîche

Whip the heavy cream until it begins to thicken. Sprinkle with the confectioners' sugar and continue to beat the cream until it makes a soft, lazy peak. Fold or gently whisk in the crème fraîche. Dollop on everything!

2 CUPS OF BLISS.

Judy Hesser's Oven-Fried Chicken

When my mother worked, this was one of her standard dinners. She would get home and before she even set down her purse, she would put her worn aluminum pan in the oven and turn it on.

My mother would sometimes put canned peach halves (homemade, not the supermarket kind, she would insist I tell you) on the chicken. She would start the chicken skin side down and once the pieces were browned, turn them and put the peach half on the browned side. It is a variation that I have only recently come to appreciate.

I sometimes add grated Parmigiano-Reggiano cheese and grated lemon zest to the flour mixture. The cheese underlines the nutty flavor you get from frying and the zest brightens the dish. It is delicious without these, too. My family likes it at any temperature and at any time of day, even cold out of the fridge for breakfast.

For years I had been frying the chicken and wondering why mine was never the same as my mother's. Then when I was home visiting recently, she told me she was making it for dinner.

"Great!" I said.

"Only this time," she said, "I didn't have time to soak the meat."

"Soak the meat?"

"Yeah," she said casually, "it firms it up and makes it better."

"Somehow, you forgot to tell me that part."

"I did?" she said, her hands digging into a bag full of flour and chicken. "Whoops, well, now you know."

I had been skipping the one real trick to this recipe, which is to soak the chicken in salted ice water for a few hours before cooking. It seasons the meat and tightens the flesh, so the skin crisps better and the seasoning permeates the meat. My mother would put the chicken in the water and chill it while she was at work.

Her other trick is to use good farmers' market chickens, which taste better and have less fat, so the chicken fries in a film of oil rather than a bath of fat.

3 tablespoons sea salt

8 chicken thighs (organic or natural, not Perdue or somesuch)

2 tablespoons unsalted butter

1/2 cup all-purpose flour

1 teaspoon coarsely ground black pepper

1. In the morning, combine 2 tablespoons salt and about a cup of warm water in a large bowl or container. Stir to dissolve the salt. Trim the chicken of excess skin and fat. Add the chicken to the bowl. Cover with very cold water and add a tray of ice cubes. Swish around with your hand to disperse them. Chill in the refrigerator until dinner time.

2. Preheat your oven to 400°F. Remove the chicken from the fridge and pat dry completely with paper towels. Put the butter in a roasting pan large enough to fit the chicken in one layer. Place the pan in the oven. In a 1-gallon freezer bag, pour in the flour, remaining 1 tablespoon salt and the pepper. Give it a good shake. Add the chicken pieces two at a time and shake them until thoroughly coated. As you lift them out of the bag, shake them off vigorously. This is vital. You do not want a gummy coating. Line them up on a plate, and repeat with the rest.

3. Lay the chicken pieces in the roasting pan, skin side down, and oven-fry until a chestnut brown and crisp on the bottom, about 40 minutes (sometimes it takes as long as an hour). Don't flip them until this happens. Use a thin spatula to scrape them up off the pan and turn them; cook the other side the same way. Remove the pieces from the oven as they finish cooking, and place on a plate lined with paper towels. Just before serving, grind fresh pepper over top and sprinkle lightly with sea salt.

FRIED CHICKEN FOR 4, OR FOR 3 BIG EATERS.

Pork Braised in Milk and Cream

I learned this recipe from Gabrielle Hamilton, the chef at Prune, a cramped little gem on the Lower East Side. Gabrielle's best quality as a chef is that she is in denial that she's operating a restaurant. All of her food is like home cooked food, only it's ten times better than anything you or I have ever had at home. She also has a great sense of when to be indulgent and when to show restraint. This recipe is her indulgent side. After dinner you get the restraint: when you ask for your check, the waiter may slip it on your table with a few fresh figs serving as a paperweight. You can do the same thing at home, minus the check.

She had two important tips for the pork: wash the lemons before peeling them (to rinse off the wax), and season the sauce generously in the beginning, because once the custard has formed, you don't want to have to stir it.

2 pounds boneless pork loin, larded with fatback and tied
1 tablespoon chopped fresh sage
1 tablespoon chopped garlic
Sea salt
Freshly ground black pepper
1 tablespoon good olive oil
2 cups milk
2 cups half-and-half
2 cups heavy cream
3 lemons, washed
3 tablespoons butter
20 cloves garlic (from about 2 heads), peeled and lightly crushed
20 sage leaves

1. Place pork in a lidded container, and rub all over with chopped sage and chopped garlic. Cover, and refrigerate overnight. The next morning, bring to room temperature. Scrape off and discard sage and garlic; season generously with salt and pepper.

2. Pour the olive oil into a deep, heavy casserole or Dutch oven fitted with a lid, and place over medium-high heat. Add the pork loin, and brown very well on all sides, about 15 minutes. Meanwhile, in a saucepan, combine the milk, half-and-half and cream. Bring to a boil, then shut off heat. Use a vegetable peeler to remove the peel from the lemons in long strips.

3. When pork is browned, transfer it to a plate and pour off the fat that's in the casserole. Turn the heat down to medium, and add the butter to the pan. When it foams, add the garlic cloves. Stir until lightly browned on the edges. Add the sage leaves, and stir to coat. Lower the pork back into the casserole, and pour in enough of the warm milk mixture to come 1/2 to 2/3 up the sides of the pork. Bring to a simmer, add the strips of lemon peel and season to taste with salt.

4. Partly cover, and simmer gently until an instant-read thermometer registers 140°F (about 15 to 30 minutes; cooking time will vary according

to the shape of the roast and degree of browning). As it cooks, the liquid will form a golden skin and custard around the pork. Shut off the heat, and allow the pork to cool completely. Cover, and refrigerate until shortly before serving.

5. To serve, carefully remove the pork from the milk mixture and carve into thin slices. Meanwhile, place the casserole over medium heat and reduce the liquid to a soupy custard. While the liquid is still a little loose, lay the sliced pork in the casserole and spoon the sauce on top. Heat gently. When dishing out, make sure to give each person a few slices of pork, and spoon some custard, lemon zest and sage on top. Sprinkle with coarse salt. Enjoy.

A FABULOUS DINNER FOR 4.

Tarragon Mayonnaise

Fire was great for advancing the culinary arts, but few things have brought more pleasure to the human race than mayonnaise. And if you've never had it made at home, it is time to try. I love tarragon mayonnaise because it's so handy. You can fold potatoes into it, or chicken, spread it on sliced ham or serve with cold poached salmon. I like to eat it with boiled artichokes, dipping one petal at a time, slather it on bread and put it on top of hard-boiled eggs. If you tire of it—if such a thing is possible—then simply substitute fresh basil for the tarragon.

    1 egg yolk, at room temperature
    1 tablespoon Dijon mustard
    1 teaspoon Champagne vinegar
    Sea salt
    3/4 cup peanut oil or safflower oil
    1/4 cup best-quality olive oil
    2 tablespoons chopped tarragon
    Lemon juice (about 1/2 a lemon)

In a heavy bowl that will stay put as you mix, whisk together the egg yolk, mustard and vinegar. Season with salt. As you whisk, add the peanut oil a few drops at a time, incorporating it thoroughly after each addition. Once the mixture begins to thicken, add the oil in a thin stream. A nice paste the thickness and gloss of tube paint should be forming. Whisk in the olive oil, then fold in the tarragon. Taste the mayonnaise, and add lemon juice to sharpen the flavor, and salt if needed. If it is too thick, you can thin it with milk or water. If it is too thin, add a little cream. Cover and chill for a few hours, so the tarragon flavor takes hold.

ABOUT 1 CUP MAYONNAISE, USEFUL FOR JUST ABOUT EVERYTHING.

Chapter 25

THE ENGAGEMENT PARTY

"So, do you think we need a reservation at Balthazar for breakfast?" Jennifer asked.

"Probably not. Why?" I asked.

"Deb and E.B. and I are getting together to plan the party," she said.

When you cook, you have an immediate in at parties. You get the invite and you become involved in the planning from the very beginning.

"I want to come!"

"You can't," Jennifer said firmly.

This time, it was a party for Tad and me—an engagement party—

and we were left on the sidelines. I didn't hear another peep for weeks. The day of the party, I called Jennifer and got her machine. "Are you cooking today? I feel weird not helping out," I said. "Can I do something?" She didn't call back. I imagined the three of them frantically cooking, resenting that they'd signed up for this party.

Tad put on a nifty shirt and I slipped into a new dress, blue with tiny sparkles, like a night sky. When we arrived at E.B. and Michael's apartment, the door was ajar.

"Hello?" we said. A collective "Hello!" echoed from the kitchen. Deb was working with a man dressed in livery, rolling melon in prosciutto and spearing them on long wood skewers. Jennifer, who was wearing a black polka-dot dress and pink lipstick, was sprinkling five-spice powder on quail eggs and E.B. was at her stove, steaming Chinese dumplings.

"Wow," Tad said, "We thought it was going to be beer and Doritos."

"Puh-lease, Tadsky," Jennifer said, smiling, "Give us some credit."

"I'm in awe of you," I said.

"Oh, you should have been here before," Deb said. "We had all of our kids here. They were running around playing while we were cooking."

"We got your message," Jennifer said, "and we were laughing. Oh, Amanda, she can't stand this. She wants to be involved."

"In control, right?" Deb said.

Exactly. I had never had a party thrown for me. Having three friends who have busy jobs and children go all out with a special menu, well, I didn't know what to feel. And then I did—both pleasantly irresponsible and also deeply cared for.

The babysitter walked in with E.B.'s baby, Paul, who began to cry. "Oh, please, Paul," E.B. said. She was mixing ground lamb and spices with her hands. "I wish you would self-actualize."

The buzzer rang, and the first guest arrived, our friend Josh, his bags in hand, straight from the train station. He had come down for the night from Boston. I moved next to the man in livery and began wrapping slippery pieces of melon with him. E.B. continued to pull things from her refrigerator.

"Guess what the theme is," Jennifer said.

"Park Avenue picnic?" Tad said. "Is it your '80s party?"

"The theme is foods of the world," E.B. said. "We couldn't decide on one place."

"And we practically went around the world to shop," Deb added. They had begun early the morning before, heading to Chinatown to buy shrimp and mussels, to Kalustyan's for cured beef, plump Medjool dates and nuts, to Fairway for regular groceries and even to IKEA in New Jersey for extra glassware. Meanwhile, Jennifer had gathered the wines: a Cava, a Rioja and a Pinot Grigio. It is the European way of shopping: you seek out the best places for each item.

"E.B. was the mastermind of this, really," Jennifer said. E.B.'s cooking was legendary among our circle of friends. We had been over for dinner about two weeks after she had Paul, and even then, with Paul hanging off her like a fifth limb, she cooked an impressive meal: pasta tossed with fresh tomatoes and basil, figs and prosciutto, and strawberries on homemade shortbread with whipped cream. Now, though, she was in full swing, cooking three things on the stove, directing the waiters who had just arrived and putting food out on platters. Meanwhile, she chatted away with us and drank a glass of wine.

"I aspire to be like E.B. someday," I said to Jennifer.

"We all do," she said.

Tad brought us glasses of Cava. We toasted. Within moments, it seemed, the party was under way. People streamed in by the dozen. The waiters circled and snaked through the crowd. I lost track of Tad for a while, as I caught up with friends. Sherry and Mark drove in from New Jersey, my *Times* editor stopped by and Jeffrey Steingarten came early and stayed late.

"This is a very good party," Jeffrey said, as he stuck out his arm to snag a shrimp wrapped in pickled ramps from a waiter's tray. "And the food is all well-prepared, tasty nice little things. I am impressed that you got three women cooking together without competitiveness, without ego. All the things women are no longer supposed to do."

I nodded. I hadn't thought about it that way.

"And look at you!" he added, "You're so animated and full of spunk. Have you had too much Cava?"

"No, Jeffrey," I said, "It's this strange other thing. I'm happy. And I'm really glad you came."

"Did you have one of these?" my friend Adam interrupted, pointing to the mussels in a wasabi mayonnaise. They were sublime, with a sharp, clean heat soothed by the mayonnaise. The trip to Chinatown had paid off. Hors d'oeuvres kept pouring from the kitchen. There were roasted peppers on cucumbers, chicken and ginger dumplings, roast fillet of beef with horseradish sauce on toasts, and baked wedges of flatbread covered with spiced lamb. The dining room table was spread with platters of dates, cashews and apricots, a ropy, creamy cow's milk cheese, herbed flatbreads and bowls of babaganoush. It was lavish, and a touch obscene. I loved it.

I finally caught up with Deb. "Are you having fun?" she asked.

"Yes," I said, reaching for an asparagus spear and dipping it in a basil and anchovy sauce, "although I'm not sure I've tasted everything yet, and I don't want to miss anything."

"Hey, I peeled all those ends!" Deb said, pointing to the asparagus. "You see?"

It's just the way I've felt so many times when entertaining. You want people to enjoy what you've made without it being the focus, and yet you also want them to appreciate every subtlety of your efforts. And that is the beauty of doing it yourself rather than, say, ordering in or catering.

"Delicious, and not at all stringy," I said to Deb.

Just then Jennifer, who was standing on the staircase, tapped her glass, and the crowd quieted down. I spotted Tad and wiggled my way through the crowd to him.

"Hello, everyone," Jennifer said, "Usually this is the point at which women get up and talk about the bride-to-be and say how great she is, and thank God she finally found someone, and the guys get up and say inappropriate things about past girlfriends. But I'm lucky because I knew both Tad and Amanda before they met.

"Amanda had just broken up with an *asshole*," she continued, to much laughter. "And I knew I wanted to set her up with Tad. He was in L.A. working on a story, so I called him. It was about six a.m. his time. He answered the phone with a very sleepy and cranky "Hello," and I said, "Tad, wake up! Because it's your lucky day.""

Michael spoke next. "I've known Tad for a very long time," he said. "We went to college together, and we met there because he was always prowling my dorm looking for women. Tad in college was a very intimidating figure. He was incredibly smart and even then was always writing these impressive articles, which contained at least one word that none of us would know and we'd have to look up and then it would turn out that he used it correctly. He has maintained this crisp intellect and wit, and over the years he's become a lovely person. So now it's really pleasing to me, to all of us, that he's marrying the only person in America who could make him look like a rube."

Deb's toast welcomed me into their group of friends. "We're the better for having you," she said. Then Tad stood up to thank our hosts.

"You're welcoming us into the company of married people," he said, "and you're also giving us hope that that company is well worth joining because I can't think of three better marriages. It's made us look forward to what's ahead." He paused, and just as he did, E.B. came from behind and slipped baby Paul into his arms. Tad started and blushed, and then displayed the toddler to the laughing crowd, as he and Paul looked at each other with mutual expressions of uncertainty and wonder.

"Do you have anything to say, Amanda?" Michael asked. I did, but I didn't know where to begin. I've never been good off the cuff. My thoughts swarm and then flee my brain as soon as I begin speaking. Which is why I enjoy writing: I can gather my thoughts and make them neat again. I declined Michael's offer with an awkward shrug.

The party picked up once more. Near the end, the Cava supply had dwindled. Guests emptied the platters of lemon squares, which Jennifer had made. When the servers started passing around toasts topped with warm bittersweet chocolate and fleur de sel, I felt flustered. The chocolate toasts were something I fell in love with in Spain a few years ago, and Jennifer had remembered.

Two days later, while running in Riverside Park, I thought of the perfect toast. I'd have another chance at our wedding.

An international party

Fragrant Lamb Pita

E.B. got this from her friend Liz Berger, and writes, "Needless to say, I have never made this recipe by the numbers and have varied it many times to great effect (lamb, minced preserved lemon and cracked green olives with more mint and no Dijon, for example) but the original really is best. It's supposed to be dusted with freshly grated Parmesan before you bake, but I don't feel that's an enhancement, somehow."

3/4 pound ground lamb
3 tablespoons olive oil
6 scallions, minced (bulb and a bit of the green part, too)
2 garlic cloves, minced
1/4 cup chopped parsley
1/2 cup chopped cilantro
2 tablespoons minced mint (say that 10 times fast)
1 tablespoon tomato paste
2 tablespoons Dijon mustard
Grated zest of 1 lemon
Sea salt
Freshly ground black pepper
6 pocketless pitas

Preheat the oven to 425°F. In a big bowl, mix together the first 10 ingredients (lamb, olive oil, scallions, garlic, parsley, cilantro, mint, tomato paste, mustard and lemon zest). Season with salt and pepper. Smear fairly thinly (a little goes a long way) in a circle on the middle of the pitas, leaving edges uncoated. Place them on a large baking sheet and slip them into the oven. Bake until lamb is cooked and pitas are toasted, about 10 minutes. Transfer to a cutting board and cut each pita into 8 wedges with a pizza wheel. E.B. says even scissors will do.

E.B. SAYS, "MAKES A HUGE NUMBER (48) OF CRUSTY lITTLE TREATS."

Quail Eggs with Five Spice Powder

These make a fabulous hors d'oeuvre, but writing a recipe for them seemed absurd. All you need are fresh quail eggs, good five-spice powder and coarse sea salt. Gently simmer the eggs like you would chicken eggs until they are just cooked through, a few minutes. Drain them and run cold water over top. Peel and halve them. Lay them on an attractive platter, dust them with the five-spice powder and sprinkle with some coarse salt. You can make a dozen, two dozen, or a hundred in no time.

Mussels in Wasabi Mayonnaise

French-style mayonnaise can often be found in the dairy case at specialty stores. It has more egg in it and is creamier than something like Hellmann's. If you can't find it, or don't want to bother, make your own. You can use my recipe for tarragon mayonnaise (page 203) and leave out the tarragon.

2 pounds mussels, beards removed and scrubbed
Sea salt
1/2 cup French-style mayonnaise or homemade
1 teaspoon wasabi paste, more to taste

1. Preheat the oven to 250°F. Fill a deep pot with 1/2-inch water. Season it with salt and bring to a boil. Drop in the mussels and steam until the shells open. If one doesn't open, it's probably not good; discard it. Take the mussels out of the pot and remove the mussel meat from the shells. Rinse the shells, pull them in half and spread them on a baking sheet. Place them in the oven to dry, about 10 minutes. Cool the shells completely.

2. In a bowl, whisk together the mayonnaise and wasabi paste. Taste it and decide if you want more heat. If so, add a little more paste. When the mussels are completely cool, add them to the bowl and fold them into the mayonnaise. They should have just a light coating.

3. Lay the best looking shells on a serving platter and nestle a mussel in each one. Take the platter out to the party.

ABOUT 40 TO 50 HORS D'OEUVRES (EASILY DOUBLED OR TRIPLED).

Lemon Curd Bars Cockaigne

Adapted from Joy of Cooking *by Irma S. Rombauer, Marion Rombauer Becker, and Ethan Becker (Scribner, 1997)*

These bars have a lovely crumbly crust and a tart curd. Generating this much lemon juice may seem daunting, but do not substitute bottled lemon juice. Fresh juice makes a huge difference in the flavor. During Meyer lemon season (approximately November to March), use them!

2 cups all-purpose flour
1/4 cup confectioners' sugar
12 tablespoons (1 1/2 sticks) cold unsalted butter, cut into small pieces
6 large eggs
3 cups sugar (2 1/2 cups if using Meyer lemons)
Grated zest of 1 lemon
1 cup plus 2 tablespoons fresh lemon juice (about 5 lemons)

1. Position a rack in the center of the oven. Preheat the oven to 325°F. Sift 1 1/2 cups flour and the confectioners' sugar together into a large bowl. Toss in the cubes of butter and, using your fingertips, cut in the butter—I do this with small pinching motions—until the mixture is the size of small peas. Tip the mixture into a 13×9-inch (or equivalent) pan, then use your fingers to pat and press it into the base and 3/4-inch up the sides to avoid leaking during baking. Bake until golden brown, 20 to 30 minutes.

2. While it cools on a rack, reduce the oven temperature to 300°F. Whisk together the eggs and sugar in a small bowl. Stir in the lemon zest and juice. Sift the remaining 1/2 cup flour over the bowl and fold together until smooth. Pour this batter over the baked crust and put in the oven once more. Bake until the top is set, about 35 minutes. Remove the pan to a rack to cool completely before cutting into bars.

ABOUT 18 3×2-INCH BARS.

Toasts with Chocolate and Fleur de Sel

Turn on your oven to 350°F. Put a thin baguette (not sourdough) on a cutting board and slice it thinly and diagonally so that you get 1/4-inch wedge-like slices. About 20 will do. Lay them on a baking sheet. Top each slice with a thin square of the best bittersweet chocolate you can find. It should be no bigger a piece than what you would normally bite from a chocolate bar. Slip the baking sheet into the oven and take it out when the chocolate is melted but still holding its shape. Quickly move them to a serving platter and sprinkle the slices first with a few drops of the best extra virgin olive oil you own, then with fleur de sel or coarse sea salt. (To get the right amount, try one and taste it, before doing the rest. The salt should enliven the flavor of the chocolate, not make it salty.) Distribute quickly to hungry guests.

20 CHOCOLATE TOASTS.

Chapter 26

FINE DINING IN THE SKY

I was going to Spain for a story, and I had a lot on my mind. I had to arrange interviews with winemakers, find hotels, secure restaurant reservations and figure out how to do it all when I don't speak Spanish. I'd work that all out. I was more worried about what to eat on the airplane.

As it was an overnight flight there were several issues to consider. I would need dinner and dessert and perhaps a little something for just before arrival. I have a few parameters, developed over years of air travel: the food must be compact and light, yet it cannot be skimpy. It must include favorite foods like cheeses, cookies and olives, and it should in some way be lavish. This is because when I fly, I am convinced that I will die. So I put a lot of energy into creating a kind of cocoon around myself. I wear Bose headphones, which block out the roar of the engines (and any signs of malfunction), wrap myself in a blanket, and wear one of those blow-up neck pillows. Food in the cocoon is most important. I want the meal to be delicious and civilized: if it's going to be my last, it's certainly not going to be some rubbery chicken suffocating in tinfoil.

I pack my meal in a plastic bag, and at the airport I buy a large bottle of water. (You never get enough in coach.) Then after takeoff, when the flight attendants first bang through with their drink carts, I have my cocktail hour. I order a little sparkling water with a wedge of lemon—some flight attendants insist on calling it club soda, but I pay them no mind—and a Scotch, served neat. I fly Delta quite often, and they always seem to stock Johnny Walker Black, which isn't bad. On overseas flights, they sometimes have Glenmorangie. You must press the attendants to look for all the brands, because even if they're friendly (which is rare), they always reach for the cheapest thing they have.

I suggest packing salted nuts (and once in Spain, I loaded up on those delicious salted almonds for the way back). A few airlines still serve them, and some airlines have good pretzels, but I wouldn't go near those Chex Mix-like combinations.

After the cocktail hour, it's a good idea to wait for everyone else to be served their meal before beginning your own. If you don't, you will be subject to much staring. And you also won't get the benefit of a knife and butter, which you can poach from a tray. This is important for buttering the chewy country roll you bring, or slicing a nutty, soft cheese. You may also like to have wine with your meal. It will be no Château Petrus, but it won't be the rotgut of years past either. Airlines, though still in the dark ages on food, have smartened up about wine. I recommend reds because the extra tannins in cheap reds are more bearable than the heavy, flabby oak in cheap whites.

For the main course, I often bring a sandwich. They were designed for eating on the road, after all. A good sandwich contains the best foods in the world: excellent cured meats and cheeses, aged vinegars, nut oils, roasted onions, herbs and homemade mayonnaise.

One of my favorite sandwiches for the air is a thin baguette spread with sweet butter and draped with prosciutto. I also love a similar version with olive oil, roasted red pepper and creamy mozzarella cheese.

This time, since I was on my way to Spain, the land of ham, I needed to think outside the box. It was spring, and the season's first asparagus was popping up, so I leapt on it at Fairway. There, I also picked up some fresh goat curd (regular soft goat cheese would have been fine), blood oranges and arugula. I bought big, plump Medjool dates and a ripe pear. For breakfast, I chose an almond croissant from a nearby pastry shop.

A few hours before my flight, I blanched the asparagus and let it cool, then sliced it into inch-long pieces. I whisked blood orange juice and vinegar with a few teaspoons of Dijon mustard, salt and pepper, dripping in grapeseed oil a little at a time. It was sweet and a moody shade of purple, which stained the arugula and bled all over the lumps of goat curd. I could have added tuna instead of goat curd, and some green beans or chickpeas, but I liked the salad's simplicity, its tangle of pure vivid flavors. I packed the salad in a plastic container and brought a napkin and a real fork (which, disturbingly, makes it through the X-ray machine every time).

For dessert, almost any tart, cake or petit four may be packed. Don't bother making anything. Buy a treat. It will give you something to look forward to, deep into the flight, after being forced to watch "Shallow

Hal." I picked up some cornmeal almond biscotti and dark chocolates and went on my way.

For those hours that stretch between meals, I sometimes bring along sliced fennel, radishes, olives or figs. And for breakfast, I like to have a ripe banana, yogurt (my own; the stuff on planes is loaded with stabilizers), plums and a small, decadent pastry. A humble bagel will not do.

One issue to consider is sharing. While I don't like talking to the person sitting next to me, I do like to share food. I've offered asparagus spears, tuna sandwiches, wedges of St. Marcellin and caramel-filled chocolates to fellow travelers. Without words, you make a friend and a companion who will happily put up with your bulky bag in his foot room.

One final tip is to ask to sit near the front, as near as possible to first class. I learned this recently when flying back from Florence. On my last day there, I had gone to a tiny gourmet food store and stocked up for my trip home. I told the clerk it was for the plane, and with this information he became inspired, packing an enticing array of cured Tuscan meats (*salame Toscano*, *coppa* and *finocchiona Toscana*), *mostarda di Cremona* (a sweet and gently spiced fruit preserve) to go with the meats, *pane Toscano*, pecorino cheese, olives, marinated artichokes, a crisp flatbread brushed with olive oil, and *brutti ma buoni*, the local almond cookies, which translate as "ugly but good."

On the plane, I went through my usual cocktail hour. When it was time for lunch, I laid out my tiny plastic containers of olives and *mostarda* and meats on butcher paper. When I ordered red wine, I was given a bottle of Friulian Merlot. I thought I was doing pretty well.

The tannins were tough to take, though, a bit like chewing on a shoe. I was letting it roll around my mouth when the first-class attendant passed my seat, then stopped in his tracks. He inspected my spread, pointed to it and gave me two thumbs up. A few minutes later, he returned. Glancing side to side, he slid a cup of red wine onto my tray. "Chianti," he said. "Much better." And it was in glass, not plastic.

Later on, he reappeared, this time with a napkin. He set it down in front of me and lifted the napkin to reveal a truffle, a cream filled pastry and a *gianduja* chocolate wrapped in foil.

It never hurts to be a fussy gourmet, even in coach.

Dinner, a few miles up

Roasted and Salted Almonds

In addition to being an excellent *amuse-bouche* on the airplane, these are a great snack to serve at home. If I'm serving a large meal, I will sometimes forego hors d'oeuvres and just serve these with Champagne, chilled Fino sherry or even beer. You can jazz them up with spices like cumin, paprika and coriander, but I prefer them with salt alone, which brings out their fragrance and butteriness.

You may also prepare these over the stove, filling the base of a medium pan with half an inch of oil. Heat the oil, then add the almonds, and keep them moving with a spoon so they toast evenly. Remove them with a slotted spoon to paper towels and shower with salt.

2 cups peeled almonds
1/4 cup peanut oil
Coarse sea salt

Preheat the oven to 350°F. Place the almonds in a bowl, pour over the peanut oil and toss to coat. Add more if needed. Spread on a baking sheet and bake, shaking the pan every few minutes, until lightly browned, fragrant and sizzling, about 10 minutes. Remove from the oven, season with salt and let cool. Once cool, season again, if needed.

2 CUPS ROASTED ALMONDS.

Prosciutto and Butter Sandwiches

You must disabuse yourself of the belief that a sandwich is not a sandwich without lettuce, tomato and mayonnaise. And do resist the temptation to put on more prosciutto. This is not about sustenance. It is about pleasure.

4 six-inch-long pieces of thin, crispy baguette, split down the middle
6 to 8 tablespoons unsalted butter, room temperature
8 slices prosciutto

Spread the insides of the baguette with the butter. Lay 2 slices of prosciutto in loose folds inside each baguette. Press the baguette closed.
4 RICH LITTLE SANDWICHES.

Asparagus and Goat Curd Salad with Blood Orange Vinaigrette

If you are feeling ambitious, replace the asparagus with artichoke hearts, which require a bit more work—boiling and lots of trimming. But please do not use the jarred kind. If you do, don't tell anyone where you got the recipe!

Sea salt
1/2 pound asparagus, woody ends trimmed
3 large handfuls young arugula
Juice of 1 blood orange
1 teaspoon red wine vinegar
1 tablespoon Dijon mustard
Freshly ground black pepper
1/4 cup grapeseed oil
1/2 cup goat curd, chilled

1. Bring a large, wide pan of water to a boil. Add enough salt to make the water taste seasoned. Add the asparagus and cook for 3 minutes. Drain and run under cold water. Lay the asparagus out on tea towels to cool completely and dry. Slice into 1 to 1 1/2-inch lengths. Combine the asparagus and arugula in a large bowl.

2. In a small bowl, whisk together the blood orange juice, vinegar, mustard and a little salt and pepper. Add the oil gradually, first in drops, then in a

thin stream, whisking all the while, until the vinaigrette is thick and emulsified. Taste and fix seasoning.

3. Pour the dressing over the arugula and asparagus and toss to coat. Add the goat curd, broken into lumps about the size of walnuts. Do this with your fingers. Toss gently to mix. Taste and adjust seasoning. If flying, pack into a plastic container with a tight-fitting lid.

SALAD FOR 4 (TO FEED YOUR FELLOW PASSENGERS, OR YOUR FAMILY AT HOME).

Airplane Salad

This is a fine salad for picnics on land, too.

1 head Bibb lettuce, leaves torn into several pieces
1 can (16 ounces) white beans, drained and rinsed
2 cups cherry tomatoes, halved
1/2 cup (4 ounces) smoked mackerel or smoked trout, pulled into small lumps
1 tablespoon aged sherry vinegar
1 teaspoon Dijon mustard
Sea salt
Freshly ground black pepper
1/4 cup excellent olive oil

Mix together the lettuce, white beans, tomatoes and shredded mackerel (or trout) in a big bowl. In a small bowl, whisk together the vinegar, mustard and a dash of salt and pepper. Add the oil a little at a time, whisking constantly so that the dressing emulsifies and thickens. Correct seasoning. Pour the dressing over the salad and fold it in using large spoons and digging deeply so you lift and turn the salad over itself, without crushing the ingredients. Grind more pepper over the top if you like. If flying, pack a serving into a plastic container.

A TASTY LITTLE SALAD FOR 4.

Chapter 27

THE NOT-SO-SECRET TAPAS BAR

My source, José Andrés, a chef in Washington D.C., said the magic words: no one had written about this place before. But his directions gave me pause: "It's west of Las Ramblas. After you cross Avinguda del Parallel, you will see a Pizza Hut. Turn left, and Quimet & Quimet is about fifty meters up the street."

Pizza Hut is not a promising landmark. Then he added that the bar specializes in canned foods, which brought to mind creamed spinach and baked beans.

But I was alone in Barcelona, and curious, so I gave it a go. I walked from my hotel through the Boquería, then down the dark narrow streets of an Arab neighborhood until I reached the Parallel. I spotted the Pizza Hut, its lights casting a fluorescent gloom over the street. The few shops were boarded up for the night, and the street was deserted. But I could hear music and muffled voices. Out of nowhere, a cyclist swept by me so close his elbow jabbed my side and knocked me toward a wall. I stood for a minute, shaken. A few yards ahead, a couple stepped out onto the sidewalk into a shaft of light, and I rushed toward them.

I stood in front of a tiny tapas bar that was packed like a subway car at rush hour. I wedged myself inside. The walls were a dense collage of wine bottles, colorful food tins, all neatly stacked, and old advertisements. It all looked like it had been there for decades. Behind the small bar stood Joaquín and Juana Perez, whose family has owned the place since 1914. Both have fair skin and fair eyes and short curly hair the color of dry grass. They shifted left and right, Juana pointing at customers and asking for their orders, her brother quickly filling them, sprinkling oil from squeeze bottles, reaching for little round toasts. I inched up to the bar to see what people were eating.

Nothing was in its familiar guise. There was squid, sea cucumber, ruby-colored slices of bluefin tuna, leeks in oil, bottarga, artichokes, two kinds of anchovy (white and pink), red peppers, caviar, smoked fish, foie gras and roasted pig's cheek. They were laid out in tins and on plates and trays in a large glass case, in the manner of an antipasti display at an expensive American grocery store. Everything at Quimet & Quimet is a *conserva*, or preserved food. The Perezes collect the finest preserved goods from around the world and sell them here, in the can or jar or layered into splendid tapa creations.

There was no menu, so I got Juana's attention and pointed to other diners' plates. I began with cippolline onions, preserved in oil, and fat green olives. The onions were sweet, the olives buttery.

Next, Joaquín placed a lump of pig cheek on a small round plate. He put a candied fig and chestnut beside it, and then thick slices of porcini mushroom from Italy. He sprinkled everything with white wine vinegar from Penedès, balsamic from Modena, a dash of soy sauce and orange flower water. The cheek was seasoned like porchetta with herbs and pepper, and was so tender it shredded into pieces when I pressed it with my fork.

For dessert, I had a little round toast spread with a creamy yogurt, as thick as jam, and Belgian chocolate. Juana made it this time. She placed a candied walnut from Priorato on it and doused it all with walnut oil and a touch of brandy.

I looked around. Everyone was crammed into this tiny jewel box, happily chewing. As I ate the toast, which seemed to me the best thing I had ever tasted, regret came over me. I was just scratching the surface of the broad array of tapas. I had made the grave mistake of going all out—ten courses—at lunch. I could barely eat another bite, and I had to leave the next morning. Who knew when I'd get to return?

Back home, I called my grocer to tell him to check it out on his next trip to Barcelona. And when Jeffrey e-mailed to tell me he was on his way there, I gave him all the details. "But," I told him, "you are forbidden to write about it before me."

Meanwhile, I tried to hang on as best I could to the spirit of *conservas*. Right now, most cooks are obsessed with fresh greenmarket foods. So preserved foods—pickles excepted—have been marginalized. But onions in vinegar, salted anchovies, smoked fish and candied figs have the concentrated flavor that their fresh counterparts sometimes lack. Moreover, if we hadn't developed the art of preserving foods, the human species would not have survived. Why not celebrate it?

I decided to give it a try at home, preparing a light dinner for Tad and me. When I announced my plan, he looked thoughtful, as if he were making a mental note to eat a bigger lunch.

Even with terrific specialty stores at my disposal, it was impossible to find the *conservas* I had at Quimet & Quimet. But this didn't mean that I was relegated to Goya beans from the supermarket. If you shop well, there are dozens of examples of artisanal preserved foods, waiting to be used in delicious ways. One of the best resources for these are Web sites, like www.tienda.com, which specializes in Spanish foods. There are also many devoted to Italian and French goods.

Lean toward things preserved in good oil or salt, without much seasoning. You want the ingredients pure, so that you can mix them without their flavor becoming muddled. You want to season them yourself with an excellent olive or nut oil or a delicate vinegar. It helps to think of them, as the Perezes do, in terms of their flavor role. It is really no different than making a sandwich. A cured meat, like speck, or fish, like sardines, provides richness and salt in a dish. Jarred artichokes will bring sweetness, and pickled ramps will add acidity and tartness. You can use bread as a base, if you like, or simply layer the ingredients on a plate and serve them with a tiny fork.

Preserved foods bring ease to the kitchen, too, for all you have to do is open them up and begin assembling. You don't need to chop, seed or dice, and you never need to turn on the oven. They are the perfect hors d'oeuvre or dessert for a party, and just the way to cook in the summer heat.

I began with a jar of tuna preserved in olive oil and smoked paprika, an import from Spain; *peperonata*, a creamy red pepper spread, and gigante beans preserved in oil. I spooned a little red pepper on a plate, dropped a few beans on it, and laid a piece or two of the tuna on top. Over it, I dribbled my best olive oil and an aged sherry vinegar. The vinegar pooled in droplets around the tuna.

Next, I rubbed slices of toasted baguette with a tomato half. On it I put a roasted cipollini onion, cured in oil, and a slice of serrano ham, curled like a ribbon. Our dinner was ready in five minutes.

Tad eyed up his plate with its tiny portions and poured himself a beer. "When you're all finished," I said, "tell me which one you liked best." He had three helpings of the tuna, two of the cipollini onion and then began eating the beans out of the jar. Perhaps they would be appreciated as tapas another time.

For dessert, I spread some *gianduja*, a hazelnut chocolate paste, on a toast, topped it with ricotta, a swirl of *dulce de leche* and a shower of sea salt. "Now that is tasty," he said, going back for more.

It was merely a warm up. Next time, I thought, I'll buy anchovies and tapenade, order preserved mussels, and splurge on candied chestnuts. I was relishing my scoop on tapas until a few weeks later when the August *Vogue* arrived in the mail. There it was in Jeffrey's column: Quimet & Quimet.

Canned food cuisine

Canned Tuna with Beans, Creamy Red Pepper Spread and Aged Sherry Vinegar

Serve this when you have a few friends over and can hand them a small dish with a tiny fork to eat while you're having drinks. Or when you have a large party and want a first course that you can prepare ahead and set out on the table before cocktails. Pass a basket of bread, so everyone can mop up the sauce on their plates.

12 ounces fine tuna preserved in olive oil
1/4 teaspoon Spanish smoked paprika (the sweet, not hot, variety)
3/4 cup roasted red pepper spread, preferably coarse (or canned roasted piquillo peppers, drained and pulsed in the food processor with a little olive oil)

1/2 cup marinated gigante beans or jarred white beans (also preferably in oil)
Extra virgin olive oil
Aged sherry vinegar

Begin with all ingredients at room temperature. Drain the tuna from the oil and place it in a bowl. Sprinkle over the paprika and stir gently to mix. On each of four small plates, spread a 3-inch circle of red pepper spread. Divide the tuna among them, placing it on top of the peppers. Spoon the beans on and around the tuna. Sprinkle with olive oil and a little sherry vinegar.

TAPAS FOR 4.

Sources: Aged sherry vinegar and canned tuna can be ordered from www.tienda. com. Canned tuna, white beans and roasted piquillo peppers can be ordered from www.chefshop.com.

Toasts Rubbed with Tomato, Cipollini Onions and Serrano Ham

While none of these ingredients are canned, the ham is preserved, and so are the onions, even though not for the long term. You can roast most any onion—leek, ramp, scallion—and then cover it in oil and keep it in the refrigerator for a week. You can also pickle them and preserve them in oil, which mellows the strength of the vinegar. But don't use straight pickled onions, because they're too sharp and will take over.

I recommend two variations. One would be to rub the toast with tomato jam (green or red) rather than a fresh tomato. The other is to sprinkle it with a nut oil rather than olive oil. A good serrano ham has nuttiness to its flavor; a nut oil would underline this.

These toasts make a terrific party hors d'oeuvre. They can be assembled in advance and are not at all taxing.

8 1/4-inch diagonal slices baguette
1/2 ripe tomato, or 8 teaspoons tomato jam
4 thin slices serrano ham
8 roasted cipollini onions (or any other roasted onion, marinated in oil; do not use pickled onions unless they're in oil), marinated in oil, halved
Extra virgin olive oil, or a nut oil like walnut, hazelnut or almond
Freshly ground black pepper

Lightly toast the baguette slices. While still warm, rub 1 side with the halved tomato. Pull the slices of ham in half and lay in folds on top of the toasts (tomato-rubbed side). Top each toast with 2 onion halves. Sprinkle with olive oil and coarsely grind black pepper over top.

TAPAS FOR 4.

Toasts with Salt Cod and Tomato Jam

H ere the salt cod is simply rehydrated, not cooked, so it may look translucent but it will taste cooked. If you don't want to bother with rehydrating, you may use good anchovy fillets instead of the cod. And if you can't find tomato jam, chop two ripe tomatoes and cook them over medium high heat with a few dashes of sugar and salt until pulpy and a touch sweet.

1/4 pound salt cod
12 1/4-inch slices baguette
Tomato jam
Excellent olive oil or grapeseed oil
Sherry vinegar

1. The day before, soak the cod in water and place it in the fridge, changing the water every couple of hours, about 2 or 3 times. Taste it occasionally; you want the cod to be rich and saline but not too salty. Take it out of the water when it's right. Cut into thin slivers.

2. Spread a thin layer of tomato jam on each slice of baguette. Top with a sliver or two of salt cod (just enough for a spare single layer). Sprinkle with olive oil or grapeseed oil, and a drop or two of sherry vinegar.

12 TOASTS.

Toasts with Gianduja Spread, Ricotta, Dulce de Leche and Sea Salt

T his dessert requires no whisking, folding or baking, just the spreading techniques for a peanut butter and jelly sandwich. If you cannot find *dulce de leche*, then make up for it with a candied chestnut, or fig, or chopped nuts.

12 1/4-inch slices baguette
12 teaspoons *gianduja* spread (recipe for homemade is in the recipe)
12 tablespoons fresh, creamy ricotta

12 teaspoons *dulce de leche*
Fleur de sel or coarse sea salt

Lightly toast the baguette slices. While still warm, spread each with a tea-spoon of *gianduja* spread. (If you cannot find *gianduja* spread, melt 10 tea-spoons of bittersweet or milk chocolate over a double boiler and stir in 2 teaspoons hazelnut or almond paste.) Top with a tablespoon of ricotta and drizzle with the *dulce de leche*. Then sprinkle with a pinch of *fleur de sel*.

DESSERT FOR 4.

Source: *Dulce de Leche* can be ordered from www.chefshop.com.

Chapter 28

EASTERN SHORE INTERLUDE

We hadn't left yet, and I already wanted to come home. We had planned a weekend at my grandmother's house, but I was behind on a story and would have to work while I was there. I knew this would disappoint her. I am always working when I visit. Worse, Tad had to work, too.

I called my mother to see if we would be better off rescheduling.

"I don't think you can," my mother said. "She already ordered soft-shell crabs. And she's made a lime cheesecake. Oh, and I think she special-ordered a rockfish."

"Ooh! I don't want to miss that!" I said.

"I didn't think so."

When we arrived at my grandmother's on the Eastern Shore of the Chesapeake Bay, we went inside and unpacked our things. She was out on her back porch talking with someone and could not hear us. When I poked my head out the door, she let out a little chortle.

"You made it. I was beginning to wonder about you."

"You remember Bill?" she said. Her neighbor Bill is a doctor in his forties. My grandmother looks after his house when he and his wife are away during the week. They check up on her when they're there. This weekend, not realizing she had guests, Bill had invited my grandmother, who is eighty-five, over for dinner with his old college buddies. He likes her that much. Most people do.

"You probably want some lunch," she said, opening the screen door into the house. Five minutes later, we were at the table. She had made her split pea soup infused with smoked ham hocks. We ate cucumber sandwiches, soft on the outside, crunchy in the middle. For dessert, she served us sliced canteloupe and cherry and almond biscotti.

Tad ate a lot. "You might want to pace yourself," I told him.

While we recovered, she flitted around the house, hanging laundry on the clothes line, weeding her garden, explaining to Tad the contents of every ship and barge passing before the window, and checking her blood pressure, as only people in their eighties love to do. It was pleasing to see her in her element. The last time I had spent time with her was in Rome, when we were not seeing eye to eye. I was also eager for her to get to know Tad a little better.

"Can I mow your lawn or something?" Tad asked.

"I already did that," she said.

"But you only have a push mower."

"Yes. It works."

Soon, Tad and I were on her sofa, computers in our laps, typing away. Grandmom was back at the sink, cleaning softshell crabs and talking to them as she wielded her knife.

"Oh, you don't like to have your face cut off?" my grandmother said. "Too bad."

I joined her at the sink. "I've never cleaned them," I said. "Can you show me how?"

"You cut their head off, then you have to dig out their lungs and ovary if it's a female."

"I'm taking your sex life away from you!" she said to the crab in her hand. She turned to me with her knife still in the crab and lifted out a little sack. "I like to take out this water sack. Otherwise you get it in a pan and it explodes. If someone was going fishing, it would make good fish bait."

Tad came up behind us. "It reminds me of marking sheep in Australia," he said to my grandmother. "I worked on a sheep station there for a while."

She looked up at him, confused. I knew she had the impression that he had been sheltered, going to good schools and being handed things, taking it easy.

"We'd castrate the sheep and snip their ears to tag them. The sheep didn't care at all about their testicles. You ripped out their genetic future and they lay there like 'Whatever.' But when you touched their ears, they would bleat and kick. That's a dumb animal."

She chuckled. "So how are your wedding plans coming along?" she asked.

"Fine," I said. "We're getting into the more fun stuff now. Choosing our menu, flowers, things like that. What did you eat at your wedding?"

"Chicken salad. Mom killed the chickens that morning. I went to get my hair done and when I came back we picked the meat off the bones and made salad with it. We had potato salad, chicken salad, and Poppy bought beer. It was 1938, the Depression years. No one had money. When mom and I bought our dresses, I think hers was ten dollars and mine was twelve or something. Our hats were a dollar ninety-eight. Poppy bought a quarter-barrel of beer. It was five dollars."

"It all sounds kind of appealing," I said. "Weddings are so complicated now."

My grandmother had taken a block of cream cheese, put it in a pan and set it on the back of her stove, where it was warm. The phone rang, and she answered it and just kept on working, rolling out pie dough.

"Here's your job," she said, covering the phone receiver briefly and handing me a spatula. I was supposed to be working, but I couldn't resist. I get an urge to bake, an almost itchy feeling, whenever I visit. Her kitchen is so accessible and well worn, like a soft old chair that you sink into. I want to spend all my time standing in it. On the counter was a recipe written in her curly script: "Double-Good Blueberry Pie." The blueberries were coated in sugar and cooking down with cornstarch. When she got off the phone, she peered over my shoulder.

"Come on. Clear up. Get thick," she said to the pan. The blueberries are ready when their thickened juices clear up like Jell-O.

Together we sorted through the blueberries selecting ones to fold into the thick base. She kept poking her crooked fingers through the pile until she found a big, plump berry. Then she'd pop it in her mouth. She said to me, "I come across a big berry and I say, 'No one is going to notice this big berry in a pie,' so I eat it!"

Meanwhile, she had the pie base baking and cooling. She showed me how to season the cream cheese, now room temperature, with sugar, vanilla and cream, and then spread it on the base of the pie. "I don't do it this way all the time. It keeps the blueberries from sinking into the crust." We plopped the blueberry mixture on top and carefully nudged it to the edges. The double-good pie was complete.

"Grandmom," I said, "I think it's cocktail time."

"Sounds good to me. You know what I like."

She only drinks when someone makes her a cocktail, and it is always the same. Gin and tonic over ice. Light on the gin, heavy on the ice, and served in a low-stemmed glass that says "Pussycat." She wraps a napkin around its base to catch the sweat.

"I just thought I'd get these beans started."

"Helen," Tad said, "why don't we all sit down for a minute?"

"She doesn't know how to sit down. It's not in her DNA."

"I can see that," Tad said.

"Oh, I suppose I could try it," my grandmother said.

We sat in her living room, overlooking the Bay.

"I don't understand these people who go out to breakfast," she said after a moment. "My friends invited me out the other week to this place in town. They go every weekend. The service was terrible," she said, pronouncing "terrible" like "turble." Tad nudged me happily whenever she said this word. She didn't notice, continuing her diatribe, "My egg was overcooked and the bacon was soggy! I said to them, 'Thanks very much, but next time why don't you come over to my house. I'll show you how an egg should be cooked.'"

Tad looked at me. "How did you ever become so opinionated about food?"

"We're a tough crowd," I said.

Soon after our cocktail hour ended, my grandmother had corn with basil simmering in a pan, the softshell crabs sautéing and yellow beans cooking on the stove.

"Spit! Spit!" she said to the crabs, which were popping and crackling in the pan. "I'm glad I cleaned out the water sack. Imagine if I hadn't!"

"Grandmom, I want to see how you do your yellow beans."

"This is one of the things I make by guess," she said. "This is Mimi's way of making yellow beans." Mimi was her mother-in-law. She died when I was a small child and my memories of her are sketchy. She was a short but large woman, who as far as I could tell at the time, took too many naps and seemed mute.

"It makes yellow beans just a little bit different," Grandmom said. "This is the way Poppy used to like them." She began with a roux of butter and flour and browned it well. Then she seasoned it with salt, cider vinegar and sugar, adding a little milk to get the consistency she wanted, that of a thick vinaigrette. Then she dropped the blanched beans into the sauce, turned them once or twice, and flipped off the stove.

"Enough of that. Done," she said.

The phone rang again. It was my mother.

"We're about to sit down to dinner," Grandmom said into the phone. "Yes, we're having softshell crabs. Tad liked watching me clean them." Pause. "We're having a fine time. They've been working the whole time at their computers." Tad and I smiled at each other.

At the table, my grandmother began telling stories about her courtship with Poppy. I think having us at hand, near to starting our married life, made her miss him.

"Our first date was an accident. Poppy came over with my cousin Stan to drink beer because they knew my pop always had beer in the house. When I first saw him, on the couch drinking beer, I thought, 'Oh, where did Stan find him?' Stan said, 'Let's go rollerskating,' and so I went with them. We ended up at the Mannachor, and while Stan stayed at the bar, Poppy stayed with me and Stan's girlfriend Naoma. On the way home, Stan was so drunk, he was driving his car up on the curb in Doylestown, and he was so busy trying to kiss Naoma that he lost control of the car and we ended up in the middle of a wheat field. The car sunk, so we got out and walked home, singing 'I'm Gonna Walk My Baby Back Home' at the top of our lungs."

Tad and I were eating our beans and crab, captivated. "The next weekend they were supposed to take us to Sunnybrook where all the big bands played," she said. "I was married to that man for sixty years and I never made it there. Later on, since we didn't have a car," she said, "we'd just doubledate with my parents." Tad's eyes widened in horror.

"So you had some trouble with transportation on your dates," he said.

"I suppose so."

After dinner, Tad hopped up to do the dishes. He washed and she dried. While I was wiping up the table, my grandmother said to Tad, "You're a good dishwasher. Amanda is going to be lucky to have you around the house."

He smiled at my grandmother, and said, "Amanda thinks I'm a turble dishwasher."

A few of Helen's treats

Mimi's Yellow Beans

My grandmother fully cooks the beans so they are soft, tangy and rich. I always loved them with sautéed perch or striped bass.

1 pound yellow wax beans, trimmed
Sea salt
1 tablespoon butter
1 tablespoon flour
1/3 cup milk
1 1/2 tablespoons cider vinegar
Pinch sugar

1. Place a pot of water over high heat and season the water with a good deal of salt, so that it tastes salty. When it boils, add the beans and cook until they are firm but no longer crisp, about 4 minutes. Drain.

2. In a medium pan, melt the butter over medium heat. When it gets foamy, sprinkle in the flour and stir with a whisk until the flour begins to toast and brown. When it's the color of a hazelnut shell, pour in the milk and stir to dissolve. Let it cook for a minute, then season it with salt and add the vinegar and sugar. It should be the consistency of a thick salad dressing and tangy. Add more milk to thin it out, or cook it down to thicken. Taste it. When it's just right, add the beans and fold them over a few times to coat in the sauce.

BEANS FOR 4.

Helen Getz's Double-Good Blueberry Pie

The recipe for the dough makes enough for four pies. You can divide the recipe if you like, but you may want to do what my grandmother does. She puts three portions in the freezer and one in the refrigerator. "Then you're always ready to make a pie," she says.

Also, my grandmother notes that she often uses frozen blueberries for this pie. I would add that this is fine as long as you picked them when they were fresh. The recipe won't turn out well using frozen berries from the grocery store.

For the pie dough
4 2/3 cups all-purpose flour
1 tablespoon sugar
2 teaspoons salt
1 3/4 cups Crisco vegetable shortening
1 tablespoon apple cider vinegar
1 large egg
1/2 cup cold water

For the cream cheese filling
4 ounces cream cheese, at room temperature
3 tablespoons sugar
1/2 teaspoon vanilla extract
1 tablespoon heavy cream

For the blueberry filling
3/4 cup sugar
3 tablespoons cornstarch

1/8 teaspoon salt
1/4 cup water
4 cups blueberries
1 tablespoon lemon juice
1 tablespoon butter

1. Prepare the dough: In a large bowl, mix together the flour, sugar and salt. Cut in the shortening until it is reduced to tiny granules. My grandmother uses a pastry blender, but you may also use a fork. In a separate bowl, beat together the vinegar, egg and cold water. Make a well in the center of the flour mixture and pour in this liquid. Mix it with the pastry blender, drawing in the flour from the sides, until a dough forms. Divide the dough into 4 balls and flatten them slightly into disks. Wrap each disk in plastic wrap. Cover the ones going in the freezer with foil (or seal in a plastic bag), too, then place in the freezer. Put the one you will use for this pie in the fridge to chill for at least 30 minutes.

2. Preheat the oven to 450°F. Roll out the dough between lightly floured sheets of parchment paper or plastic wrap into a circle about 1/8-inch thick. Line a 9-inch pie plate with the dough. Trim the edges, leaving about 1/2-inch overhang. Fold under this overhang and crimp the edges. Prick the base of the dough with a fork. Line the pie dough with foil and pour in pie weights or beans. Bake for 10 minutes, then turn down the heat to 350°F and bake for 10 minutes more. Remove the foil and pie weights and bake another 5 minutes to dry the surface. Let cool completely before filling.

3. Prepare the cream cheese filling: With a hand mixer or a whisk, blend the cream cheese, sugar, vanilla and heavy cream until light and smooth.

4. Prepare the blueberry filling: Put the sugar, cornstarch and salt in a medium pan. Add the water and 2 cups of the blueberries. Cook over medium heat, stirring constantly. The mixture will seize up and thicken and, after a minute or two, turn clear. Take it off the heat and stir in the lemon juice and butter. Pour in the remaining blueberries and stir until coated.

5. Assemble the pie: Spread the cream cheese mixture over the bottom of the cooled pie dough. Drop the blueberry mixture over the cream cheese in large spoonfuls, then gently spread them around, trying not to mush the cream cheese layer. There should be two distinct layers. Chill in the refrigerator for a half an hour or so to set. Let it come to room temperature before serving.

A PIE THAT MAY BE CUT INTO 6 OR 8 SLICES.

Chapter 29

CHANGING PLACES

It was a cruelly hot June day. I had my cart packed with groceries—fresh fish, fava beans, potatoes, basil—and when I got to
Jennifer and Ed's building, a few blocks away, they did not answer.
Strange, I thought. They're never late. A trusting older woman let me
into the building and I sat on a bench in the lobby. Lobbies of prewar
buildings are often cool, like cathedrals.

Echoing down through the staircase was a woman's voice ebbing and
flowing, as if she were reading verse. It was Jennifer. When I got to the
fifth floor, she was sitting in the hallway, a stroller and its contents
strewn to the side, reading a story to a young boy kneeling beside her.

"Oh, hi!" she said, "I locked myself out of the apartment and Ed is out riding his bike."

"Where's Hannah?"

"At the neighbors', harassing their kids. I got Joseph, their son."

I sat down on the floor beside her. It felt like college for a moment, sitting in hallways to socialize. I wish I had known Jennifer in college, I thought as she continued reading.

Tad and I were moving to Brooklyn in just a few days. We'd go from living around the corner to an hour subway ride away. We were all pretending it was just another Sunday. But it would be the last casual visit. Jennifer and I could no longer hang on the phone, peering into our refrigerators, figuring out how to pull together a meal. Now it would become a more typical New York get-together. Dozens of e-mails comparing schedules, shopping alone, cooking for one another, hurrying home.

The elevator door opened and Ed pushed his bike out. "Forget your keys?" he asked in his calm, dry manner.

Inside, I got to work, unloading my groceries, while Jennifer and Ed settled in. Jennifer, who is usually charged up and eager to conquer a new recipe, was uninspired, so I took over.

I am never quite satisfied with the fish I cook at home. Sautéing it doesn't produce the crispness you get in a restaurant. Roasting works but seems hard treatment for delicate fish like trout or sole. And poaching, I worry, reminds people of a country club buffet. Then there is the problem of sauce. Poaching sauces are a pain in the neck: I'm not going to boil down the cooking liquid and whisk in butter to thicken it. And I'm not going the other way and serving my fish with some ludicrous salsa. I just want a great piece of fish, perfectly cooked, sprinkled with a buttery olive oil and served with vegetables, real vegetables.

I had bought two branzino, a white-fleshed Mediterranean fish that is often stuffed with fennel and lemon and roasted or grilled whole. It's a sensible preparation but not what I was going for. I had the branzino filleted, and picked up fava beans, haricots verts, asparagus, tiny red potatoes and basil.

I dug through Jennifer and Ed's cabinets selecting pans, and realized that I now knew their kitchen as well as my own. I know which pans I like and which ones I avoid. I know where the cutting board is tucked away and which oils are freshest.

Hannah's footsteps slapped through the living room, and screeched to a halt at the kitchen door. She stared at me.

"I have Piglet," she said. "Wanna see?"

"Sure. Who's Piglet?"

"Pooh's friend," Jennifer said.

"Ah."

"Hannah, show Amanda Piglet, but then come back here and we'll make cupcakes, O.K.?" Jennifer and Hannah do a lot of cooking. Hannah, who is three, has always loved the noise of the hand mixer.

"What recipe is it?" I asked Jennifer.

"I can't tell you."

"Why?"

"Because you'll think I'm ridiculous."

"No I won't," I said, thinking that she'd found it on the back of a box. Back-of-the-box recipes, like Quaker Oats' "Vanishing Oatmeal Cookies" and Chex party mix can be excellent. "So, where?"

"*InStyle.*"

"What?! Why?"

"Oh, I don't know," Jennifer said, "I was reading about some stupid celebrity bridal shower and the cupcakes caught my eye."

"We're having J.Lo's cupcakes?"

Jennifer measured the flour, sugar and cocoa into the bowl, while Hannah climbed up on a stepladder. She was now at the same height as

Jennifer, about five feet from the ground. They held the mixer together, whirring round and round, and every now and then a wad of batter flew onto the microwave or one of our shirts.

"So we were at some friends' house the other week," Jennifer said, "and all they fed their children, and thus mine, were Fruit Loops. It was awful. By the end of the day, Hannah was a mess."

"Hannah, do you remember that? That day that all you ate was Fruit Loops?"

Hannah watched the batter spin, and shook her head "No."

"It's not a good idea to eat multicolored sugar, is it?" Jennifer asked.

"I think it's O.K. to have multicolored sausages," Hannah said.

"Hm. Interesting," said Jennifer.

Hannah turned to me, "I have frogs," she said.

"O.K. now, we have to finish our business," Jennifer said, pulling Hannah from frogs back to cupcake icing. "Let's make sure we've got everything in here. Butter."

"Check!" yelled Hannah.

"Sugar."

"Check!"

"Gross pink coloring."

"Check!"

"Butter, butter, butter, butter," Hannah said as the mixer spun through the icing. I leaned over. "It's the color of Piglet," I said.

The doorbell rang. "So when are you moving to Brooklyn?" Tad asked as he walked in. He has taken to urging everyone we know to move there.

"Ed and I have decided we're moving to Queens, where real New Yorkers live," Jennifer said.

"We have?" Ed said.

Jennifer and I moved on to the main course and began peeling fava beans, one of the best tasks on earth. The skins are like slippery shells and from them pops a soft, kidney-shaped bean.

We blanched asparagus, haricots verts and tiny red potatoes. We swirled together a basil sauce and then simmered the fish in olive oil, over a whisper of a flame. Eventually, the fish, vegetables and sauce were merged on dinner plates, everyone helping, eight arms criss-crossing the stove.

At the end of the evening, after we packed up my cart, Ed said, "So this is it."

"The end of an era," Jennifer said. "It's over. I'm so depressed." I was depressed, as well. But I was also excited to move in with Tad.

"It's not over," Tad said, "Brooklyn isn't that far."

"Yeah, you say that," Jennifer said. "But then it's Sunday, you're tired. Long subway, blah, blah."

"Well, you're moving to Brooklyn soon anyway," he said, "so what does it matter?"

"Ha!" Jennifer said. "Tadsky, you're too much."

After we moved, I called a touch anxiously to ask them over for a visit. Would they do it out of a sense of duty? Would we all pretend that things were normal and try to keep up our Sunday ritual?

They were free. "Come out for lunch, so it doesn't get so late with Hannah," I said. "And we can go for a walk to the playground. It looks out over the harbor." I was selling too hard.

They arrived at noon. Hannah marched up the red-carpeted steps of our brownstone and into our apartment. We gave them the tour. Our belongings were mostly unpacked, except for our books, which were in boxes piled high in Tad's office, waiting for us to build them shelves. I realized as we were walking around that they had been to my old apartment only once, and never to Tad's. It must have been like walking into some strangers' home. They were quiet. Maybe they didn't like it. I began pointing out what we would like to change, then stopped myself. Who cares?

I had cooked chicken salad with beans and potatoes on the side. I made mayonnaise for the salad, whisking in corn and olive oils to thicken it and stirring in a bunch of chopped basil. I was a little behind when they came, still poaching the chicken, so I folded it into the mayonnaise and served it warm.

Jennifer searched the kitchen drawers for serving pieces. She laid the dishes of food and bread on the table. We sat down. Our table and chairs were some of the only furniture we had. In my fantasy life, I would have stone floors and a rustic table. My guests would eat from worn plates and feel free to pull pieces from a baguette to spread cheese on or to mop up a sauce. But here I was in my new reality. The floor was walnut and our table was a formal mahogany one passed down from Tad's grandparents. As we tore apart the bread, crumbs bounced across its shiny surface like pearls.

Hannah ate a few carrots, then asked to watch television. Our only functioning T.V. was in our bedroom, next to the bed. To watch it, we had to sit on the floor, cross-legged like children. Hannah opted to flop on our bed.

Jennifer ate slowly at first, then blurted out: "Did I tell you I started kick boxing?" We segued to the dress she wanted to buy for our wedding (pink), then ground zero (now a tourist attraction) and real estate (how little of it we own). Tad got in another Brooklyn plug.

I was putting a bowl of cherries and a plate of oat and orange zest cookies on the table when I noticed that Ed got up, walked to the refrigerator and got himself a drink. Things would work out—they had all, in their own way, settled into our home.

Sunday lunch and dinner

Chicken Salad with Basil Mayonnaise

For lunch at the paper, I often order in a tarragon chicken salad sandwich. The tarragon perfumes the pieces of poached chicken breast. It is so flavorful that the sandwich needs, and gets, nothing else except a piece of lettuce and squishy white bread to hold it together.

I had that in mind for Jennifer and Ed's visit, but I like to use the more flavorful dark meat with chicken salad, and I adore basil. I poached breasts and thighs and combined the meat. While it was still warm I folded in the mayonnaise, streaked with minced basil. You can serve the salad warm or cool (never cold!) but always dress it warm so the flavors sink deeply.

Sea salt
1 clove garlic, smashed with the side of a knife
2 skinless chicken breasts
4 chicken thighs
1 egg yolk, at room temperature
1 tablespoon Dijon mustard
1 teaspoon Champagne vinegar or white wine vinegar
2 teaspoons lemon juice, perhaps more
3/4 cup corn or safflower oil
1/4 cup plus 1 tablespoon best-quality olive oil
1/2 cup minced basil leaves

1. Fill a large saucepan with 1 1/2 inches of water. Season with salt, drop in the garlic clove and bring to a simmer. Lower the chicken into the water, bring back to a simmer and cook gently until the chicken is almost cooked through. Then shut off the heat to let it finish cooking and cool in the water. This will keep the chicken moister.

2. Pull the chicken meat from the bones in as large pieces as possible. Add any small slivers to a mixing bowl and cut the rest into 1/2-inch cubes. Set a bowl on top of a folded wet dishcloth, to keep it steady, and whisk together the egg yolk, mustard, Champagne vinegar and 1 teaspoon lemon juice. Season with salt. As you whisk, add the corn oil a few drops at a time, incorporating it thoroughly after each addition. Once the mixture begins to thicken,

add the oil in a thin stream. A nice paste the thickness and gloss of tube paint should be forming. Whisk in the olive oil. Scrape the basil into the mayonnaise and fold it together. Stir in the remaining lemon juice. Taste the mayonnaise, and add more lemon juice to sharpen the flavor, and salt, if needed. If it is too thick, you can thin it with milk or water. If it is too thin, whisk in a little cream.

3. Add a third of the mayonnaise to the chicken and fold together. It should just lightly coat the meat. Add more if needed. Cover the chicken and chill for a few hours. Let it come to room temperature before serving. Use the rest of the mayonnaise for something else—dress potatoes with it, dip blanched green beans into it, spread it on sliced tomatoes.

ENOUGH FOR 4 AS A SALAD, 6 IF USING FOR SANDWICHES.

Branzino Poached in Olive Oil with Asparagus, Fava Beans and Potatoes

While you may snicker at food writers' fussiness about ingredients, it is simply undeniable that you will always be rewarded for using the best olive oil possible. It is particularly important here, when poaching an expensive and delicate fish. Warming olive oil only heightens its flavors. So if it's a cheap supermarket oil, you'll know it. Also, the vegetables have no other seasoning aside from salt, so the oil plays a significant role in their dressing. Go all out.

When Jennifer and I made this, we blanched the asparagus, haricots verts and potatoes, doing them one at a time in the same pan, to save dishes, and undercooking them slightly so they would be just cooked, and still a little crisp, when reheated together. I showed her how to make a quick pesto when you don't feel like pulling out a food processor or if you don't have a mortar and pestle, chopping basil finely, crushing a sliver of garlic and a few almonds and moistening the mixture with olive oil.

Then I prepared the fish, spreading the seasoned fillets in a nonstick sauté pan, large enough to fit them all in one layer. As the fish warmed, turning opaque at the edges, I began spooning the warm oil over the top, to slowly bathe the fish and allow the seasoning to stream into the cracks in the flesh. If you spoon continuously, the fish cooks so slowly that it is impossible to overcook. In the end you have a beautiful fillet glistening with oil, and you have avoided the stresses of sautéing or high-heat roasting.

1 cup (packed) basil leaves
10 almonds
A sliver of garlic the size of a slivered almond
Sea salt
Freshly ground black pepper
About 1 cup excellent olive oil
8 baby red potatoes
8 asparagus spears, trimmed
1 handful haricots verts, stem ends trimmed
8 fava beans
4 fillets branzino (no skin; about 2 pounds) or red snapper, halibut, cod
   or mackerel

1. Finely chop the basil leaves, and crush the almonds and garlic using the bottom of a heavy pan (you may want to put the almonds in a plastic bag so they don't shoot all over your kitchen). Combine them in a bowl. Season with salt and pepper. Sprinkle with enough olive oil (1/4 cup or thereabouts) to moisten the basil and create a sauce that would pour from a spoon.

2. Put the potatoes in a large pot. Cover with water and season with salt. Bring to a boil and have a large bowl of ice water ready by the stove. Add the asparagus and cook until just starting to get tender but still quite crisp (you will cook them more later), about 3 minutes, depending on their thickness. Use tongs to lift the asparagus from the boiling water and plunge them into the ice water. Keep the pot water boiling. Add the haricots verts next and cook them, too, until they show the first signs of tenderness, then transfer them to the ice water. Do the fava beans the same way. Check on the potatoes. When they are tender, remove them to a plate.

3. Lay the asparagus, haricots verts and fava beans out on a dishtowel and pat dry. Cut the asparagus into 2-inch lengths and peel the fava beans from their pods and shells. Slice the potatoes into quarters. Combine them all in a medium saucepan and sprinkle them with olive oil so they're ready for their last step.

4. Season the branzino with salt and lay it in a nonstick skillet large enough to fit the fish in one layer. Pour in enough olive oil to barely half cover the fish. Set over medium low heat, and adjust it as the fish cooks so that it is always just gently bubbling. When the fish begins to turn opaque on the edges, begin spooning the warm oil in the pan over the fillets. Do this continually until the fish is just cooked through.

5. Meanwhile, place the vegetable pan over medium heat, season with salt (if needed) and let heat for a few minutes. Gently fold them together once, heat for another minute and serve (they do not need to be steaming hot).

6. To serve, lay a fillet on each of 4 plates. Arrange the vegetables around the fish and spoon on some of the basil sauce.

A FRESH SUMMER MEAL FOR 4.

Frosting Minus the Cupcakes

This tasty frosting is adapted from *InStyle*. Jennifer and Hannah added some pink food coloring. In the end, we decided the cake part was too dry. Jennifer plans on going back to her other cupcake staple, the 1-2-3-4 Yellow Cake from *Joy of Cooking*. For chocolate, I'm going back to the Dump-It Cake (page 195), and pouring it into greased, lined cups (in a muffin pan) and baking them for about 20 minutes.

Cupcakes, like fish, can overcook quickly. It's best to test them with a cake tester or toothpick, pressing it into the center of the cupcake. They are done the moment it comes out clean.

Here's the frosting:

1 box (16 ounces) confectioners' sugar
6 tablespoons unsalted butter, softened
3 tablespoons milk, more if desired
1 teaspoon vanilla
2 to 3 drops pink food coloring.

Beat together the confectioners' sugar, butter, milk and vanilla until smooth. If the frosting seems stiff, add another tablespoon of milk. Beat in the food coloring until blended and monochromatic.

ENOUGH FOR ABOUT 2 DOZEN CUPCAKES.

Chapter 30

CHEZ WHO?

In my old apartment, my kitchen was a tricky space. Everything was stacked, piled and squeezed. To get to my stockpot you first had to crouch down like a monkey, then remove a pile of casseroles, while trying not to tip over a row of baking sheets. Although it depressed me on occasion, I had grown used to the system and had even come to love my cramped closet-like space.

The first time Tad helped me put dishes away he was up on a stepladder lifting a platter into place, when he turned to me, and declared: "We have to get you a new kitchen!"

I thought, "We have to get us a new kitchen, living room, bathroom and bedroom."

I was tired of lugging bags back and forth from his apartment and tired of coming home after a few days at his apartment to find the fruit on my counter moldy and the milk sour.

But now we had finally bought an apartment in Brooklyn Heights, and we were about to move in together. We had a few things to sort out. Tad's decorating style is worldly WASP; tattered Persian carpets and old family furniture worn at the edges, mixed with Buddha heads, art from Indonesia and a table from Morocco. Mine was more urban mini-malist, with a Herman Miller credenza, a crimson mohair sofa and sisal rugs.

It wasn't going to be a seamless merger of styles. A few weeks before we moved, a small miracle occurred. A reading lamp above Tad's brown, masculine, drab sofa fell onto it and burned a large hole in the back cushion. I did a bad job concealing my glee.

When I suggested he burn a few other items, Tad growled. Our belongings, shabby as they were, quickly became symbols of our free-dom. Tad was loathe to part with his desk, which was made out of a door set on top of filing cabinets. I was unwilling to give up my Eames chair, which Tad had never used as anything more than a footrest. We purged as much as we could bear to, then, suddenly, the moving trucks showed up.

I had no idea what would be in store. I had lived in my apartment the entire time I have been in New York. I could walk to Fairway and Zabar's, and lived close to the park. I was friendly with my neighbors. We actually borrowed sugar and milk from each other. I gave them stews and cakes and soups that I tested for work, and their kids raced into my apartment whenever I left the door open.

"Amanda!" Charlotte, who is seven and is one of those kids, shouted from over the boxes in the hallway.

She wrapped her arms around me. "Don't leave," she said. "I want you to stay in New York City."

"Charlotte, Brooklyn is part of New York City."

"Really?" she said. "Oh, but don't go."

"I'm getting married. I have to!"

"Don't get married," Charlotte said.

Later, I sat on my sofa, surrounded by moving men, and watched as my belongings were plucked from their places like weeds. As my apartment emptied, it seemed to shrink. The walls looked narrower. The gray paint turned cold and grim. I had come to know the tiny stove with its plastic knobs as if it were another limb. Now my whole kitchen looked slight and powerless.

I called Tad, whose apartment was being packed at the same time. Before I could say anything, he cried, "I can't believe how dingy and small my apartment is!"

"Let's go eat lunch," I said.

"Good idea," he responded.

I was famished. All week, as our move progressed and as we closed on our new home, a powerful hunger set in. I became desperate for good food. It was all we had. The blur of logistics was like a vacuum sucking up every inch of mental space. I was anxious to be settled, anxious about my bank account, and anxious about the transition in my life. Food was a source of calm.

For one night between moving out and moving in, we had nothing but the bags we were carrying. Practically everything we owned was out of our hands.

We showed up at Maiken and Tim's to crash. "You guys look like you've been through a war," Maiken said, greeting us at the door.

"We have been," Tad said, lugging bags full of our clothing for the week, our mortgage paperwork and our computers.

We ordered in fusilli with eggplant and ricotta, and sat on the floor, mechanically feeding ourselves while Maiken, who was eight months pregnant, laid on her sofa across the room.

"I am so over being pregnant," she said. "These women who savor it, I don't get it."

Finally, we signed the papers and it was ours. And when our taxi pulled up in front of the brownstone on our new leafy street, we were still giddy. Inside, we weaved among the piles of boxes, trying to take it all in. It was so much larger, so much more adult, than what we had had.

I stood in our new kitchen, staring around. It was embarrassingly polished. There were dark marble counters, cherry cabinets, a Viking stove and a Sub-Zero fridge. But there was an abundance of storage space, I reminded myself, and there was a dishwasher. I could warm up to it.

Surrounded by boxes, we collapsed in bed, and fell asleep to the sound of rain. In the morning, we could hear birds chirping and foghorns in the harbor.

I began cleaning the apartment in a frenzy of nesting. Tad stayed home that day, opening boxes in what seemed like a leisurely manner, and actually went to work for a few hours the next day.

As I scrubbed the floors, I began having arguments with him in my head. I knew this feeling of anguish, but could not pinpoint the source. I was happy. We were together. But I was the one cleaning! I washed windows, ran errands, unwrapped dishes and grew angrier. Then a more horrifying thought crossed my mind.

He was abandoning me. Just like my father had so often abandoned my mother. Her way of dealing with it was by cleaning, by washing dishes, by ironing our jeans and vacuuming in straight lines. I was wiping down the moldings. I couldn't stop myself!

And this enraged me. I didn't want all of those clichés. What I adored about Tad was that he was evolved, understanding, considerate.

I knew that all I had to do was talk to him about it to find out what he was feeling, but I couldn't bring myself to. I wanted to be angry. So, I regressed. I stopped making eye contact with him. When he made the bed, I fixed it. When he put the mail on top of my cutting board, I threw out his old pillows. When he spilled soda on the counter, I made sure he knew that I had cleaned it up. I guarded the kitchen like it was my kin. If he was going to slack on unpacking, I was going to defend my only turf.

We did have a few good moments. After unpacking the kitchen, for instance, we took turns diving into the pile of packing paper and banded together to haul out our mass of garbage. We invited our friends Deb, Paul, Katie and Harry over for dinner, hoping their company would encourage us to get past these hurdles, or ignore them for a little while.

I stopped cleaning to bury myself in cooking. I prepared a tiny starter course of fresh mozzarella hidden beneath asparagus spears, fava beans, roasted shallot, an arugula leaf and a few basil leaves, all sprinkled with olive oil, sea salt and a few drops of an aged wine vinegar.

Just before everyone arrived, I asked Tad to put a special bottle of Champagne in the freezer to chill it down quickly.

"So how's it been going?" Paul asked Tad. "Are you learning lots about each other?"

"Well, yes," Tad said crisply. "Amanda loves ammonia. I'm thinking of buying stock in it."

We showed Deb and Paul the apartment. Each room to them was more exciting than the last. Their enthusiasm was infectious.

"You probably didn't have to clean very much," Deb said. "This place is in great shape. It's got so much room. You could live here forever."

"Now that we've signed our lives away, we may have to," I said.

For the main course, I roasted capons with lemon and garlic shoots and served potatoes cooked with smoked paprika. We had pannacotta and strawberries stiffened with a dash of balsamic vinegar for dessert. It was at once soothing and brisk. Dinner turned out very well, with bubbly conversation and laughter.

After they left, Tad started the dishes.

"Their enthusiasm brought back all the happy feelings I had about this place when we arrived," I said.

"I knew they would like it," Tad said, as he rinsed the wine glasses. "Go get ready for bed. I'll finish up."

I did. But when I came out to get a glass of water, I noticed that some of the dishes were still greasy. Fury welled up inside me. I thought we had resolved this long ago in my old apartment, but here it was reappearing, like so many issues, in our supposedly new adult lives. Once again, I would be stuck with these in the morning. So I began rewashing them all.

After a few minutes, Tad came back in. I could feel his breath on my ear.

"You know, it doesn't do you any good to have the kitchen be exactly the way you want it if, as a result, I never want to set foot in it," he said, then turned around and went to bed.

The next morning, the dishes were clean but Tad was barricaded in his study. I opened the freezer to find the bottle of Champagne—a Bruno Paillard that I had saved for several years—shattered. It was just how I felt.

Sustenance for weary times

Fresh Mozzarella with Green Leaves, Spears and Beans

This does not merit a recipe, but a few tips might help. Think of this as a composed salad, with cheese as the main ingredient. You should only make this if you can buy great, freshly-made mozzarella. Slice it thinly and place a slice on each plate. Lay one or two spears of blanched asparagus over the mozzarella, and drop on a few cooked fava beans. I used French torpedo shallots, which are about 6 inches long and sweet, and roasted them until they were as soft as a ripe plum. If you can't find these, use a sweet onion like Vidalia and roast it, cut into wedges. Arrange the roasted shallot or onion to one side of the cheese.

Continue layering: mingle an arugula leaf or two and a basil leaf or two with the asparagus and beans. It should be a collage of white and green shapes. Pull out your best olive oil and sprinkle it over the top, letting it drip in some spots, pool in others. Do the same with your best aged vinegar—balsamic, sherry, or something else with a little sweetness—using a bit less vinegar than oil. Splash a pinch of sea salt and grind fresh pepper over it all, and serve it up to hungry guests.

Potatoes with Smoked Paprika

This is also not quite worth a recipe, but I'm giving it anyway for fear that you may not try it otherwise. Smoked paprika is a recent obsession of mine. If you have the impression, as I had, that paprika is a 1970s spice, it is time to try the smoked. Even a good plain paprika from Spain is lovely, but the smoked, which comes primarily from the Extremadura, is seductive. It has warmth and depth and makes you want to sprinkle it on everything. There are both hot and mild varieties. I prefer the mild, which is also called sweet or bittersweet.

1 1/2 pounds baby white potatoes
2 tablespoons peanut oil or olive oil
Sea salt
1 tablespoon smoked paprika (mild), perhaps more

Preheat your oven to 350°F. Toss the potatoes with the oil in a large bowl. Season with salt and sprinkle over the paprika. Toss again and tip the potatoes into a roasting pan. Roast until the potatoes are soft and creamy inside, about 40 minutes, stirring them up now and then. Taste a potato to see if it has enough salt and paprika. The paprika should stand out but not be overwhelming. Add more, if desired, and toss to coat the potatoes evenly.

POTATOES FOR 4.

Pannacotta with Strawberries and Aged Vinegar

This is an amalgam of recipes, but it relies mostly on one by Mario Batali. I was drawn to it by his use of goat's milk yogurt. Pannacotta made with pasteurized cream is often flat; here, the yogurt gives it a lively tang. I also cut the vanilla and black pepper, used confectioners' sugar rather than granulated, and halved the amount of heavy cream, adding whole milk in its place. If you want to see his original recipe, it's on www.epicurious.com.

1 1/4 teaspoons unflavored gelatin
1 cup heavy cream
1 1/2 cups plain goat's milk yogurt or whole cow's milk yogurt
1 cup milk
1/2 cup confectioners' sugar
2 cups small, ripe strawberries, hulled and quartered
1 tablespoon sugar, perhaps more
About 1 tablespoon aged sweet vinegar, such as a very good balsamic,
    sherry or ice wine vinegar

1. Put 2 tablespoons of water in a small bowl. Sprinkle over the gelatin and let it soften for a few minutes. Whisk together the heavy cream and yogurt in a large bowl. Pour the milk into a small saucepan, add the confectioners' sugar and place over medium heat. Stir once or twice and remove from the heat as soon as bubbles form around the edge. Pour the gelatin into the hot milk and stir until it's fully dissolved. Whisk the milk mixture into the cream and yogurt and blend until smooth. Pour the mixture into a pie dish or a casserole dish. Let cool, then cover with plastic wrap and refrigerate for a few hours or overnight.

2. An hour before serving, fold together the strawberries and sugar. Taste one to see if they need more sugar. Take the pannacotta from the

refrigerator and let it warm up a little. Scoop up the pannacotta with a spoon, as if it were ice cream; distribute it among six bowls or parfait glasses. Spoon some strawberries and juices over each and then sprinkle with a few drops of vinegar.

A LIGHT, TANGY DESSERT FOR 6.

Chapter 31

MOMENTARY LAPSES

After a few heated fights and a session with my therapist, Tad and I had begun to work things out. One morning I opened a kitchen cabinet to find that he had arranged all of the spices alphabetically, beginning with ajowan and ending with white poppyseeds.

"Thanks for doing that," I said.

"Sure," Tad said, pouring himself coffee. "I wanted to be sure I could always lay my hands on the dried sumac."

I had let go of the ammonia bottle and stopped vacuuming the moldings. And Tad was back to his old self, readily offering to help out, and no longer hunching his shoulders when I asked a favor. We kept the

Eames chair and the door desk and focused on enjoying our new home and exploring our new neighborhood.

While there were a few things we missed about the Upper West Side—like combat shopping at Fairway, and our morning coffee group—life was much better in Brooklyn. Now we had coffee out on our deck, shaded by a large, leafy maple.

We were also acquiring a new identity, as one does in every neighborhood in New York. When I told a friend where we had moved, right near the Brooklyn Bridge and the Promenade, he scoffed, "That's sissy Brooklyn!" But we liked sissy Brooklyn. It had restored old houses with window boxes overflowing with flowers, quiet lanes and a healthy population of birds. We had found a restaurant we loved called Noodle Pudding and it was just around the corner. We could walk to the movie theater and by subway quickly be in the Village.

I settled into my new office. My old office was a table in my bedroom. The new one was a former nursery and had marching elephants on the walls. But it had a pocket door and I could close it behind me when it was time to put my work to rest.

I warmed up to the kitchen, too, although it took a few tries. The first time I used the professional stove, I was frying potatoes and had a stack of paper towels set up next to it. When I turned my back to get salt, the paper towels ignited and flew up in the air in a great ball of fire.

It is a small kitchen, a cozy square with counters all the way around, efficient as—but larger than—a galley kitchen. (Many New Yorkers scorn their galley kitchens, but they are actually a superb design. You have to move very little to get things done, and you have a lot of counter space.)

The former owners had also made excellent design choices. On one side, there is a lower butcher-block counter, the perfect height for the average person. Beneath it is a drawer containing garbage cans, so you can trim chicken, celery or peaches and simply scrape the waste into the garbage. I have space for a dish of salt, a canister for utensils, and an actual freezer. I can make ice cream!

Meanwhile, Tad was relishing having new spaces to read and lots of light in his office. He bought flowers for the house and was quick to initiate a small renovation—building bookcases, painting the walls and recovering some ratty old chairs. It felt like our new life together was taking hold. All we needed to do was pick up a few last bits of furniture from our parents.

We headed first to Tad's parents' house, near Philadelphia. His parents were giving us some beautiful pieces, including our wedding present, an old bow-front chest of drawers that they had had refurbished. After we arrived, we began packing it into our rented Ryder truck. Everyone was helping out.

Elizabeth pulled us aside to ask us to look at some chairs upstairs. Tad was not interested, and when she pressed her case, I could see his shoulders slouch and his face muscles tighten, just like when I ask him to do something he doesn't want to do. I touched his shoulder and urged him along. We took the chairs, too.

When the truck was all packed, we gathered around the table. Elizabeth had arranged a beautiful lunch, with bright red tomatoes juxtaposed against blue and white plates that were set on top of varied blue Provençal linens. In the center was a Mediterranean blue bowl piled high with ripe mangoes. It reminded me of a Gauguin painting.

"It looks like someone coordinated all the colors of this meal," Dorie said. "Who could that be?"

"Oh, I don't know, someone," Elizabeth said. "Yes, I chose this mango to go with the tomatoes."

We began with bruschetta mounded with tiny diced tomato and, after, had her broccoli salad, which was balanced cleverly with yellow raisins and sunflower seeds. Both were simple dishes, but because she had presented them in such an original way, they felt sumptuous.

As we ate lunch, Tad amused his parents by telling them about registering for gifts for our wedding. In his story, I drag him around for hours on end, we have a tête-à-tête in the middle of Barneys and when he politely asks to skip the last store, I have the nerve to call him a five-year-old.

But before I could butt in to tell my side, Elizabeth cried, "You were heroic! Amanda, you were lucky he went at all!"

He was safe at home, and getting out his residual tension.

A few hours later we drove to my mother's. As we pulled into her driveway, I began having overwhelming urges to ride my old bicycle and flop on my old bed. I ignored Tad's presence while I helped my mother do laundry and showed her the large box of my belongings that Tad and I had agreed to shed.

We stayed overnight and the next day she made us fried egg sandwiches for lunch. They were my father's specialty. Whenever my mother was away, he'd make us fried egg sandwiches. He was particular about every step, and usually did it while singing and humming and doing a shuffly dance to Bonnie Raitt or Ray Charles. He would toast the bread and fry up bacon. He'd thinly slice a tomato and an onion. He would spread Miracle Whip on the toast, and sometimes, for himself, add a dash of horseradish. The egg would be laid across first, then the bacon, tomato and lettuce.

I hadn't had one in years, perhaps since my father had died. It was just as I had remembered it and this made my heart ache.

But it was time to go back to our new home, so rather than let my emotions flow, I focused on doing the dishes and making the kitchen neat and orderly again. Tad stayed at a safe distance, talking to my mother's boyfriend, Neil.

The ride home was quiet, and we were both relieved, I think, when we finally turned onto our street. Tad's brother Pier and sister-in-law Sara were waiting to help us carry the furniture upstairs. Their son Wil tore through our apartment, juice box in hand. I was excited to show them around and found myself pointing out my favorite pieces of furniture. They were all Tad's.

We all went out to dinner and afterwards Tad and I walked home along the Promenade, which offers a view of the Brooklyn Bridge, Lower Manhattan and the Statue of Liberty. It is such a breathtaking cityscape that a kind of euphoria came over me. I was happy to be there with Tad, and tired of us being mad at each other. So rather than run home and scrub the floor with a toothbrush, I decided to bring it up.

"I'm sorry for being so tough on you lately," I said to Tad. "It's not intentional. I feel like my mother is haunting me, like I've become her clone. And the worst part is that I'm not even as good at washing dishes as she is."

"That may not actually be the worst part," Tad said, smiling.

"I know it's not intentional," he added, more seriously. "We've both regressed. I've certainly been treating you like you're my mother."

"And I've been treating you like you're my father," I said, pausing. "Ew."

"Let's stop doing it, O.K.?" Tad said.

I hugged him and laughed, "O.K. Dad, I mean Tad."

Family classics

Elizabeth's Broccoli Salad

Elizabeth got this recipe from her friend Jeanne Cortner. The salad is great for picnics because it can be easily scooped up with forks. Elizabeth once served it for a beach picnic with roasted chicken and sliced tomatoes.

Sea salt
3 cups broccoli tops in small buds
1/2 cup yellow raisins
1/2 cup roasted, unsalted sunflower seeds
5 slices bacon, cooked (in the oven or in a skillet) and coarsely chopped
2 tablespoons chopped onion
1/2 cup mayonnaise
1 1/2 tablespoons cider vinegar
1 teaspoon sugar

1. Fill a large pot with 1/2 inch salted water. Fill a steamer with the broccoli tops and place it in the pot. Bring to a boil and steam until the broccoli has brightened and is just soft around the edges, but still quite firm. Let cool.

2. In a serving bowl, combine the cooled broccoli, raisins, sunflower seeds, bacon and onion. In another bowl, whisk together the mayonnaise, vinegar and sugar. Pour this over the broccoli and fold together.

A SIDE SALAD FOR 4. EASILY DOUBLED OR TRIPLED.

Tom Hesser's Fried Egg Sandwiches

My father used regular yellow cooking onions but you may want to try something a little sweeter, like Vidalia, particularly if you plan on talking to anyone for the rest of the day.

4 slices bacon
8 slices country bread
4 eggs
Sea salt
Freshly ground black pepper
Miracle Whip
8 thin slices ripe tomato (4 slices will do if the tomato is very juicy)
2 slices of a medium onion, rings separated and divided between the
    sandwiches
4 romaine leaves (from the heart)

1. Place an iron skillet over medium heat. Lay the pieces of bacon across its surface. Render the fat and brown the bacon on both sides, turning it just once. Meanwhile, toast the bread. Drain the bacon on paper towels. Pour off all but 1 tablespoon of the bacon fat and place the skillet over medium heat.

Crack the eggs into the pan and break the yolks. Season lightly with salt. Grind pepper over top. Fry until the bottoms are bubbly and browned on the edges, then turn and cook the other sides for a minute. Remove from the heat.

2. Spread the toasted bread with Miracle Whip. For each sandwich, lay an egg on top, break the bacon pieces to fit over top. Cover with tomato, onion and lettuce, then top with another piece of bread and press down with your palm to compress. My father liked to eat his with a beer. Try it. It's good!

4 DELICIOUS FRIED EGG SANDWICHES.

Chapter 32

MUST INTERVENE

I am not the kind of woman who has been planning her wedding since she was eight. I only knew what I would not do. I would not wear anything that reminded me of meringue. I would not have a "sushi station." I would not let our families dilute our vision—whatever it would eventually be—with the weird wedding requests all families make, such as finding dog-free hotels or insisting on chicken for the main course "because everyone will like it." And I would not plan a wedding all alone.

The wedding would be ours. And when it came time, it was. Tad was so into planning it that for the first few months, I was scrambling to keep up. While he forged ahead, getting permits for our party and working out with the caterer the tent's dimensions and the number of waiters we would need, I floundered with my few small projects: shopping for a dress, getting our invitations ready, finding a florist.

Eventually I got cracking, and everything went remarkably well. We had our caterer, our band, our florist. Our invitations were finally out. Then my friend Paula, who had moved to Texas to work on a ranch with her boyfriend David, said she was coming to town.

Paula was in our wedding party, and as Tad was away for the weekend, I invited her to come shopping with me for a slip for my wedding dress. It was late July, and so hot that talking made you sweat. But we had so much catching up to do!

"When you said lingerie shop," Paula said as she walked in the door, "my eyes turned into dollar signs. I love La Perla."

Our day was mapped out. We'd go to the greenmarket and swoon, shop for the slip, go to a gourmet store, buy too much food, then come back and cook it. David would join us for drinks and dinner on the deck.

"How are you feeling about the wedding?" Paula asked as we entered the greenmarket. "Are you nervous?"

"Well, since we're having it outdoors, I'm having hurricane dreams but nothing worse than that," I said, stopping next to a pile of zucchini. "And Tad's been amazing. He's planned more of the wedding than I have."

"How about the food? Have you decided on a menu?" she asked.

"No. I think of that as the least of my worries. I know I can do that. What I can't do is buy a dress. I told you about my dress saga, right?"

"No," Paula said. And so I began, as we stood in the middle of the market, people nudging around us. A few months before, my mother had come to the city to help me shop. We had a sublime lunch at Frank, a tiny Italian place in the East Village: a smoky lentil soup and a prosciutto sandwich on a crusty baguette with slow-cooked tomatoes, arugula and goat cheese. It was all a little too sublime, perhaps. By the time we reached the first dress shop, all I wanted on my body was a smock.

A few hours of power walking around Bergdorf's and up and down Madison Avenue worked it off, and we were back in action. I was determined not to buy a traditional wedding dress. And since I was going to shop for a stylish party dress, I wanted to go to all the stores I normally only read about. I fell in love with a very expensive Valentino gown covered with yellow orchids and draped with a silk sash. When my mother left I bought it.

Thirty seconds later buyer's remorse hit me like a tidal wave. I stood on Madison Avenue, unable to move my feet. I didn't know what to do. I couldn't go home, because I was too embarrassed to tell Tad.

What I needed to do, I told myself, was to shop for shoes. I owned a new dress that cost as much as a Viking stove, and I needed shoes for it. So I walked north at a zombie's gait. Before I knew it, I was in Prada, standing in a different dress, even more torn about my purchase.

At home I flung myself on my bed, unable to move or eat for a day.

Then Tad swept in and convinced the salesperson at Valentino to take the dress back. And at Prada, when I came out of the dressing room and he got misty-eyed, I knew I had made the right choice.

"Mostly, though," I continued to Paula, as we piled cranberry beans in a bag, "I've been enjoying the process. And it's interesting, psychologically, how people respond." My mother had recently called up in tears to say she thought that our wedding was going to be "odd."

"What do you mean 'odd'?" I asked her.

"Well, nothing you're doing is normal!" she cried. "You're not wearing a wedding dress, there is no cake, no flowers, no church!"

"And no chicken, either!" I said.

"How about some cherry tomatoes?" I asked Paula, who, like many good cooks, caressed every vegetable she passed.

"Sure. I get to markets like this and just get dizzy with ideas."

After dropping our bags from the greenmarket at our apartment, Paula and I headed to Madison Avenue.

"Then one day I got a voice-mail message at work from a woman who called herself Caroline," I said as we crossed the Brooklyn Bridge in a cab. "She said that she knew all about my affair with her husband, Philippe, and that now that I'm getting married, she hopes 'some little slut' like me won't sleep with Tad. I don't even know a Philippe!"

"That *is* weird," Paula said.

At the lingerie store, Paula helped me put on my dress. I hadn't been in it for several months, and knew it needed altering. I knew I also needed to buy a bra, deal with the purse issue, and wear in my shoes. I've never been good at embracing feminine rituals.

"Ooh," she said. "You need a different pair of underwear." I blushed. They *were* granny underwear.

The slip I tried on took away my dress's gossamer quality. And the flaws in the dress, though minor, were noticeable. I was also breaking out and having a bad hair day. I walked out of the dressing room in tears. I'm a terrible bride and I'm going to look awful!

Paula took pity on me and dragged me back to Prada, where she found me a better slip and got the alteration in motion. I was still tense until she pointed out a piece that should be taken in to the store's barrel-shaped Hungarian tailor. The woman looked deeply insulted and snapped, "I know what I do!"

Paula and I cracked up.

From Prada, we marched to Agata e Valentina, which felt like an oasis. Seeing the piles of exotic fruits, prosciutti hanging from the ceiling and heaps of cheeses put me at ease. I know what I do! I thought.

"What's that?" Paula asked, pointing to a giant square cheese with its top rind peeled back to show its soft creamy interior.

"It's Teleme," the man behind the counter said. "Would you like some?"

"I'd like to dive into it and swim around. Sure, let's get some."

We also picked up burrata, which is like mozzarella only much creamier.

When we got home, I opened a bottle of Prosecco, poured it over fresh berries from the market, and took a gulp. I needed a drink. Then we started cooking.

"David, wait until you see Amanda in her dress! She looked so beautiful!"

"Thanks, Paula," I said. "It needs a little work yet."

"Just a little strategic altering, and it will be perfect."

"Keep talking. I need coaching. You saw me at my weakest, wearing bad underwear, feeling like an awkward teenager."

"It would have been worse if you were alone."

We shelled cranberry beans together, took turns chopping, stirring and tasting. In a stream of gossip, we assembled the meal—fried zucchini blossoms, the cheeses with a corn and tomato salad, roasted poussin stuffed with an onion, cranberry bean gratin, and honey ice cream with fresh berries. It was such a treat to cook with her, something we've done in fits and starts, but never a full meal. I felt like I had been cooking with her my whole life. Then she, David and I sat outside for hours, sipping and nibbling until the heat wore us out, or the rosé was gone. I can't remember which.

A week later, Paula dropped by with a gift: a Cosabella thong from La Petite Coquette, meant for a good dress. We giggled.

"I couldn't help it!" she said. "I took one look at what you were wearing and was like 'Must Intervene.'"

A dinner that puts everything back in perspective

Paula's Corn Salad

Adapted from Paula Disbrowe

After Paula went back to Texas, I asked her about her recipe. She wrote, "The corn salad was a take on the corn pico de gallo that I do at the ranch. It was fresh corn and cherry tomatoes. I usually add serranos (unseeded, people in Texas like things hot, don't cha know), which we couldn't find at Agata's, so we used a fresh jalapeño instead. We also added a little thinly sliced onion, I believe, and fresh cilantro (another nod to Texas). At the ranch, I usually do a sprinkle of cumin, and add lime juice along with sherry wine vinegar and oil." Here, I've given the recipe for what we did at my house. Feel free to try the ranch recipe by adding a little cumin and lime.

4 ears corn, husked
2 cups cherry tomatoes (a mix of yellow, orange and red, if possible;
    Paula said we used sweet 100's)
1 jalapeño pepper, minced (use less if you don't like heat)
1/2 small red onion, thinly sliced
1/4 cup chopped cilantro
Sea salt
1 tablespoon red wine vinegar
1/4 cup extra virgin olive oil

1. Bring a large pot of water to a boil. Drop in the corn and let cook for 3 minutes, then fish the ears out of the water and let cool. As soon as you can hold onto an ear without burning your fingers, cut the kernels from the cob and scrape off any excess pulp and juices by running a knife edge down the length of the cobs.

2. Gather the corn and juices in a bowl. Halve the tomatoes and add them, along with the jalapeño, red onion and cilantro. Season with salt. Sprinkle in the vinegar. Fold the salad together, using a large spoon and turning the bowl as you scoop and lift. Pour over the oil and fold again, until the corn glistens. Taste the salad and add more salt, vinegar or jalapeño if desired. Let the salad sit for a good 30 minutes, then taste again before serving.

SALAD FOR 4.

Paula's Cranberry Bean Gratin

Adapted from Paula Disbrowe

Cranberry beans are tough to come by unless you have a garden or a farm stand nearby. You may substitute almost any kind of firm fresh bean. Dried beans like white beans or chick peas will work, too. Soak them overnight and simmer them in water until they're faintly tender, then begin at step 2 using 3 cups of the par-cooked beans.

3 cups shelled cranberry beans
Sea salt
1/4 pound pancetta, cut into thick lardon-size dice (about 1/4-inch thick cubes)
Extra virgin olive oil
1 onion, chopped
2 cloves garlic, smashed and minced
1 tablespoon chopped rosemary
1/2 tablespoon thyme leaves
1/2 teaspoon crushed red pepper
1 28-ounce can peeled San Marzano tomatoes, with juice
1/2 cup toasted fresh breadcrumbs

1. Preheat the oven to 300°F. Fill a medium pot with water and put it over high heat. Season the water with a good deal of salt, like for pasta water. When it boils, add the beans and cook them until they are just beginning to turn tender. Don't let them overcook after all your tedious shelling! Drain.

2. While they cook, start the tomato sauce. Put the pancetta cubes in a sauté pan and place them over low heat. Render the fat and brown the pancetta so it's nice and caramelly on the edges. Remove the pancetta to a plate and try not to eat it all before you need it again. You need about 2 tablespoons of fat in the pan, so if you have more, drain off some. And if you have less, supplement with olive oil. Place over medium heat now and add the onion to the pan. Sauté for a few minutes, until softened on the edges, then toss in the garlic, rosemary, thyme and crushed red pepper. Cook for a minute or two, then add the tomatoes, squeezing them into pieces with your hands over the pan. Add the juices from the can and the reserved pancetta, as well. Let this simmer for about 20 minutes, until the sauce is nicely melded

but not reduced and thick. Season generously with salt and pepper. Fold in the par-cooked beans.

3. Coat a gratin dish (large enough to accommodate the contents of the pan) with olive oil. Pour in the bean mixture and pat it around evenly. Spread the breadcrumbs on top and put it in the oven. Bake, checking it every 15 minutes or so to be sure there is enough liquid in the pan. It should be moist, not soupy; add more liquid—chicken broth or water—as needed. Cook until the beans are creamy and the sauce is bubbly, about 2 hours.

BEANS FOR 4 WITH WONDERFUL LEFTOVERS.

Chapter 33

GUESTS IN OUR OWN HOME

We began with the best intentions. Rather than having someone throw us a shower, Tad and I thought we'd invite our wedding party, our parents and my grandmother all to dinner. We didn't need an iron and a roasting pan, and I wouldn't be caught dead in one of those ribbon bonnets. We were more interested in having those close to us get to know each other before the big day.

We set a date in early August, about six weeks before our wedding. It felt just right. Until it got near, and it began to sink in that we had to feed twenty-three people. Both of our families were traveling from Pennsylvania, and they were not expecting burgers on the grill.

Most people have a natural number that they feel comfortable cooking for. For me, that number is eight. I like a sense of abundance. Potatoes for four seems stingy and small. No matter how hard I try to cook for four or six, I always end up with enough food for eight. But now I had to triple my natural number in a new kitchen and in a new neighborhood where I didn't know the stores very well. I was determined not to have a meal that felt like it was designed for a large group. I wanted the meal to feel special, as if each plate were carefully constructed, not spooned from a hotel pan. We weren't going to have lasagne or stew.

Meanwhile the temperature in New York City shot up into the '90s, and the flowers on our deck—where some guests would have to eat—shriveled like raisins. Lamb, which I had intended on, was not going to work. But cod would. So I planned a Spanish-influenced meal around it. We'd begin with Prosecco while everyone tasted hors d'oeuvres like figs wrapped with Serrano ham; toasts with ricotta, garlic chives and corn; deviled eggs with smoked paprika; and big bowls of pistachios. Then we'd sit down and have slow-roasted cod with Romesco sauce, a tomato salad and roasted potatoes with pancetta. We'd drink a crisp rosé with hints of peaches and melon. For dessert, I'd make one of Elizabeth's desserts, a peach slump, but with tiny, sweet apricots from the greenmarket. I'd churn some honey ice cream to spoon on top.

Normally, I don't discuss my menu with anyone. I decide what I will serve, I shop and I cook while it is all tucked away in my head. But it was summer time, the greenmarket was full of beautiful produce and I was feeling blissful. I began taking an informal poll on the ideas fluttering around in my head. I recited my menu to Sofia, a Spanish friend over lunch, and searched her for signs of wincing.

"Do you think it's weird to serve Romesco sauce with roasted cod?" I asked her. "I mean, would a Spanish person shriek?"

"Well, no," Sofia said. "But they probably wouldn't have deviled eggs with it." Interesting, I thought. But I'm stubborn.

A few days before the party, I had lunch at Frank with my friend Nancy. She ordered chicken liver crostini and it came spread thin on a thick piece of *pane pugliese*. You had to fight the bread with your teeth to get a bite, but it was terrific: creamy and peppery with a nice splash of hot pepper. I shoehorned it onto the menu.

I had a fantasy of an old-fashioned party, where I would shop at the fishmonger and greenmarket and have our wines delivered. It was all possible in our new neighborhood. But between moments of calm and confidence, I experienced flashes of panic. Tad and I had gotten over our initial moving-in conflicts, but I worried that the stresses of a large party might cause us to slip up. I couldn't do this whole thing on my own. So I decided to preempt.

"Tad," I said, "The party this weekend, I think we—"

"I know," he interrupted, "I'm here. I'm totally into it. I'm ready to help." Then he squeezed my hand, and said, "You know, everyone who is coming cares about us, so there's no one to impress and nothing to worry about."

That was too easy.

"How about E.B.?!" I blurted. "She's such a good cook!"

"You are, too. Anyway, I've been thinking about the seating." He had made placecards, and divided them among three areas: the living room, dining room and deck. We didn't want our guests to come all this way only to sit next to someone they already knew. Spouses were separated, and he made each group a balance of storytellers, inquisitive types and the shy.

Seating people, and the right number of people, is one of the great challenges of a successful dinner party. I recalled a conversation that Tad and I had had with an older southern man named Louis, who was an avid cook. One year he entertained twenty nights in the month of June, and did all the cooking. When I asked him the best number for a dinner party, he leaned in close, his blue eyes sparkling. "Well, the best number for a dinner party, of course, is two," he said drawing out the word "two." Then he pulled back, and said, "Otherwise six is the magic number."

"Why not eight?" I asked.

"You lose the common ground," Louis said.

Tad added, "It's like a Venn diagram where the common subset is too small."

But we would have to try groups of eight. We only had three tables.

"Do you think people in the living room will feel like they're in Siberia?" I asked Tad.

"It won't be Siberia. I'm going to sit there. There will be witty remarks, parlor games, and a ceaseless flow of laughter."

"O.K."

The morning of the party we walked to the greenmarket together. I selected an assortment of tomatoes while he chose the flowers. I spotted purslane and bought some of that, too. I went to my new fishmonger and picked up eleven pounds of cod.

While I whirled together the slump in my mixer, Tad cleaned up the house, arranged flowers and laid down the placecards.

"We own exactly twenty-three chairs," Tad said, as he joined me in the kitchen.

"It's a good thing we kept my Eames chair," I said.

He very carefully composed a large bowl of tomatoes—tiny orange globes, large heirloom tomatoes sliced into wedges, red cherry and yellow pear tomatoes. He mixed in the purslane.

Meanwhile, I roasted tomatoes and garlic for Romesco and hoped Rhoda, our upstairs neighbor, was not home. When we moved in she told us that the former owners always cooked with garlic and she couldn't stand it. Garlic for twenty-three might knock her right out.

Tad took a break to read the paper and pour himself a drink.

"What's that you're having?" I asked.

"Peach Snapple."

"In a glass?"

"Yes, I think it tastes better in a glass on ice," he said.

"I didn't know it had such nuance."

"Some day you will recognize what a refined palate I have."

So many times before when I've cooked for parties, I would reach a point—somewhere between setting the table and making dessert—where I would begin doubting myself. Doubting the amount of time it takes to blanch beans, or second-guessing that the cake is done. That feeling was conspicuously missing today. Tad had put it into perspective. No one was coming to judge me. And he was there by my side. This was our party.

The afternoon skipped by. I finished my work and actually had enough time to change. Tad's father, Dorie, arrived early, parched from a long walk in the heat, but elated to see our new place. Then my mother arrived, looking smashing in a bright skirt and ruffly black sleeveless top. At sixty, she still turns heads.

Tad began pouring Prosecco and his arm was like a spigot for the next hour as guests arrived. Jennifer and Ed, John and Aleksandra, my sister Andrea and her husband Tony, escorting my grandmother. She was dressed up and carrying a purse.

I made my rounds with the hors d'oeuvres, one of my favorite parts of hosting a party. You get to float from group to group, picking up bits and pieces of conversations, sensing the mood. I heard Jennifer telling Sherry about her first few months of breastfeeding. "I was like a prisoner of war, with sleep deprivation," she said. "I was in jail!" Sherry, who just had a baby, was hypnotized. Jennifer added, "At one point I just laid down on our kitchen floor and sobbed!"

My brother Dean, who is a car dealer, was discussing BMWs with Dorie. I heard Elizabeth, Tad's mother, prodding my mom about her feelings about how we were arranging our wedding. I ducked quickly to another group.

It was pleasing to see how people responded to our new space. Many of them were drawn to the one room that has no furniture, our den, which has a large leaded-glass box window.

When the cod was ready, suddenly, almost spontaneously, everyone who I've cooked with before showed up in the kitchen, and a production line formed. I put the fish on the plate. My mother scooped up the potatoes, Deb dolloped on the Romesco sauce and Tad and Jennifer handled the tomato salad.

"Now Tad," I could hear Jennifer saying as they passed plates, "Did I tell you about our Douglaston, Queens plan? It has the best school district in the city."

Tad groaned, "You're never going to see anyone if you move there. You're going to be shuffling through the streets talking to yourself."

"It's real New York! I hate Upper West Siders!"

"You're in denial—you're one of them. Move to Brooklyn."

Tad had me seated in the dining room with my grandmother, Ed, Elizabeth, Mark, Dean, Tony and Tad's brother Pier. We exchanged wedding stories. One couple had been married the week after September 11th. Days before the wedding, they had to change venues for their rehearsal dinner, switch florists and find a new rabbi.

I told the story of our friend Will, who in a mix-up had to hitchhike to his ceremony wearing his tuxedo. When he appeared at the altar, fifteen minutes late, he was pale and sweating and wild-eyed.

Then, somehow, we segued to White Day in Japan where, Pier told us, men give women white chocolates, marshmallows or white under-wear. The latter is so popular that you can find them in vending machines.

When it was time for dessert, Tad directed our guests to switch tables, so that they'd have a chance to talk to new people. I was helping him when I noticed desserts coming from the kitchen. I hadn't asked anyone to help with dessert. A flash of my old self came over me: I need to do it so it's done right! I rushed to the kitchen, crying "Wait!" as I rounded the corner.

Jennifer, John and Deb looked up, then ignored me.

"You shouldn't watch this!" Jennifer said.

I gathered myself. "Why?" I said, "This is the new me. I'm now free and easy."

"Free but not easy, that's what everyone says," Jennifer said as she spooned apricot slump onto plates.

"Hey!" John chimed in, as he scooped the honey ice cream, "you're taking up the whole plate with your slump. How about my ice cream?!"

"My slump is more important than your ice cream," Jennifer said.

After dessert, a group in the living room passed Julia, Sherry and Mark's baby, around the room. I thanked Jennifer for taking charge of dessert. "I didn't do anything," she insisted. "Who came up with the idea of seating everyone? It was brilliant."

"Tad."

"I've been meaning to ask you. When you open a dry salami, do you have to refrigerate it?"

"No."

"And did I tell you that I've rebonded with my Cuisinart? You'll have to come over so we can make puree."

I passed Tad in our den on my way to the kitchen. The room was empty. He laid a big kiss on my lips. I hugged him.

I continued on to the kitchen where E.B., Michael and Aleksandra were crowded by the stove, dipping leftover roasted potatoes into a bowl of Romesco sauce.

"Do you mind that we're in your kitchen stealing food?" E.B. asked as she bit into a potato. "You know, your kitchen is just so inviting."

"It has the perfect proportions," Michael said. "You just want to stand around in here."

I didn't mind a bit. It was the best feeling I could imagine: good friends wanting to keep eating in a space so dear to me.

Food for a happy union

Chicken Liver Pâté

I prefer to spread it on slices of lightly toasted country bread ahead of time. Otherwise, a bowl of pâté gets very sloppy looking.

1 tablespoon extra virgin olive oil
1/2 onion, chopped
1 clove garlic, peeled and smashed with the side of a knife
Large pinch of red pepper flakes
1 pound chicken livers, trimmed of veiny membranes
Sea salt
1/2 cup Fino sherry
30 1/4-inch slices crusty country bread (cut into pieces small enough to hold in your hand at a party), lightly toasted

1. Coat the bottom of a sauté pan (one large enough to fit the livers in one layer) with the olive oil. Place over medium-high heat. When the oil shimmers, add the onion and garlic and sauté for a minute. Flick in the pinch of pepper, continue cooking until onions are softened. Add the chicken livers and cook for a minute. Season with salt and turn them. Pour over the sherry and reduce the heat so that it simmers gently. Cook, turning the livers occa-sionally, until they are just cooked through, about 20–25 minutes. There

should be a little broth in the base of the pan but the livers should not be swimming in it.

2. Pour the contents of the pan into a blender. Holding the lid on, pulse the mixture to get it started, then puree on high until very smooth. You will need to stop to scrape down the bits on the side with a spatula. If the mixture is too thick, add a little olive oil. Taste it. It should be rich and highly seasoned because you only spread a thin layer on the bread. Also, note whether the hot pepper is strong enough for you. Add more if you want.

3. Sprinkle the slices of bread with olive oil and use a knife or spatula to spread them with pâté. The spread should be no thicker than a lemon peel.

ABOUT 2 CUPS PÂTÉ, FOR 30 SLICES OF BREAD.

Deviled Eggs with Smoked Paprika

When Dorie put one of these into his mouth, his eyes lit up. "I love deviled eggs," he said, "but the smoked paprika is remarkable. It's subtle but what a difference!" He won the favorite guest award.

1 dozen eggs
2 tablespoons Hellmann's mayonnaise
2 tablespoons Dijon mustard
Dash of hot sauce
Smoked paprika (mild), from Spain

1. Bring a large pot of water to a simmer. Lower the eggs into the water and simmer gently for 9 minutes. Drain the pot and run cold water over the eggs for half a minute. As soon as the eggs are cool enough to touch, peel them and halve them. You want to mix the yolks with the other ingredients while they're still warm. Place the yolks in a mixer fitted with a whisk. Add the mayonnaise and mustard and blend until smooth. Add a dash of hot sauce and mix again. Taste the yolks, and add more mayonnaise, mustard or hot sauce to your liking.

2. Arrange the halved egg whites on a colorful platter. Pipe or spoon the yolk mixture into them. Sprinkle a pinch of smoked paprika over each. Make a test one to see how much you like before seasoning all of them.

24 DEVILED EGGS.

Toasts with Ricotta, Corn and Garlic Chives

20 1/4-inch slices of a thin baguette (not sourdough)
1 clove garlic
1 tomato
2 small ears of fresh corn, blanched in boiling water for 3 minutes
1 1/2 cups sheep's milk ricotta, or regular ricotta mixed with fresh goat
    cheese (half-and-half), at room temperature
1/4 cup thinly sliced garlic chives
Sea salt
Freshly ground black pepper
Excellent olive oil

1. Preheat the oven to 350°F. Toast the slices of bread on a baking sheet. As soon as they begin to color, take them out. Once they're cool, rub each toast gently with a garlic clove. Then slice the tomato in half and rub the toasts again with the tomato.

2. Cut the corn kernels from the cob using a small sharp knife, then scrape the cob to collect any juices. Stir together the ricotta, corn kernels and juices, and garlic chives. Season with salt and pepper.

3. Spoon a small mound of the ricotta mixture onto each toast. Sprinkle with olive oil and arrange on a large, decorative platter.

20–25 TOASTS.

Slow-Roasted Cod for a Large Party

You do not need a recipe for this, and it is an excellent main course for a party. Because you're slow-roasting the fish, there is almost no time pressure. The fish cooks at such a leisurely pace that it gives you great allowance to extend your cocktail hour or push back dinner if the potatoes aren't cooked through yet. You can check it casually, every so often, and once it's done, you can just turn down the oven heat and leave it in there. It won't change a thing.

I bought cod (a tiny bit less than 1/2 pound per person) and cut it into serving sizes. It would be nice if you could get only the thickest parts of the fish but no self-respecting fishmonger would let you. So you can fold the thin ends under, or don't worry about them. They won't overcook with this method. Coat a roasting pan with a thick slick of olive oil. Season the fish all over with sea salt and lay the pieces about an inch apart in the pan. Sprinkle with more olive oil and place the fish in a 250°F oven. It should take about 30 minutes for cod, less for a thinner fish. I like to baste it now and then with the oil collected in the pan, so the fish soaks up the oil and doesn't dry out on any part.

If you want to have Romesco sauce, too, that recipe can be found below.

Romesco Sauce

Adapted from Bill Devin

If you want one terrific, versatile sauce in your arsenal, this is it. I was introduced to it by Bill Devin, who invited me to join his family for a *calçotada* outside Tarragona, in Spain, last year. At the outing, we grilled *calçots* (wintered over onions) over a fire made with grape vine trimmings. Then Bill handed me a mug filled with a sauce the color of a carrot and as thick as mud. It was *Romesco*. When I dunked the *calçot* into the sauce, and put it in my mouth, my life improved measurably.

Romesco is a synthesis of the best local ingredients: tomatoes, chilies, garlic, olives, nuts and wine vinegar. Each is first elevated beyond its natural state. The tomatoes and garlic are roasted. The chilies are soaked. The olives are made into oil. The nuts are toasted. Then they are all blended into a puree.

During my trip, I had the sauce in many versions, sometimes loose and sweet, sometimes coarse and thickened with bread. Once it was served alongside mayonnaise with a plate of fat, firm asparagus spears. Another time it was spooned over braised cod. And in several instances, it was dolloped on a salad of frisée with black olives, a scattering of white beans and slivers of salt cod that had been rehydrated and served cold so that they were like sashimi.

This is Bill's version.

5 ripe, baseball-sized tomatoes, cored and halved
8 large cloves garlic
Olive oil, preferably from Arbequina olives (see note)
Sea salt
1/3 cup blanched almonds
10 blanched hazelnuts
1 dried ancho chile pepper (soaked in very hot tap water for 20 minutes)
2 fire-roasted piquillo peppers

Aged sherry vinegar

Red wine, preferably from Priorato or Rioja

1. Preheat the oven to 400°F. Lay the tomatoes cut-side up in a medium roasting pan. Place the garlic cloves near the middle. Sprinkle olive oil over the tomatoes and garlic. Season with salt. Roast for 15 minutes, then reduce the heat to 350°F and continue roasting another 60 to 75 minutes, rotating the pan once or twice. (The garlic should be soft after 20 minutes; remove from the oven and let cool.) Remove the tomatoes from the oven.

2. Meanwhile, coat the bottom of a small sauté pan with 1/8 inch olive oil. Place over medium heat. When the oil shimmers, add the almonds and hazelnuts and cook until toasted a golden brown, about 2 minutes. Stir them as they cook or they will toast unevenly. Remove the nuts from the oil with a slotted spoon and cool on paper towels.

3. Split open the ancho chile and carefully remove the seeds; discard. Using a small knife, scrape the thin layer of flesh from the skin. Add this pulp, along with the tomatoes, nuts and piquillo peppers to the bowl of a food processor. Squeeze the garlic from its skin, and add it, too. Pulse a few times to blend and grind the mixture a little, then leave the processor on, pouring olive oil through the feed tube in a thin stream. The sauce should become thick and creamy like a mayonnaise. About 1 cup of oil should be enough. To sharpen it up, season with salt and add a tablespoon or two of vinegar and red wine.

ABOUT 2 CUPS SAUCE.

Note: Arbequina olive oil and fire-roasted piquillo peppers are available at www.tienda.com.

Apricot Slump

The original recipe is called "Pears in Mascarpone Custard" and comes from *Under the Tuscan Sun: At Home in Italy* by Frances Mayes. Elizabeth makes it with peaches and calls it a slump, which, in my view, has a much better ring to it and evokes more accurately its slouchiness. I made it with apricots for the party by buttering every casserole dish I owned and packing the base of each with a layer of apricots (split in half, not peeled) sprinkled with sugar. I quadrupled the mascarpone mixture and divided it among the casseroles. I also baked it ahead of time and I recommend this. It gave the slump time to settle and meld.

284   A M A N D A   H E S S E R

4 tablespoons unsalted butter, softened
About 1 pound ripe sweet apricots, halved and pitted
1/2 cup plus 1 teaspoon sugar
1 egg
2/3 cup mascarpone
2 tablespoons flour

1. Preheat the oven to 350°F. Wipe the inside of a large shallow casserole dish (a 10-inch ceramic quiche dish works well) with a generous amount of butter. Lay the apricot halves, cut side up, in the bottom. You should fill the base with a single, snug layer. (If you have leftover apricots, use them for something else.) Sprinkle them with 1 teaspoon of sugar.

2. In a mixer fitted with a paddle, cream the 4 tablespoons butter and the rest of the sugar. When it's nice and fluffy white, beat in the egg, then the mascarpone. Lower the speed and stir in the flour. Mix well.

3. Pour this mixture over the fruit and bake until the center is just set, about 20 minutes. Let cool.

SLUMP FOR 6.

Chapter 34

SINGLE CUISINE

Tad had gone to Vermont for an annual golf outing. He and a dozen friends play thirty-six holes a day, eat too much beef teriyaki at a bad restaurant called "Vinny's" and go to bed at nine. Not my idea of a good time, but he likes it.

Our apartment seemed hollow without him. Already I had grown used to seeing him reading at our dining room table when I came in from work. I had come to love when our hands bumped reaching for the toothpaste at the same time, and the sound—clink!—of him setting a pan of milk on the stove for our morning coffee.

One day while he was away I was working at home and was having a difficult time focusing. The restaurant that I had reviewed had changed its menu just before publication and I was struggling to get another story to unleash itself onto the page. For hours, I clicked back and forth between e-mails and a blank screen.

For a change of pace I went out on our deck to water the flowers. I heard rustling below, where our garbage cans are kept. Our garbage had recently been ransacked and our bank information had been used in a scam. So I leaned over the railing to take a look. A man was lifting a bag of our garbage from the can.

"Hey you!" I shouted. "Hey, you! I see you picking our garbage!!"

The man turned and looked up at me. "What's that, m'am?" he said.

"I *said*, I caught you picking our garbage. Now get out!!"

"Oh, miss. Are you the new tenant, Ms. Amanda?"

"Yes," I said, warily. I now noticed that he was neatly dressed in jeans and a fitted polo shirt, "Why?"

"Oh, hello. I'm Gilbert," he said with a French Caribbean lilt. "Welcome to the neighborhood!"

Gilbert, I knew, was the man who has taken care of our building for years. But we hadn't yet met.

"Thank you. Nice to meet you," I said, and slunk inside.

Thoroughly humiliated, I definitely could not write. So I did the only thing I knew would relax me: I went grocery shopping. I walked slowly through the aisles of our local gourmet store, Garden of Eden, taking in bottle after bottle of olive oil, the neatly stacked tins of anchovies and sardines, and the display of cheeses. I picked up eggs and a long loaf of bread. At the greenmarket nearby, I bought garlic chives, fresh figs and a head of butter lettuce that was as tight as a fist. As I shopped, it occurred to me that the menu I was dreaming up was nothing I would ever cook for Tad or for friends. It was less structured and more self-soothing—separate entities tied together by nothing more than the fact that I liked each part. With anyone else, I would feel obliged to make a meal with a beginning, middle and end, a meal that would cohere.

There was nothing guilt-making about the foods I had chosen. They were simply flavors and textures that I love.

My habits are not eccentric. I know many women who have a set of home-alone foods. My friend Aleksandra, for instance, leans toward foods that are white in color. Her signature private dish is polenta. "I cheat and use the five-minute kind," she says. "But I cook it with a broth made from porcini bouillon cubes. When the polenta starts to form a mass, I add a splash of heavy cream and some Parmesan. If I have truffle butter in the house, I add that. If not, I drizzle the polenta with white truffle oil, off the heat. If I want something really mild—and white—I cook the polenta in milk instead. It is like breakfast, that way, but better. If I were rich, I'd use white truffles and shave them copiously over the polenta. Or maybe I'd wait for John."

Aleksandra also makes grilled cheese sandwiches with Gruyère and a sprinkling of white wine (before broiling), sliced comice pears sautéed in butter and sugar, coconut sticky rice, pasta with "just a little butter, Parmesan and black pepper," and before bed, a mug of hot milk sprinkled with freshly grated nutmeg.

My own sister, Rhonda, favors things like rich cheeses, fried chicken, and goose liver pâté on toasts. Her specialty is spaghetti with fried eggs. She fries two eggs and a clove of garlic in oil while she boils spaghetti for one. When the pasta is done, she puts it back in the pot, drops the eggs on top and showers it all with pepper and grated cheese. Then she tosses it with a little pasta water and as she does, the egg yolks crack open and dress the strands of pasta, making it like a rustic, simple carbonara, minus the bacon.

Ginia, a friend from work, has created a dish, which she calls, jokingly, "single girl salmon." She simmers tiny green French lentils and seasons them with white wine vinegar, lemon juice, salt and pepper. She fries shallots with a dash of sugar until they're caramelized, then sautés the salmon. The dish gets layered like an entrée at Union Square Café, and she even garnishes it with parsley. It is a model for all single women because it is at heart about taking the pains to treat yourself well.

Another woman I know says that even if she orders in, she always sets her table with a place mat, china, silverware and linen napkin. I have a similar ritual. I do not eat standing up, and I do not watch television. And when I cook I refuse to use more than one pan. A great meal alone is joyous but ending it with a lot of dishwashing diminishes the effect.

My home-alone dinners are often composed of one or two flavors, prepared in a way that underlines their best qualities. Eggs are high on the list. I rarely eat breakfast but I adore eggs and there are very few opportunities to eat them at other times of day. So I might poach one and lay it on a nest of peppery or bitter greens. I might toss a poached egg with pasta, steamed spinach and good olive oil, and shower it with freshly grated nutmeg and cheese. Or, I might press a hard boiled egg through a sieve and sprinkle the fluffy egg curds over asparagus.

It's not traditional comfort food, but it works for me. I like rich, full flavors paired with clean bitter ones—a gentle lull and a bracing finish. I might boil pasta and toss it with grated cheese, nutmeg and butter, and follow up with a baby arugula salad. When artichokes are in season, I will steam one and dip its leaves one by one into homemade mayonnaise. It's a messy, time-consuming dish to eat, but no one is there to fidget. I am the cook, waiter and dining companion.

In the winter, I have made hearty salads of smoked mackerel and redskinned potatoes and accompanied them with braised leeks. I like to sauté sausages and eat them with a mound of broccoli rabe, a lemon wedge and olive oil; and assemble platters of prosciutto, mortadella and duck liver pâté with a tuft of parsley and caper salad. I might roast carrots and beets, and dip them into ricotta seasoned with olive oil and sea salt.

Dessert is a must. Sometimes I'll buy a Pithivier or cherry and almond tart, or toss peaches with sugar and sour cream. I might have cookies, and I am a sucker for caramel ice cream. But my preferred dessert is a bar of dark bitter chocolate and a glass of Cognac.

This night, I was looking for foods to soothe my embarrassment about Gilbert. I had been daydreaming about the truffled egg toast from 'ino, a paninoteca in Greenwich Village. It's a thick piece of white bread blanketed under a layer of gently cooked eggs and a cloud of truffle oil.

I dropped a nugget of butter into a sauté pan the size of a saucer. I whisked a few eggs with a little crème fraîche and poured it into the pan. Then I began stirring it over low heat, stirring in circles and zig-zags and figure eights. The eggs warmed and turned a lemon yellow on the edges.

I remembered a story I once did about making scrambled eggs with Daniel Boulud. He prepared his in a double boiler, whisking the entire time, so that the eggs became more like a custard than like any scrambled eggs I had ever seen. They were extraordinarily delicate. I like to treat myself well, but as I mentioned, I do have a one-pan rule. I wasn't about to pull out my double boiler. My effort to improvise was working fine, anyway. The eggs, with patience, formed into fluffy curds. I put a slice of bread in the oven to toast, and when the eggs were ready, piled them on top of it. I sprinkled on the truffle oil and then let it sit for a minute so the heat from the eggs would moisten the bread.

I left the butter lettuce as whole ruffly leaves and turned them in a bowl with sliced garlic chives and a gentle dressing. I poured myself a glass of pale yellow Fino sherry; the glass began to sweat instantly in the summer heat. The toast calmed my nerves. I carefully ate my salad, carving the leaves into manageable pieces. I heard a door shut outside but otherwise it was silent.

I'd had so many meals like this since I moved to New York. Sometimes they were glorious feasts. Sometimes they were a chore; I would force myself to cook to fortify my independence and to commit to a satisfying life on my own. From now on, they would become an infrequent occurrence. I would miss the dinners, but not life alone.

For dessert, I dropped a spoonful of *dulce de leche* over vanilla ice cream and placed an orange zest cookie on top as if it were a *tuile*. Then I went out on my deck and ate it with a small spoon. I couldn't duck Gilbert for the rest of the time we lived here, I thought. I should bake him cookies or a cake to apologize. I'd ask Tad about it. He was coming home in the morning.

My last night home alone as a single woman was nearly over. The next time I would be married.

Dinner for you, when there's no one to share with

Truffled Egg Toast

1 teaspoon butter
3 eggs
1 teaspoon crème fraîche
Sea salt
1 slice country bread (not too chewy, not too sour, but sturdy)
White truffle oil

1. Melt the butter in a tiny skillet over very low heat. Whisk together the eggs and crème fraîche. Season with salt. Pour this into the skillet and use a whisk or wooden spoon to stir it, making sure to cover the entire bottom surface. This will take at least 10 minutes, so be patient. If you do it too fast,

the egg will dry and the curds won't be as silky. Toast the bread and put it on your favorite dinner plate.

2. As soon as the eggs have formed soft curds and are loose but not raw, spoon them onto the toast. If some of the egg tumbles off, that's fine. Sprinkle with truffle oil, and let sit for a minute before digging in. (Eat with a fork and knife.)

DINNER FOR 1.

Single Girl Salmon

Adapted from Ginia Bellafante

Ginia came over one night to show me how she makes this dish, a marvelous confluence of salmon, lentils and shallots. Tad was home, too. We stood close by with glasses of rosé in hand as she went to work, chopping shallots, peeling garlic, tipping lentils into a pan. She moved quickly like a line cook who was dressed like a model, in heels and a vintage dress. Ginia is a fashion writer.

"One of the reasons I like this dish," she said, "is that it's so easy. 1 garlic clove, 1 shallot, 1 bay leaf, 1 piece of salmon."

"It's like a pound cake," I said. Pound cakes are always even proportions of butter to sugar to flour.

She began by simmering lentils, and when they were done, she seasoned them with an alarming amount of salt. "You can never have enough salt," she said. "Vinegar, too. I sometimes add lemon juice as well, to create a complex acid." She's no slouch when she's alone.

Next she sautéed coarsely chopped shallots in a pan with oil and sugar, stirring vigorously as if she were washing a window. When the shallots were done, she returned the pan to the stove.

She turned to me: "What happens now is the following: we stick in our little salmon friends and then we sear them at a high heat so we can get the skin off." Ginia has made the salmon often enough to fine tune it. Salmon renders a lot of fat and the skin just gets in the way, so she figured out a way to quickly render the fat and then swiftly scrape up the skin, leaving the salmon to finish cooking. She could ask for skinless fillets, but then she wouldn't have enough fat to fry the salmon. This way, the fat serves as a cooking medium and the skin protects the fish for most of the rigorous sautéing.

When the salmon was done, Ginia laid it on top of the lentils and began layering shallots, parsley and a generous squeeze of lemon juice. The lentils were bright with acidity, the salmon was sweet and that sweetness was echoed in the shallots. Tad and I toasted Ginia, then dug in.

1/3 cup tiny green French lentils
1 clove garlic
1 bay leaf
Sea salt
Freshly ground black pepper
2 tablespoons olive oil or walnut oil
1 tablespoon white wine vinegar
1 tablespoon lemon juice
1 large shallot, chopped
Pinch sugar
1 7-ounce fillet salmon, cut from the center (ask to have a square piece, rather than a skinny slice)
1 teaspoon chopped flat-leaf parsley
Lemon wedge

1. Rinse the lentils then pour them into a small saucepan with the garlic clove and bay leaf. Cover with water (about 1/2 inch above the lentils). Set a lid on top, slightly askew. Bring to a boil, then adjust the heat so it is at a simmer. Cook until the lentils are just cooked through but still have a little bite, 15 to 20 minutes. Ginia does hers so they are like firm peas or al dente pasta.

2. Drain the lentils and put them in a bowl. Season generously with salt and pepper. Pour in 1 tablespoon of olive oil, the vinegar and the lemon juice. Fold and stir the lentils for a minute, so the seasonings blend well, then taste them. They should be quite tangy, because salmon is fatty and you will need something to sharpen it up. Ginia continued tasting the lentils every few minutes and adding more lemon juice as she prepared the shallots and salmon.

3. Place a small skillet over medium heat. Swirl in the remaining 1 tablespoon of olive oil and add the shallots. Drop in a pinch of sugar, then stir as the shallots cook, turning them over and over, until they're soft and have a glazed and golden look. Transfer to a plate and place the pan back on the stove over medium-high heat. Season the salmon with salt and lay it skin-

side down in the pan. Let it cook for 1 minute. It will begin to render its fat and the skin will crisp and stick to the pan. When it is crisp, use a spatula to scrape up the skin. Ginia scrapes it up, quickly turns the fish and removes the skin from the pan. This may take one or two tries the first time around. Continue sautéing until the salmon is cooked on the edges and has just a thin line of pink running through the center.

4. To serve, spoon the lentils onto a plate. Lay the salmon fillet on top, and dab on the shallots. Shower with parsley and squeeze over a wedge of lemon.

A FINE FEAST FOR ONE. DOUBLE IT IF YOU HAVE A GUEST.

Chapter 35

COOKING, ON SCHEDULE

My mother and I were in her kitchen preparing dinner. She had cleaned a pile of mushrooms and I was slicing them while she changed the laundry, organized papers, looked over my shoulder, fiddled around. It was, as always, a seamless dance. I know that she doesn't like to make sauces or sauté, so I jump in for those tasks. She knows that I dislike cleaning up, so she follows me around with a warm soapy dishcloth. We chitchat. Dinner gets on the table. Then she washes the dishes and I dry. She wipes down the counters and tucks her cutting board behind the coffee machine. I toss the damp dishtowels onto the laundry room floor.

When we cook together I never feel put out with my mother. If anything, I feel guilty for not helping more. She is a dynamo, constantly churning the household machine.

"So, you're leaving me," she said. "You're going off and getting married."

"That's right," I said, "I may never visit you again."

"You think so, do you?"

Well, no, I didn't think that. In truth, I had always thought that one got married and simply gained a second family to please. But as Tad and I were learning, it wasn't easy to embrace each other's families while trying to avoid the feeling that they were living down the street. Our plan was to establish our new family—Tad and me—so that my mother would no longer believe she should have a say in where we went on vacation or whether our answering machine message was thorough enough, and Tad's parents would no longer seek to override our paint choice for our kitchen.

One-liners with my mother were easy. I was having a harder time with Tad's family. Mind you, I like them tremendously. They do not scream, argue or emote. They use sarcasm, but gently. Mostly, they are extremely polite. I was having trouble telling them that I *hate* one of their family routines—a routine that had the potential to infect summer vacations for the rest of our lives.

Every summer, they spend the last two weeks of August at their house in Wainscott, on Long Island. With everyone together, there are about eight people—eight people who like to eat well, but do not much like to cook or shop. So they have devised a system to limit the pain. Each person is assigned a night or two to cook, and every few days two people go shopping. The night you cook, you don't do dishes, and once a week there is a leftover night.

Last year, the first time I joined them for their annual vacation, I resented this arrangement. A system was clearly needed, but this one's consequences were dreary. Everyone stayed out of the kitchen and you were stuck there all alone, laboring over dinner like hired help. Having had jobs that bordered on servitude, I felt the solitude acutely.

I was sad that the kitchen did not have a warm core, where someone acted as the foreman and people pitched in happily. It made me frustrated, nervous and homesick. You couldn't depend on anything being in stock and you couldn't count on starting to cook with a clean slate. There might be lunch dishes in the sink, mayonnaise smeared on the counter, and someone boiling an egg at the stove when you needed to use the burner. I wanted to impress Tad's family with the dinners I cooked, but by the time it was my turn at the stove, I was completely out of sorts.

I made one decent meal that vacation: pasta with roasted tomatoes and peas. The other was a train wreck. When I'm uneasy, I tend to complicate my menu. I made a green sauce for roasted striped bass (that I overcooked) but then decided to put basil and chive blossoms in with the green beans and nasturtium in my salad. It was all a green nightmare. By the end of the two weeks, I was plotting a campaign to hire a cook for the following summer and thinking of reasons not to go at all. I worried that every year was going to leave me with this same sinking feeling. And that every year, the evil system would reinforce Tad's resistance to cooking.

As the months passed I became more rational. I could see that the system was fair. And I had come to like so many other things about Tad's family—their consistent interest in each other's lives, their regular calls and thoughtful gifts. This seemed like a minor bump in the road.

Plus, I reasoned, this year would be different. I was now nearly a family member. This made it both better and worse. Better because I cared for them more now, and instead of wishing merely to impress them, I genuinely wanted to please them with a good meal. Worse because the situation was permanent.

I decided to take an optimistic stand. I would help everyone with his or her meal, especially Tad, who finds timing a meal very stressful, and I would treat the kitchen like my own. After I got the first scroll-like shopping list, though, I clamped down like a threatened oyster. I was in the kitchen beginning my first dinner, seething, when Tad came up behind me and kissed my neck.

"What can I do?" he asked.

"You're going to help me?"

"Of course."

Of course! I thought. I was disappointed. I had been moping, enjoying the dissatisfaction. Enjoying thinking how my family would do it better.

"Well that would be totally great," I said, snapping out of my spell. "You're saving me."

He set the table, opened the wine, sliced tomatoes and acted as my taster.

"Hey, how's it going?" Timmie, Tad's sister, asked as she walked in with her boyfriend, Scott. "Do you mind if we make mojitos?"

"Please do," I said. The kitchen was warm and jovial all of a sudden. Maybe it had been last year, too, and I had refused to see it.

Meanwhile, I roasted striped bass again, this time leaving it plain, and served it with a simple baked zucchini dish and a rice salad.

Dinner was, as it always is with Tad's family, an animated mix of humor, wit and world news. "This dinner is so good," Elizabeth said, in her warm, supportive way.

"Thanks!" I said.

"I just keep eating it," she continued. "Tad, you are so fortunate."

Tad's family is always complimentary about meals cooked for them, but I never heard it so clearly before. The compliment did not mean, as I had previously imagined, "Thanks for relieving me of the drudgery." As opposed to my family, to whom I had invidiously been comparing them, the Friends respond less with offers to chop onions or set the table at the beginning of a meal than with vociferous appreciation at the end.

We were finishing up dinner, eating my peach tart. "This is the first thing you made for me," Tad said.

"Is that what you brought over as an excuse to see him?" Timmie asked. "Did you really just drop by?"

"Pretty much," I said.

"What did you say, Tad?" asked Timmie.

"I said, 'The Masters is on TV. Leave it outside,' " Tad said, kidding around.

"What did you do in return?" Elizabeth asked Tad.

"I dropped off a haiku," Tad said.

"What did it say?" Elizabeth pressed on.

Tad paused, then began,

> "I really loved your peach pie
> It was to die
> For

Thank-you-so-much," stringing these last words together like a lounge singer.

"A haiku has to have seventeen syllables," Timmie said.

"It also has to have nature in it," his brother Pier added.

"It has peaches!" Tad cried. Pier shook his head. "O.K., then," Tad said,

"I really loved your peach pie
The soft peach blossoms swept down
My gullet."

Everyone began clearing the table.

"Good dinner," Dorie said. I smiled, thoroughly pleased.

"Wait until tomorrow for a culinary treat," Pier, who was cooking the following night, said. "It will be a palate cleanser."

"The sorbet intermezzo?" Tad asked.

"You could say that. We're having pizza, so put in your requests."

Dinner, when you're cooking for eight

Baked Zucchini with Herbs and Tomatoes

Adapted from Paola di Mauro

I must have had Italy on my mind when I set out to cook in Wainscott, because it influenced everything I made. This is a borrowed recipe. It comes from Paola di Mauro, a winemaker outside of Rome who is so well known for her cooking that chefs in America beg to visit her to divine her secrets. I was lucky to spend a day with her for a story for the paper. Paola, who is seventy-eight, cooked eight dishes for me in two hours.

This one captures her style. She sliced tiny zucchini, an onion, scallions, celery and basil leaves into a colander. She sprinkled flour over them and worked it all together, pushing and twisting like she was kneading dough. In her palm, she sliced tomatoes into chunks and let the chunks drop into the colander. She poured it all into a shallow baking dish, doused it with superb olive oil and put it in a roaring hot oven. It sounds very straightforward, but Paola is a wise cook and she knows that the flour makes this dish. Flour disappears in the baking while it subtly melds the vegetables, making them silky, like eggplant in a good ratatouille. Without it, the dish would be a watery mess.

This is the kind of dish that you can only make during one or two months of the year, and it will vary each time you make it. Don't even think of it when tomatoes are out of season. When I prepared it for Tad's family, I used cherry tomatoes instead of the plum tomatoes Paola used and my zucchini yielded more moisture than hers. I may have used less flour, too, because it was all a bit wet. No one seemed to mind; it vanished from people's plates.

10 firm baby zucchini, or 5 small zucchini, ends trimmed
1 small onion, chopped
2 scallions, white part only, thinly sliced
Leaves from 3 inner stalks celery
6 basil leaves
About 1/4 cup flour
Sea salt
2 whole ripe plum tomatoes, cored and coarsely chopped, or 1 cup tiny
    cherry tomatoes
1/3 cup extra virgin olive oil (the best you can find)
Freshly ground black pepper

1. Preheat your oven to 425°F (if you have a convection option on your oven, use it and reduce temperature to 400°F.). Slice the zucchini lengthwise into 1/4-inch-thick, 2- to 3-inch-long sticks. Scrape the sticks into a colander. Add the onion and scallions. Tear celery and basil leaves into small pieces and scatter on top. Season lightly with salt, and sprinkle flour over all. Using one hand, press and toss ingredients together until well mixed and lightly coated with flour (it will get a little moist, but should not get gooey). Add the tomatoes, season again with salt and toss once more.

2. Coat the bottom of a medium baking dish or ceramic pie plate with half the olive oil. Fill the dish with the zucchini, then grind pepper over it. Sprinkle the remaining oil on top, and put the dish in the oven. Bake for about 20 minutes, or until ingredients are just cooked, but firm, and the edges are browned.

A SIDE DISH FOR 4; OR 6 IF THERE ARE SEVERAL OTHER DISHES.
DOUBLE FOR 8.

Arborio Salad with Pine Nuts and Lemon Zest

This recipe began in a very different form. I first had Arborio rice salad when I was working at a restaurant in northern Italy. Francesca, the daughter of the owner, who was my age, would often make a salad of Arborio rice mixed with sliced cornichons, capers, red peppers and olives. Over it, she would pour olive oil the color of a sunflower. Her father, who was a traditionalist about risotto, tolerated the dish, but just barely. She and I lapped it up.

I was thinking of her rice salad when I made this dish. The lemon zest and vinegar act in the same manner as the cornichons and capers. The pine nuts were an experiment. I think you will like them.

The rice, a rounded pearly grain, soaks up the flavors and, because it's firm, holds together like little beads.

I served this one night with slow-roasted striped bass and the vegetables (above). The leftovers made an excellent salad for the lunches that followed.

Sea salt
2 cups Arborio rice
3 tablespoons best-quality olive oil
3 tablespoons red wine vinegar
Zest of 1 lemon
Freshly ground grains of paradise, or mixed peppercorns
1/4 cup pine nuts

1. Preheat the oven to 350°F. Fill a large pot with warm water and season it with enough salt so that you can taste the salt but it's not salty. Bring to a boil. Stir in the rice and cook until the rice is just tender but is still firm. You should have to chew it; it shouldn't mush under your teeth. Drain the rice and tip it into a serving bowl. Sprinkle over the olive oil, vinegar and lemon zest. Grind pepper over top. Use a spatula to fold the rice over itself again and again. Let sit for an hour (or for up to 8 hours in the fridge) so the flavors meld. Stir every now and then.

2. While the rice sits, pour the pine nuts into a small baking dish and toast in the oven, 4 to 5 minutes. You want the nuts to turn golden brown, but not get too dark. Remove from the oven and let cool.

3. Before serving, bring the rice to room temperature and stir in the pine nuts. Taste once more, adding more oil, vinegar, and salt and pepper as you see fit.

RICE FOR 8.

Penne with Roasted Tomatoes and Corn

This is another nod to Paola di Mauro. It is her recipe entirely, except for the corn. It was summer on Long Island, and having a dinner without corn seemed tragic.

1 1/2 pounds small, sweet cherry tomatoes, halved
1/2 cup extra virgin olive oil, plus 2 to 3 tablespoons for tossing
Sea salt
Freshly ground black pepper
1/ 3 cup freshly grated pecorino Romano cheese, more for serving
1/3 cup coarse breadcrumbs (preferably homemade; storebought are too
    fine)
4 ears corn, husked
1 pound penne

1. Preheat the oven to 425°F. Line the bottom of a baking sheet with the tomato halves in a single layer, halved side up. Pour 1/2 cup olive oil on top. Season with salt and pepper. Dust the tomatoes with the cheese and bread-crumbs. Bake until the tomatoes have wilted and the ones on the edges are caramelized, about 30 minutes.

2. Meanwhile, bring a large pot of water to a boil. Season the water with enough salt so that it tastes like sea water. When it comes to a boil, add the corn and turn off the heat. Let sit for 3 minutes. Take the corn from the water, and scrape the kernels and any juices from the cobs. Collect the kernels and juices in a bowl. Bring the water back to a boil and add the penne. Cook until al dente (it should be pliable but like a fresh piece of gum in the center; it will continue to cook so it should not be soft). While it cooks, scoop out a cup of the pasta water and reserve.

3. Drain the pasta and add back to the pot. Scrape the tomatoes and any pan juices into the pot, along with the corn. Place over medium heat and fold tomatoes, corn and pasta together, adding another few tablespoons of olive oil, until it is melded like a well-composed salad. Check to see if it needs more salt. It will continue to soak up liquid on its way to the table, so add a little pasta water to loosen it up, if you think it needs it. Serve in shallow bowls and pass a bowl of grated cheese at the table. A dash of cheese is desirable, but don't smother it.

DINNER FOR 4. DOUBLE FOR 8.

Chocolate Chunk-Pecan-Coconut Cookies

When it came time to clean out the pantry, Sara and Timmie pitched in and made these cookies. This recipe grew out of my mother's recipe for chocolate chip cookies. Hers is basically toasted and chopped walnuts and chocolate chips held together by a thin swath of dough. This is the same recipe, adapted to the contents of the pantry. There were very few chips but a chunk of dark chocolate, pecans instead of walnuts and a bag of grated coconut.

Sara chopped the chocolate creating a mixture of chunks and fine shreds, and combined them with a small amount of chips. The chunks created big pockets of chocolate and the shreds melted into the dough. With the pecans and coconut folded in, they were like magic cookie bars.

2 sticks unsalted butter, softened
1 cup sugar
1 cup packed light brown sugar
2 teaspoons vanilla extract
3 large eggs
3 cups all-purpose flour
1 teaspoon baking soda
Pinch sea salt
24 ounces best-quality bittersweet chocolate, chopped into chunks,
    shreds and all
2 cups toasted chopped pecans
1 cup grated coconut

1. Preheat the oven to 325°F. Grease 2 large baking sheets. In a mixer fitted with a paddle or whisk, cream the butter with the sugar and light brown sugar until it's good and fluffy like a mousse. Add the vanilla and eggs and keep beating until it's smooth.

2. In a small bowl, stir together the flour, baking soda and salt. Add it to the mixer in small portions, beating it on low until blended in before adding more. Once the dry ingredients are all in there, pour in the chocolate, pecans and coconut. Fold them in by hand, with a spatula—it is a bit of a workout, but the best way to coat the ingredients evenly.

3. My mother likes to chill the dough a little (30 minutes or so) before baking, which helps the cookies hold their shape better when baking. Then

she uses an ice cream scoop to drop the dough onto the sheets. She flattens them lightly with her fingers, so they spread evenly. They should be about 1/2 inch thick and 2 inches around before baking. Bake for 12 to 15 minutes, until lightly browned on the edges and cooked in the center. Cool on racks. Store in a cookie tin.

TWO DOZEN LARGE COOKIES.

Chapter 36

THE TART THAT TOOK A YEAR TO BAKE

It began last summer when we had dinner at the Earles'. They are friends of Tad's parents and had invited Dorie, Elizabeth, Tad and me to dinner. Alix Earle served up a splendid meal: grilled lamb and a ratatouille that melted on your tongue. For dessert we had a delicious summer pudding, which was like a berry terrine, bound together with bread.

Alix is modest, and whenever Elizabeth or I praised her, she simply replied, "Oh, it was from *Cook's Illustrated*," as if she had no part in it.

Elizabeth had never heard of *Cook's Illustrated*, a curiously lovable food magazine with no photographs and text as dull as a washing-machine manual. So I sent her a subscription. Months passed and I didn't hear a word from her. I asked Tad to prod as subtly as possible, to see that she was actually getting it.

"I talked to my mom," Tad told me a few days later. "The news isn't good." For months she had thought the bland-looking magazine was junk mail and just tossed it in the garbage.

Elizabeth then called me before our vacation together on Long Island. She wanted to know if I would like to help her make a tart recipe. "It's from *Cook's Illustrated*," she said, "I managed not to throw this one out."

I was delighted and amused that she called me. I am still unaccustomed to her Emily Post ways. My mother would ask Tad for help with a tart by yelling from the kitchen. So far, all of the cooking Elizabeth and I have done has been for each other, a polite but formal exercise. I hoped the tart would be a bonding experience.

The recipe was a poached pear and almond tart. I was mildly opposed to it being pear since it was August and not yet pear season. When I suggested peaches, Elizabeth resisted. She did not want to mess with the recipe, a trait I've recognized in Tad, who does not like improvisation. But when we weren't able to find Bosc pears at the store, I got my wish. We went to a farm stand and bought peaches instead.

We began in the late morning, which seemed plenty of time to allow for preparing a fruit tart for dinner. We assembled the dough first, putting the dry ingredients into a food processor and pulsing the butter into it.

"It says here, Elizabeth, to 'pulse to cut butter into flour until mixture resembles coarse meal, about twenty one-second pulses.' You ready?"

"That is some precision," she said, as she began pulsing, "One Mississippi, Two Mississippi."

It felt ridiculous standing together, counting mechanically, but they know what they're doing at that magazine. At the twentieth pulse, the mixture had the nubby texture of coarse meal. The dough then melded to a smooth paste with the help of egg yolk, cream and vanilla.

Elizabeth and I worked together well, each fetching ingredients and sharing measuring cups. I opened a drawer to look for a lemon juicer for her. The drawer was filled with odd gadgets, many of them so ancient they were made with wood handles.

"This house has an amazing array of kitchen equipment," I said. There is an antique set of Le Creuset, a wall of strainers and pots and a butler's pantry filled with old crystal stemware and countless platters.

"Well, you have to remember that this house has pretty much been in operation since 1914." That was the year her grandfather had bought this cedar shingle house overlooking the Atlantic. Elizabeth has been coming here since 1934 and Tad has come every year since he was born. Over the years it has remained relatively unchanged. There is a kitchen garden and a rose garden in the back, and rooms upstairs that were once for maids are now bedrooms for family. At night we eat at a broad oak dining table that has been there since the beginning.

"That's interesting," I said, "because I just wrote about a tapas bar in Barcelona that opened in 1914. It's funny to think of both places being built at the same time."

"A topless bar?" Elizabeth said. "Well, what with World War I, a topless bar in Spain was probably just what was needed in 1914."

Tad, who was passing through the room, said, "Tapas bar, Mom. Not topless bar."

"Well, that, too," Elizabeth said.

We had prepared the dough and set it in the fridge, where it was supposed to chill for an hour, at least, if not overnight. We were on a tighter schedule. This was for dinner tonight.

"How does the dough feel now?" I asked.

Elizabeth was in the next room. I could hear her opening the door of the fifty-year-old G.E. ice box.

"It feels like your spleen," she said as she approached me, cradling this lump of plastic and dough in her hands.

"You've never felt my spleen," I said.

The phone rang. It was for Elizabeth. She sat down at the kitchen table and fiddled with the plums in the fruit bowl while she talked. Meanwhile, I measured almonds and sugar and cut butter into small pieces.

"It's two by three by five!" Elizabeth cried. "Is it a baby grand?"

When she got off the phone, she said, "That was Jane Smith and she would like to know what kind of car you'll be driving home from the wedding. She has a big present for you."

"Really?" I said. "Great. I wonder what it could be."

"A chainsaw-carved grizzly bear?" Timmie, Tad's sister, said.

"Yes, and we're going to regift it to you!"

We got back to the task at hand, crawling through the instructions, preparing the frangipane and the poaching liquid for the peaches.

The pastry shell was in the oven. The frangipane was ready to go. The peaches were simmering in their poaching liquid. Elizabeth began removing lamb from a marinade for dinner.

"How is your aunt doing?" she asked. My mother's sister, Nora, was losing her battle with cancer.

"I think until I saw her last week, I was in denial about how sick she is," I said. I had gone to visit her in the hospital where she had had brain tumors removed. When I arrived, she was ignoring her lunch, a piece of meatloaf that had all the appeal of a scab. A nurse came in behind me and asked her why she hadn't eaten anything. She said, "Would you want to eat that?"

"She still has her sense of humor," I said to Elizabeth. "But she is really very sick, and it is so sad to think we might lose her. You know, my grandfather died of lung cancer not long ago."

I hadn't talked about this with anyone and was just bleeding all of the thoughts on my mind. Elizabeth was at the sink beside me listening. When I turned, she had tears streaming down her face. "I'm just so sorry for your aunt," she managed to say. "It's such a brutal, awful illness."

Elizabeth had had a bout of breast cancer before I met Tad, and she is so healthy now that I sometimes forget that she had it at all. She had undergone a grueling experimental treatment, and it had worked.

"It was so cruel," she said. "First I lost my hair and then my taste buds. I couldn't eat and in the hospital there's so much activity I couldn't sleep for two weeks. I reached a point where I really wanted to die." She paused. "I guess I didn't mind losing my hair so much. I used to have great bushy red hair, and I must say that I do have a rather handsome skull."

We laughed and hugged.

"I suppose we should get going with this tart," Elizabeth said. "It's supposed to be radiant when it's done. I'm not sure we'll be radiant by then."

"O.K.," I said, "now the recipe says to breathe and to place one foot in front of the other. Then slice the peaches. Our leper peaches," I said. When they simmered, an ugly brown ring formed wherever they peered out of the water.

"Our Bosc peaches," Elizabeth said.

Dorie dropped by. "I'm just coming in for some human warmth," he said. "How is that old tart going?"

"It's sitting there looking at us reproachfully," Elizabeth said. "They should say at the beginning that if you start on Tuesday, you might be able to have it done by Saturday night."

Just before we sat down to eat, a few more family members swept through the kitchen to see how the eternal tart was going.

"It looks good," Timmie said.

Elizabeth cried, "Well it better be the best tasting tart you've ever had in your life or I am going to throw myself on the sword!"

It was pretty darn good. The crust was dense with butter, the frangipane delicate and the ugly peaches were plump, fragrant with vanilla, and still warm.

"Is there marzipan in there?" Tad asked.

"Yes, there's almond in everything this year," Elizabeth said. Both Timmie and I had made almond-scented desserts earlier in the week.

"Well, almonds must be back," Dorie said, "because the '70s were the years of the lemon and the '80s were the years of the almond."

"What were the '90s?" I asked.

"Not sure," Dorie said.

"Lattes?" Tad suggested.

Meanwhile, the tart that took a day to bake was eaten in six minutes.

A baking project for two

Poached Peach and Almond Tart

Adapted from Cook's Illustrated; *for the full-blown three-page poached pear and almond tart recipe and analysis, see issue number 58, September & October, 2002.*

The original recipe calls for pears, not peaches, and white wine, not rosé. But we went our own way on a few details. The recipe points out that you can prepare this in stages. You can, for instance, poach the peaches, make the almond filling and line the tart pan with the pastry up to three days in advance.

Also, save the poaching liquid—it's delicious! A few nights later, Elizabeth simmered blueberries in it, and spooned the berries over her almond cake (page 70).

For the poached peaches
1 bottle rosé wine
2/3 cup sugar
2 tablespoons juice from 1 lemon, plus 4 or 5 large strips zest removed
    with vegetable peeler
1 3-inch stick cinnamon
15 black peppercorns
3 whole cloves
1/8 teaspoon salt
1/2 vanilla bean, split in half lengthwise
6 or 7 small ripe peaches, halved and pitted

For the tart pastry
1 large egg yolk
2 tablespoons heavy cream
1/2 teaspoon vanilla extract
1 1/2 cups unbleached all-purpose flour
3/4 cup confectioners' sugar
1/4 teaspoon salt
10 tablespoons very cold unsalted butter, cut into 1/2-inch cubes

For the frangipane (almond filling)
4 ounces (1 cup) blanched slivered almonds
1/2 cup sugar
1/8 teaspoon salt
1 large egg plus 1 large egg white
1/2 teaspoon almond extract
1/2 teaspoon vanilla extract
6 tablespoons unsalted butter, cut into 6 pieces and softened

1. Poach the peaches: Combine the wine, sugar, lemon juice and zest, cinnamon, peppercorns, cloves and salt in a large, nonreactive saucepan. Scrape the seeds and pulp from the vanilla bean pod and add seeds, pulp and pod to the saucepan. Bring to a simmer over medium heat, stirring to dissolve the sugar. Slide peaches into the simmering wine; cook for 5 minutes, then turn the peaches and shut off the heat. Let peaches cool in liquid.

2. Prepare the tart pastry: Whisk together the egg yolk, cream and vanilla in a small bowl. Combine the flour, sugar and salt in a food processor with four 1-second pulses. Scatter butter pieces over flour mixture; pulse to cut butter into flour until mixture resembles coarse meal, about twenty 1-second pulses. With machine running, add egg mixture and process until dough comes together, about 12 seconds. Turn dough onto sheet of plastic, press into small disk, and wrap with plastic wrap. Refrigerate for at least 1 hour.

3. Roll out the dough between lightly floured sheets of parchment paper or plastic wrap to a 15-inch round. Transfer dough to 11-inch round fluted tart pan. Working around circumference of pan, ease dough into pan corners by gently lifting dough with one hand while pressing dough into corners with other hand. Press dough into fluted sides of pan, patching breaks or cracks if necessary. Run rolling pin over top of tart pan to remove excess dough. Chill in the freezer for 30 minutes.

4. Meanwhile, adjust the oven rack to middle position and heat the oven to 375°F. Set the dough-lined tart pan on baking sheet; lightly spray one side of a large piece of heavy-duty aluminum foil with nonstick cooking spray. Press foil, greased side down, inside tart shell and fill with metal or ceramic pie weights. Bake until dry, pale gold, and edges have just begun to color, about 20 minutes (rotate the pan halfway through baking). Pull from the oven and carefully remove foil and weights. Set on a wire rack and cool completely.

5. Prepare the frangipane (almond filling): Pulse the almonds, sugar and salt in food processor until finely ground, about twenty-five 2-second pulses; process until as finely ground as possible, about 10 seconds longer. Add egg and egg white, almond and vanilla extracts; process until combined. Add butter and process until no lumps remain. Scrape bottom and sides of bowl with rubber spatula and process to combine thoroughly.

6. Reduce oven temperature to 350°F. Remove peaches from poaching liquid. Use a small paring knife to peel off their skins and set them cut-side down on triple thickness paper towels. Pat dry. Cut each half crosswise into 3/8-inch slices; do not separate slices, and leave peach half intact on cutting board. Repeat with all peaches. (Save the poaching liquid for another dessert.)

7. Spread the frangipane evenly into the cooled tart shell. Slide an icing spatula under a peach half and, steadying it with one hand, slide peach onto the frangipane in the center of the tart. With the remaining peaches, gently

press to fan them slightly then place them on the frangipane to make a flower-petal pattern off the center peach.

8. Set the tart on a baking sheet and bake until the crust is a deep golden brown and the almond filling is puffed, browned and firm to the touch, about 45 minutes, rotating the baking sheet halfway through the baking time. Cool the tart on the baking sheet on a wire rack for 10 minutes.

10 THIN SLICES OF A FINELY COMPOSED TART.

Chapter 37

AND SO TO WED

The weeks leading up to our wedding were a frenzy of work. Every minute was taken up with lists and duties. Aside from occasionally considering the remote possibility that a hurricane could whirl in and wash out the event, I wasn't anxious.

Things were going fine. Tad went over the song list with the band, worked out the details of the ceremony and found two college students to park cars. I convinced my mother to bake her delicious chocolate chip cookies for the wedding weekend, finalized the menu and wore in my heels.

A few days before we left for our wedding weekend in Wainscott, an acquaintance called. She had just been married, she told me, and an hour before her ceremony, someone had accidentally spilled a bottle of red nail polish down her dress. "Ooh," I said. "That's bad." It can't get worse than that.

Then the phone rang. It was Pete, the caterer for our rehearsal dinner, which would be nearly as large as our wedding—120 people, lobster rolls, beer, and a bonfire on the beach. "I'm not going to be at your party," he said.

"What?" I said. "Yes, you are."

"No, I'm not. I've got Rocky Mountain spotted fever. I don't look very good and I feel like crap."

"Wasn't Rocky Mountain spotted fever wiped out with polio?" I said. "Can't you get better?" I was incredibly unsympathetic. "The food has to be great!"

"It will be fine," he said, sounding half-dead.

"Fine" was not the word I wanted to hear. I got the number of his partner, John Dee, who would be replacing him, and grilled him on every detail.

"By the way," I asked, "how will I recognize you?"

"I look like a Marine," John said. That was reassuring, somehow.

An hour later, my hairdresser canceled on me. I took an appointment with her assistant, whose hair looked like it had been put through a meat grinder. When she lifted her scissors, I closed my eyes.

The day we were leaving for our wedding, my sister Rhonda called. "Mom's going to be a little late picking you up," she said. "Grandmom ironed Mom's wrap for the wedding and it melted. Then Mom locked herself in the bathroom, sobbing. But everything's O.K. now. They're speaking again. And they're on their way, about an hour behind."

We eventually made it out to Tad's family's house. On Friday morning, we got up at six to play golf. When I turned on the faucet to brush my teeth, there was no water—no water in the house where our wedding would take place the next day. Tad calmly scribbled a note to his sleeping family: "There is no water. Please fix A.S.A.P."

"Like I said," he said to me, "it's a great day to play golf."

And then bad things stopped happening. The wedding began to swell like a well-conducted orchestra. There were trucks arriving with linens, men hanging Japanese lanterns in the tent, Tad's cousin, Eliza, who is a florist, in the garage assembling our centerpieces—a large round button of hydrangeas in a glass bowl filled with sea stones.

Our wedding-planner-cum-drill-sergeant, Irene, gathered the wedding party that afternoon and led us through our rehearsal. We would walk on a path cut through sea grasses to the end of the lawn where a small birdbath stood. The pond was just a few feet away, the ocean a few hundred yards in the distance. Guests would gather around us, most of them standing.

Suddenly, we were at the beach, that night, greeting guests as they drank Red Stripe beer and nibbled steamed mussels and clams with butter, and oysters on the half shell. Jeffrey arrived with his wife, Caron. "Where is your mother?" he demanded, mischievously. "I want to have a word with her about Bern's Steakhouse. I wonder if she'll feel badly about all the mean things she said about the place now that Bern is dead."

"I doubt it," I said. My mother and Jeffrey, like me and Jeffrey, disagree about a few things.

Sherry and Mark, Jacob and Deborah, Nan and Tony, relatives and old friends from Italy were arriving in droves. Some had flown in. Others had taken ferries. Still others had braved Route 27. I could see Tad a few yards away laughing, and I caught a glimpse of John Dee, who did look like a Marine. The sun was setting, plump and orange like a clementine, and a strong breeze was blowing eastward. It was fun to see friends and family who had never met now mingling, their feet deep in sand. We sat on blankets at low tables inside a circle of tiki torches. I ate a lobster roll, with its squishy sweet bun holding lumps of fresh lobster, celery, chives and mayonnaise. It was more than "fine." I thought of Pete, all spotted up, and regretted my behavior. Then I kept on eating. John Dee had provided a feast: there were also Brooklyn "D" hotdogs, sliced tomatoes from a local farm stand, and green beans in vinaigrette. For dessert, there were my mother's cookies, s'mores and sliced watermelon. Afterward, everyone gathered around a large bonfire for toasts that went late into the night.

On Saturday afternoon, Jennifer and Deb, who were in our wedding party, arrived at the house. "We're going to blow out your hair," Jennifer announced. Soon, I was sitting in a chair, Deb pulling my hair into a tight curl and Jennifer working the hairdryer. Tad, already in his suit, sat across the room, his legs crossed, peering at his watch every few minutes. We were late.

From our corner room on the second floor, we were able to watch our guests arriving, and finding their way down the lawn to the birdbath.

"Susan looks fabulous!" I said. "Oh, there goes my therapist, talking to my mom!"

"Who's that man in Kissinger glasses crashing our party?" Tad asked.

"It's my uncle."

When we lined up to walk the path, the sky was a piercing blue and the sunlight golden. I could feel the breeze flapping the little cap sleeves on my pink silk chiffon dress.

"Hey, slow up!" I said to Tad, who was striding ahead toward our guests. "I want to take it all in."

"I'm excited," he said. "Here we go!"

At the ceremony, Tad and I spoke about why we were marrying each other.

I said, among other things, "I love that after September 11th, your first instinct was to reread *War and Peace*. I love that you can open a bottle of Champagne without flinching and are the first to fill others' glasses. And I am marrying you, Tad, because you put a spring in my step, because you make me want to be as generous as you are, because I can trust you to know me. And because our relationship has made me happier than I ever knew I could be."

Then Tad said, "I love your passionate conviction that each day is incomplete without a bowl of ice cream. I love how you've taught me that greasy Vietnamese takeout is not! not! not! a meal and that talking late into the evening, over a glass of red wine, is among the most satisfying of life's pleasures. And I am marrying you, Amanda, among many other reasons, because my heart jumps up with gladness whenever I see you."

Our friend Maia read William Carlos Williams's "This is Just to Say," a favorite of ours. (*I have eaten / the plums / that were in / the icebox / and which / you were probably / saving / for breakfast . . .*) I thought of a friend who had told me how important she thinks it is to have a wedding, to have family and friends there to witness that milestone in your life. I didn't understand what she meant at the time. But I did now, and it moved me so much, I was beyond tears. I felt that Tad and I were truly loved.

Many people have told me how they didn't remember their wedding, that it was all a blur. For me, it was like clear snapshots. I remember talking to my friend Wade about American architecture while we ate the first course: tomatoes stuffed with dried tomatoes, orange marmalade and tomato parfait, and tomatoes filled with eggplant and anchovies, all eaten with your fingers. I remember the aroma of wet stone and flowers in the Con Class Rueda we drank with it. And I remember the rest of dinner: the sliced hamachi on an intense green sauce made with green peppers, green tomato, scallions, zucchini, tomatillos, avocado and parsley water, served with chopsticks; the lobster touched with smoke and served in a corn and clam chowder; the Rosa del Golfo rosé; and the plum coupe with layers of plum pit pannacotta, plum compote and a plum cookie that was eaten with a long thin spoon. I recall showing my friend Corby my wedding band and asking for his thoughts, and the memorial candle we lighted for family members, like my father, who we wished could have been there.

I remember our friend Andy's toast, and how everyone laughed when he said, "This summer, I noticed that Amanda started doing the $25 and Under reviews. Tad was pissed. He was like, 'I thought I was marrying Jean Georges, not the Afghan Kebab House.' "

I remember Tad spinning me around on the dance floor, my mother beaming in her poppy-colored dress, our friend Binky giving me a giant hug.

I remember our toasts to our parents and the long, mad, sweaty hora that our friends started and that went on for 20 minutes. We're not Jewish, but so what? Raised up on the chairs, we waved our napkins exultantly.

Hours later, the band was packed up and the tables put away. Tad's tie was loosened and my heels were off. We were on the porch saying goodbye to the last lingering friends, when my grandmother asked, "So now what's happening?"

"Well," I said, "everyone has gone to bed. It is 1:30 in the morning."

"I guess I'll go to bed then," she said. "I was ready for more."

Tad and I kissed her goodnight, then drove down the misty lane to the neighbors' house. They had invited us to stay in their guest room, which seems to float on top of the ocean waves. We climbed the stairs as quietly as we could, and noticed light flickering from the doorway. Turning the corner, our room was aglow with dozens of votive candles. Our friends had lit the candles and left piles of fresh figs and jars of honey around the room.

We sat on the window seat, taking it all in. We could hear the waves crashing outside our window. Sea breezes swept in through the window cracks, making the candles flicker. The light danced on the walls.

"Are you tired?" Tad asked. "Because I'm not tired at all."

"I don't know," I said. "I'm just so elated." I bit into a fig, and turned to Tad. His eyes were shutting.

"I'm very tired," he said, and we laughed. "I think we need to sleep now."

Favorites from our wedding feasts

Lobster Rolls

1/4 cup Hellmann's mayonnaise
1/4 cup finely diced celery
1 tablespoon sliced chives
1 tablespoon chopped parsley
1 tablespoon Dijon mustard
Juice of 1 lemon
Sea salt
Freshly ground black pepper
2 cups steamed or poached lobster meat, cut into 1/2-inch cubes
4 hot dog rolls
Melted butter, for brushing

1. In a large bowl, stir together the mayonnaise, celery, chives, parsley, mustard and half the lemon juice. Season generously with salt and pepper. Fold in the lobster and add more lemon juice, salt and pepper to taste. Cover and refrigerate for at least an hour, to let the flavors blend.

2. When you're ready to serve, let the lobster salad warm up for a half hour or so. Preheat the broiler. Split the hot dog rolls and toast them lightly on their cut sides. Brush with butter and fill each with a few spoonfuls of the lobster salad.

TECHNICALLY 4, BUT SERVES PROBABLY JUST 2.

Polenta with Marinated Pepper Salad

Adapted from Dan Barber, Blue Hill Restaurant

These looked like tiny buttons, some served on plates that were set atop round green stones, and others lined up on plates that were set on a bed of lavender flowers. The peppers and shallot should be chopped so finely that they are almost minced.

8 ounces quick-cooking polenta
1/4 cup heavy cream
2 tablespoons unsalted butter
Sea salt
Freshly ground black pepper
1 red pepper, seeded and finely chopped
1 yellow pepper, seeded and finely chopped
1/2 orange pepper, seeded and finely chopped
1/2 green pepper, seeded and finely chopped
1 shallot, peeled and finely chopped
2 1/2 tablespoons best-quality olive oil
2 tablespoons basil oil (optional)
2 1/2 tablespoons sherry vinegar
1 1/2 teaspoons balsamic vinegar
Baby basil leaves for garnish.

1. Line a large rimmed baking sheet with parchment paper. Cook the polenta according to the directions on the package and stir in the cream and butter at the end of the cooking time. Season with salt and pepper. Immediately pour the polenta onto the parchment and spread it around so that it is about 1/2inch thick. Set aside to set and cool.

2. Combine the peppers and shallot in a medium bowl. In a small bowl, whisk the oils and vinegars until smooth and season with salt and pepper. Pour this dressing over the peppers and let marinate, 20 to 30 minutes.

3. Cut out 24 3/4-inch diameter rounds from the polenta with a cookie cutter. Top each polenta button with a tiny mound of marinated peppers and garnish each with a basil leaf.

TWO DOZEN BLISSFUL HORS D'OEUVRES.

Tomatoes Stuffed with Eggplant Puree and Anchovies

Adapted from Dan Barber, Blue Hill Restaurant

P art of the reason I wanted Dan to cater our wedding is that he is a great proponent of seasonal cooking. Our September wedding happened to be right in the middle of the best season for cooking in the northeast. Corn and tomatoes are still at their prime, plums are ripening, and the lobster is delicious. Our entire menu was planned with this in mind. There would be no asparagus or artichokes on guests' plates.

These plum tomatoes, filled with a silky eggplant puree and swathed with a single, plump marinated anchovy, were served as one of a trio of stuffed tomatoes, all to be picked up and eaten with your hands. Poised next to it was a green tomato filled with crab salad that was seasoned with a white balsamic vinegar, mint and tarragon. The third was stuffed with dried tomatoes, orange marmalade and a tomato parfait.

1 large eggplant
Sea salt
4 tablespoons garlic oil
Freshly ground black pepper
1 small onion, peeled and finely chopped
1/2 cup (about 2 ounces) finely chopped button mushrooms
2 cloves roasted garlic (roast alongside the eggplant to save time)
2 tablespoons balsamic vinegar
2 tablespoons mayonnaise
Juice of 1 lemon
6 small plum tomatoes
12 marinated anchovies

1. Cut the eggplant in half lengthwise and score the cut surfaces with a knife (in a lattice pattern). Sprinkle with salt and let sit for 1 hour.

2. Preheat the oven to 350°F. Wipe the moisture from the eggplant with paper towels. Line a small baking sheet with foil and place the eggplant on

top. Drizzle the eggplant halves with 2 tablespoons garlic oil and sprinkle with pepper. Bake until tender and buttery soft, about 1 hour. Carefully scoop out the seeds from the eggplant and peel away the skin. Place the flesh you are left with in a strainer set over a bowl. Let drain for 1 hour.

3. Heat 1 tablespoon garlic oil in a skillet over medium heat and add the onion and mushrooms. Cover and sweat until tender, about 7 minutes.

4. Scrape the onion mixture into a food processor and drop in the eggplant. Puree, adding the roasted garlic, vinegar, mayonnaise, lemon juice and remaining garlic oil through the feed tube. It should become thick, smooth and light as whipped cream. Season with salt and pepper.

5. Cut the tomatoes in half lengthwise and scoop out the seeds. Fill the halves with the eggplant mixture and top each with an anchovy.

HORS D'OEUVRES FOR 6.

Smoked Trout Salad with Quail Eggs

Adapted from Dan Barber, Blue Hill Restaurant

Our friends are still talking about this hors d'oeuvre. Dan served each cup of salad in a miniature iron skillet on a flat woven tray covered with herbs. Guests snapped them up. In a single bite, you get a crisp shell, the lightly smoked salad, seasoned simply with oil and chives, and then the egg, whose yolk cracks open and spills out, dressing the salad like an old fashioned *frisée aux lardons* with a poached egg nestled in the center.

Applewood chips
2 rainbow or brook trout, filleted, skin on
Sea salt
Freshly ground black pepper
Juice of 1 lemon, strained
3 tablespoons excellent olive oil
3 tablespoons thinly sliced chives
1 package spring roll wrappers
1/4 cup melted unsalted butter, plus additional butter for frying
24 quail eggs

1. Place about 1/4 cup applewood chips in a cast-iron skillet or wok (or put the chips in a smoker and follow manufacturer's directions). Heat until smoking and blackened over medium-high heat, about 8 minutes. Turn on your stove fan!

2. Meanwhile, oil a rack that will fit in the skillet or wok and place the trout skin side down on the rack. (You may need to do this one trout at a time if they don't both fit.) Sprinkle lightly with salt and pepper. Place the rack over the smoking chips, cover and smoke, regulating the heat, until cooked through and well flavored with smoke, 5 to 6 minutes. Repeat with remaining trout if cooking one at a time.

3. Peel back the trout skin and gently flake the trout meat into a bowl. Sprinkle it with the lemon juice, oil and chives and fluff with a fork to mix. Season to taste with salt and pepper. Cover and refrigerate.

4. Preheat the oven to 350°F. Cut the spring roll wrappers into 48 3-inch rounds with a cookie cutter. Butter 24 small muffin cups (about 2 inches in diameter). Brush one wrapper round with some melted butter, place another on top, brush with butter and place in a muffin cup, pressing the folds to the side. Repeat with the remaining cut wrappers and butter. Bake until golden brown, about 7 minutes. Remove the spring roll cups from pans to cool.

5. Fry the quail eggs sunny-side-up in butter in a large nonstick skillet. (You may want to do this in two batches.) The yolks should still be soft. Spoon some smoked trout salad into each spring roll cup and crown with a fried quail egg.

TWO DOZEN HORS D'OEUVRES.

Index

Index to Recipes

Page numbers in **bold type** refer to recipes.